BEAST

An Erotic Fairytale

Omnibus Edition

ELLA JAMES

FROM HOLLYWOOD ROYALTY…

At twenty-one years old, third-generation movie star Cal Hammond is on top of the world. He has more money than God and more women than any man could need. But when a night of debauchery ends in tragedy, he forfeits a life of luxury for a ten-year prison sentence at La Rosa, California's most violent prison.

TO BRUTAL BEAST.

Eight years later, a ruthless man runs La Rosa from the inside. He is known simply as Beast. All the wardens fear him. All the gangs obey him. He speaks to no one but his inner council. What he says is law.

ONLY SHE CAN SAVE HIM.

Annabelle Mitchell's stepfather is the warden at La Rosa. He deals as dirty as his trustees, and after years of smooth relations with Beast and the gangs he runs, Holt lands on the powerful prisoner's hit list. That very afternoon, Annabelle pays a surprise visit to her father's work, hoping to use her new counseling license at a place she thinks she could make a difference. When she catches Beast's eye, he releases the warden and grabs the girl he recognizes from the worst night of his life. The price for the warden's betrayal is not death. It's his precious Belle.

BEAST

Volume 1

CHAPTER 1

Annabelle
October 2006

IN ALL MY LIFE, I've never done anything crazy. It's true, I'm only seventeen, but I've had a few occasions. Like when Mom brought home that sleazy guy named Joe, who tried to get into my bed with me. Or when Mom forgot to pay our rent—more than one month in a row—and we got kicked out of the apartment on Rhode Street, and we didn't even have enough money to go to a motel. We slept in the Trans Am for four days, and I had to brush my teeth without water. And then right after that, my friend Rita gave me a baggie full of pot and told me I could start selling. There've been times in my life when I could have done some stupid things—and I didn't. Because I'm responsible. Because I'm Annabelle.

Tonight, that's changing.

Tonight, I'm not Annabelle. My fake ID says my name is Belle Hammond, and I'm twenty-one years old. I grin down at the gleaming piece of plastic, cupped like a jewel in my palm. This ID, made by my friend Julian's older brother, cost me one hundred and fifty dollars. Practically a fortune. I was only able to get it because Holt, my Dad, put three one hundred dollar bills in the ash tray of my new VW Bug—along with a post it note that said, "Never use this ash tray."

Yeah, that's right. I got a brand new, super shiny, never-scuffed-up, good-smelling car three days ago, on my seventeenth birthday. Because my Dad is awesome. Even though he doesn't live with me, and we only see each other sometimes, he loves me. He says I've earned a nice car. Why? No reason. Just because I'm me.

I slip the ID back into my denim clutch and step to the window of my room, so I can look down into the apartment complex parking lot and make sure my precious Baby Blue is still in her spot. I'm relieved to find she is, and giddy to behold her beauty from a bird's eye view. The orangey sunset reflects off her royal blue roof, making her look like she's been ordained.

She has, kind of.

Tonight, Baby Blue will be my chariot.

I flop down on my bed, hug my pillow to my chest, and pull out the magazine I keep tucked under the sheets. I thumb to page fifteen, where his picture is, and run my eyes over the face I know almost as well as my own.

I let out the breath I've been holding.

Suck in another one.

I hope tonight will be perfect.

I know my plan more than a little crazy, but that's what being young is all about…right?

I leave the apartment at 9:45 and pick up Alexia first. She lives a few blocks from me, in a condo with her older sister, who just so happens to be spending the night with her boyfriend down in Downey.

Alexia saunters off the stairs and into the paved lot wearing butt-tight jeans and a white tube top, her long brown hair bouncing, stick-straight, around her shoulders. She glances covertly left, then right, as if she's worried one of the neighbors will see her, then slides into the front seat and raises her eyebrows.

"Damn, girl." She knocks her knuckles on the dash. "I can't believe this is your ride."

"I know." I bite my lips to suppress a grin. "Me either."

"Baby Blue, our pumpkin carriage on the way to the ball."

I nod, struggling to keep a proud look off my face.

Alexia doesn't have a car, and she probably won't until she's a lot older. Her sister is a secretary, her mom is dead, and her dad is in La Rosa—the prison where my dad works as a guard.

On the way to Carolina's house, Alexia tells me about her sister's latest Match.com disaster, and we make guesses as to what Carolina will be wearing.

Carolina lives with her mom and stepdad and her little sister, Danielle, on the outskirts of La Placita, in a little beige house with a nice, fenced yard. As I pull up to the curb in front of the front walk, Baby Blue's headlights gleam against the smooth, yellow and red plastic of a Little Tikes car. Carolina's stepfather manages the night shift at a nearby electronics factory, and her mother can't sleep without Lunesta, so as long as Danni doesn't squeal, she's safe sneaking out. As if on cue, I see a shadow bounce against the left side of the house. Then Carolina is flying through the side yard, trailing what looks like pale pink silk.

She rushes to the passenger's side door, and Alexia mutters a curse as she fumbles with the lever to make the seat pop forward. Carolina tugs the door open and practically sails over Alexia's head, into the backseat.

I hear a ripping sound and then "shit!" She bobs up into my rear-view as I pull out onto the street, all curly blonde hair and huge blue eyes. She holds out one arm, confirming that yes, she is wearing a flappy, pale pink dress.

"I tore my sleeve! Does someone have a safety pin?"

"I don't."

"I might," Alexia says.

As the two of them suss that out, I drive to the next neighborhood, where Anya lives. But when I dim my lights and pull up in front of her little gray brick house, I see the red plastic thing on her mailbox sticking up. It's a signal that her dad is up late drinking, and she won't be able to sneak out.

I point us toward the interstate that will take us toward Malibu and send some good vibes to Anya. Her dad is an asshole. I hope he leaves her alone tonight. I juice the bug up to eighty miles an hour, pleased with its getup, and listen to Alexia and Carolina talking about all the VIPs we might see tonight.

"Carolina, I hope you give your Dad a big kiss next time you see him."

She shrugs. "It's about time he did something cool."

Yeah…like really cool. "I can't believe we're doing this. Are you guys sure we won't get…I don't know…kicked out?"

Alexia grins, her round face illuminated by the glow of my orange dashboard lights. "I think someone's gone chicken. That's you, chica." She looks pointedly at me. "Did you wax and shave the way I said?"

I smirk, then nod. It feels strange confessing details like that, even to my BFFs.

"You're too old to be a virgin," Carolina says, kicking her feet up between the driver and passenger seats. "I just hope he'll take you."

"*Take* her," Alexia says, "like in the romance novels."

I've got my eyes on the road, but I can feel my cheeks go hot. My hairline prickles with sweat, and for a second, I want to turn right back around and watch *Mrs. Doubtfire* with Mom and her smart ass boyfriend, Bobby.

"I think you should take *him*," Carolina says. She spanks an invisible butt and arches one thin eyebrow. "He'd look good all tied up."

"Oh yeah. Kinky," Alexia says.

"Shut up," I tell them.

I've talked a big game with "The Cherry Poppin' Plan," but the truth is, I don't know if I can pull this off—at all. Alexia's father, Bruce McLeer, a TV producer, got us on the guest list for the party, and I look pretty good in my tight, black dress, but it may not be enough.

He's Cal Hammond. I'm just me.

The party is at the home of Perri Adams, a pretty, blonde nineteen-year-old who stars in *Shifting Sands*, this melodramatic, scripted TV show about high school seniors living in Bel Air.

On the show, Perri lives in her parents' home, a massive grey stone up in the Hills, but after the success of *Shifting Sands* last year, she bought a house of her own in Malibu. It's a huge, whitewashed two-story, perched on some rocks that jut out over the ocean, nestled in the back of a traffic-laden cul-de-sac.

I inch forward, my sandaled toes pressing gently on the brakes, then stomping as I see a slot between a black SUV and a little Porsche convertible. I put on my blinker, idling while traffic spills around me. Then I throw the bug into reverse and point my bumper into the spot.

When I look behind me to navigate my way in, I feel kind of dizzy. Between all the other traffic and my car, people—mostly girls—stream toward Perri's beach house. Their dresses flutter and sparkle as they move. The cherries of their cigarettes—or joints—streak through the darkness. I see pale hair whipping in the sea breeze, tanned limbs swinging as they move: an army of ants descending on a yummy morsel. My Dad calls them "star fuckers." He doesn't know I'm one of them.

"Annabelle!"

I jump, snapping out of my daydream to find another car—some kind of very flat-looking yellow sports car—vying for the spot I'm backing into.

I cut my car closer to the space, and yellow sports car honks.

Alexia flicks a bird over her shoulder as I struggle to get the Bug into the space. The sports car stays uncomfortably close to me, punishing me for getting the spot that I saw first.

A few seconds later, it whizzes off. A little more maneuvering, a few more beads of sweat along my forehead, a lot of guidance from Alexia and Carolina, and I'm in.

Ricardo

It's going to be a shit night. I can tell early. My publicist, Nicci, wakes me up with a mid-afternoon phone call, in which she says I need to be photographed with Uma. That would be

Uma Thornton, my pretend girlfriend, a red-haired model who won't even blow me because she's secretly dating another douchey model.

"Don't tell me you're too hung over. Give her a buzz."

I roll my eyes and sprawl back on the custom, king-sized bed nestled at the bow of my yacht, docked at Windjammers on the coast of Santa Monica. "Aye aye, cap'n."

Almost as soon as I get my achy body settled on the bed, I hear a loud thunk on one of my windows. "What the…?" I reach the window in time to see a gull spiral down toward the water.

"Do I hear the ocean?" Nicci crows. She sounds disingenuously interested—like she always sounds, about everything. "Are you on that behemoth you call a yacht?"

"*Mistress of the Seas*, baby."

She fake-laughs. "Dock her and call Uma. Some cunt is saying you're dating a groupie from the set. Bad for your image. You know?"

I shake my head but tell her, "Yeah."

"You'll do it, then? No stalling? Wear something clean this time. I don't want you stained or torn or wrinkled. Okay, wrinkled would work."

"I'll call Uma. What time for the paps?"

"I'll tell Ronald eight o'clock at the Viceroy."

I nod. "Eight it is."

"Bye, babe."

I hang up and toss my phone onto a couch. Flop back on the bed and shut my eyes. After four years, Nicci knows me well. I *am* hung over. Last night, I hosted a party here on *Mistress*, and I got a little carried away with the Cristal.

The party was for my buddy, Guy, who was all hung up on fucking this Moroccan princess type. She came, and then she *came*, and everyone was happy, but it was goddamned boring from my vantage point.

I drag myself up to get a shower, after which I swear that I'll call Uma. I've got a towel wrapped around my waist, rubbing my hands through my dark, dripping hair, when the phone rings.

I check the screen, praying Nicci wasn't feeling crazy enough to call Uma's publicist, Sarah, and have Uma call me.

Nope.

It's Maria.

I bring it to my ear and smile into the mirror. "Old lady. How's it going?"

Maria was my nanny when I was a kid. She still works for my parents, looking after my younger sister Bea and running parts of my parents' estate.

She's the closest thing I've ever had to a maternal figure, and I've gotta admit, I like it when she calls me.

Silence spreads itself out: one second, two—and I can feel my chest get tight.

"Maria? Everything okay?" There it is: that panic in my voice. The sound I fucking hate. I gulp some air into my lungs and try to sound less like a kid. "Maria. Talk to me."

"Ricky, it's your father," she says in Spanish. Her whisper is so soft I can barely hear it. "I found him in the bathroom—with a needle."

Shit. She means he's shooting up again.

"He passed out?"

"Yes. I tried calling your mother, but she's still in Dubai, taking photos for the perfume ad. She doesn't answer."

Right. That's not surprising. "Where is Raymond?" My father's chief of security is practically worthless, a gambler my father feels he can't fire because Raymond knows all of his secrets.

"I can't find him. I looked all over the house. I called his phone two times. I called Dr. Fieldman—but I don't have time for a message. Your father, he doesn't look good."

My stomach tightens. Of course he looks bad. That's my dad for you. Lifelong addict. General disgrace. Yeah, he had a decent career, but he's pissed it all away.

"I'll call Promises. My contact there will send an ambulance."

"I don't know," Maria says. She sounds reluctant. "Your mother tells me there is no money. She says if this happens again, they will lose the house."

"You don't need to worry about that. I've got it."

That's my job. To pay for shit.

"I'm sorry, Ricky. You're a good son. I'm so proud of you."

"Thanks, Maria. He breathing okay? His pulse okay?"

"He seems stable."

"'Kay, I'm calling now. Have Sam let them in the back gate. They'll have sirens off, like last time."

All during dinner at the hotel with Uma, I'm texting with my contact at Promises, giving instructions on what to do with Dad. By the time Uma and I get up and walk out to my Lambo, I'm four million dollars lighter, and Dad has a preliminary treatment plan.

Uma is sitting in the front seat of my car, complaining about her perpetual stomach ache, when Guy calls.

I steer out of the parking lot and lift the phone to my ear.

"Guy."

"Hey dude. You up for a party?"

I hesitate only a breath before saying, "Why the fuck not?"

I haven't docked the yacht yet, so I can't go to my place in the Hills, or my beach house down in Coronado. But for some reason, I find the yacht lonely. Especially at night, when I'm the only non-employee there.

"Where's the party?"

"Uh…it's at Perri Adams' new beach place."

Perri Adams. Guy knows I'm not her biggest fan. "Miss Morocco's going, is that it?"

"Could be." I can hear the bastard's smiling.

"Royce won't be your wingman?"

"Yeah, Brody's coming. But it wouldn't be a party without you."

I snicker. Guy is an emotional mofo, never hesitating to share his thoughts and feelings. I glance over at Uma. She's got her hands folded over her stomach, looking out the window, like she'd rather be anywhere but here. Maybe she'd like to go home. I think about that time last year, at an after party. Perri, dancing on my lap, like a fucking hooker, then telling her friends shit about me when I didn't fuck her. I really don't want to see her again.

I sigh. "Give me two hours."

I hang up the phone, and Uma raises her drawn-on brows. "Are we going to a party, Hal?"

"Do you want to?"

She nods shyly.

"You sure your boy won't care?"

"We broke up." She reaches into her handbag and pulls out a plastic baggie filled with white powder. She holds it up. "You and I, we've never really…spent quality time together. I thought tonight we could have lots of fun."

She opens it, pours some blow into her hand, and leans down over my lap to work my zipper down.

CHAPTER 2

Annabelle

I'VE HAD A CRUSH ON Cal Hammond for forever. I've had crap self-esteem almost as long. I don't know how it happened. I'm not overly fat or ugly. In fact, I'm tall and thin. I wasn't teased or anything. My mom is half Puerto Rican and my dad—she thinks—was black, so I've got mocha skin and curly ringlet hair, and if I'm being completely honest, I know my face would be considered pretty by most people. But I don't know... I just...don't like myself. I don't like to be touched, because it makes me feel nervous. Kissing kind of scares me, because I'm worried that I'll do it wrong. Alexia has had sex with three different guys, Carolina four, Anya two, and here I am with zero.

As we walk from my car to the house, I'm worried I'm going to pass out. That's how nervous I am. We follow the flow of foot-traffic over knee-high grass speckled with patches of sand, around a two-story, sea blue home belonging to some unlucky soul, and when we sight Perri's lit-up, white mansion, reality hits me like a meteor. I don't think I want to lose my virginity. I don't *want* to have sex. Not even with Cal Hammond. Perfect, unattainable Cal Hammond.

He's twenty one years old, and in the last two years, he's been in eleven movies. He's a third-generation celebrity, and he's flawlessly beautiful—tall and commanding, with a huge chest and shoulders, thick, wavy black hair, and hazel-brown eyes framed by long, lush lashes. He isn't *really* Cal Hammond. His birth name is Ricardo Condor. His father is Peruvian and his mother is from Egypt.

Do you know how many photos I've seen of him? I have a collection of them, in a binder under my bed. Seventy-nine different snapshots, cut from magazines and newspapers, pasted onto white cardboard pages. I've seen him lying on a bed, standing on a boulder, hang-gliding over cliffs. I've seen every inch of his throat, his chest, his thighs. I've seen him in an underwear ad for Ralph Lauren, in old-fashioned swordsman's armor for a movie. I've seen the way his eyes crinkle when he laughs. One day he'll have laugh lines. I've seen him smirk. When I lie under the covers late at night and close my eyes, and reach under the sheets, I see his "V." You know, the sexy man version of love handles: the way his hips indent in those little lines of muscle I think I could grab onto. I know what I'd name our babies. But I don't want to have sex with him…because I don't want to have sex with anyone.

At least I don't think I do.

We step through the tall, wooden fence around Perri's house, and into the torch-lit yard, and I can taste the Peppermint Patty I had while getting dressed.

I don't want to meet Cal Hammond. It was just a joke. A silly joke that got way out of control when Carolina's father got us on the guest list for this party.

I only mentioned it because I thought that it would never happen.

I look out across the lawn, across dozens of bodies, talking and touching and swaying to the music. I look over to the porch, and there he is. I rush back outside the gate and throw up in the sand.

Ricardo

I was wrong about Uma. For the last three months, I've thought she was shy and boring. Long red hair, pale skin, thin lips. She's tall and well-proportioned, but she's kind of plain. To be honest, I didn't see how she was a model.

Now I do. It's the intensity.

She wanted to suck me off while I drove to Perri's. Guy's piece of shit Ferrari wouldn't start, so he and Royce needed a ride, which meant I had to tell her no. Still, she spread a bunch of blow around the head of my cock and licked it off, and I came in her mouth.

Maybe pretend dating her won't be so bad.

We pick up Guy and Brody, do a bunch of blow just to spice things up, and I drive us there with a pounding heart and twitching hands. We get to the beach, and I can already tell I'm too hyped up for something this crowded. Who the fuck did Perri invite? Every tween, teen, and twenty-something in this zip code?

One of the little twits steals a parking spot I'm working my way into, and I maneuver the Lambo to give her hell for it. It's an asshole move, but I'm high, and I'm feeling like a dick.

My brand new, yellow Lambo is noisy and warm. We've gone through the bag and have energy streaming out of us. Uma is talking a thousand miles an hour about some hair product she's contracted with. Guy is practically bouncing as I pop the seat to let him out. And Royce— Jesus. Fucker cannot quit talking about his hard on, and what kind of girl he wants to stick it in.

"Just no one that looks like my sister," I hear him say—to himself—as he climbs out.

"What the fuck?" Guy laughs.

I just shake my head and hold out my hand for Uma, who gropes my crotch before weaving her fingers through mine.

I consider telling her not to do that shit in public, but instead I walk a half foot ahead of her, our joined hands trailing between us. I glance over my shoulder a few times as we move. She's wearing some crazy, floral patterned blue dress that looks like it belongs on a woman from the 1930s. It flounces around her long legs as she walks.

"Cal," she coos as we walk toward the fence. Her fingers tighten around mine. "Everyone with tits is staring at you, but you're mine."

She uses a sexy, sultry voice, and gives me a sexy, sultry look, and I know I should think she's hot.

Her face is on billboards all around the country, selling lotion and all kinds of other shit. But as I look over at her, I realize I don't like it. Not my type of face.

God, there's a lot of people here. A lot of lights strung up over the fence and the lawn and the sand. This place is happening. Why did I come here?

I turn around to look at Guy. "I hope you get laid," I mutter.

Not that the new Spiderman ever has a problem. He's just picky.

He says something I can't hear because suddenly, the music is bumping. I hear the gate creak as it shuts behind us, and there we are in a sea of bodies, bumping and grinding and talking and drinking and laughing.

Normally, I'm alright with the party, but tonight, I'm twitchy. I don't like this.

I look at Brody—short, stocky Royce, whose looks don't matter because his family's old money like mine, and motherfucker is the frontman of the band Inez Irene. He's still standing funny. I look at Guy, the golden god, Brody likes to call him in jest. He's a TV actor, but he doesn't have to be, because his father owns one of the largest studios in Hollywood. Brody's still bopping, still bright-eyed and bushy fucking tailed. And then I look at Uma. Her huge, green eyes are working like little fucking lasers, trying to see through me. I just want to sit down. Lay down.

Fuck.

I'm already crashing.

I rub my eyes. Me and my fast fucking metabolism.

"Goddamn," I murmur.

"What's wrong?" Uma purrs.

I sigh. I wonder if bitch has more coke in that giant ass bag on her shoulder. I don't do coke, though. I'm not my fucking father.

I rub my head again and try to wipe the irritation off my face.

"Nothing is wrong."

"There she is," I hear Guy say. And then he's off, a lanky cowboy in ragged blue jeans, some kind of hipster boots, and a plain white t-shirt.

I watch the girls around him turn and stare, and I can tell this party is a lot of townies. Clingers and hangers on, star fuckers, although I think that term is somewhat lewd.

"Want to go inside?" Uma asks me.

Brody says, "I need a beer, dudes. Then find Britta—" his flavor of the week.

A few minutes later, the world is spinning still more slowly, and Uma keeps grabbing at my crotch.

I'm sweating, and my stomach hurts.

Why are we still on the lawn? It's so damp out here. Fucking ocean breeze.

"I gotta get inside," I say, and Uma replies in that awful, raspy voice.

She's got my elbow, and we're swimming through the human sea. Over a wooden deck, past a lit-up swimming pool, up some stairs and finally inside where it's cold and louder and the stone floor vibrates from the beats.

"I want to do some more blow," she whispers in my ear. "And then blow you."

She smiles, like she's just told me she's going to save my soul, and I nod. No, wait. I shake my head.

"Go away and find me later." I look up and down her. "This is just for show. Unless you like drinking my gizz?"

She smiles, the kind of smile that belongs on a billboard, not on a person. Then she bites her lip. "I do kinda like it. It's rich in protein, you know."

And that's so fucking sick, I turn around and walk the other way.

God, I'm such a dick. Walking about from Uma. Associating with Uma at all. Sometimes I think my life is such bullshit.

I guess that could be my comedown talking.

A few minutes later, at the bar that spans most of the first floor, I bump into Ted, my agent's son, who, ironically, offers me some blow.

I decline, even though I know it would make me feel better. "What is it with the blow tonight? Good shipment come in somewhere?"

"Oh, the best," he tells me, nodding like a Muppet. "My dealer says it's Grade A shit. I feel like nothing but air and adrenaline." He reaches into his pocket and pulls out a baggie like Uma's. Holds it out to me. "You sure you don't want a line or two?"

I shake my head. "Save it for yourself, dude. I'm good."

But that's not true. I'm stupid. I shouldn't have come here. Shouldn't have done so much powder, 'cause now I'm heavy and my head throbs and everything is dim, and I want to sit down. I'm sweating. Hope no paps are here. Nicci will be pissed if I get photographed looking like shit.

What a man-girl. Girl-man. Who gives a fuck how I look? But it's my job. I'm hardly any better than Uma.

The acting, I like. It's the other stuff that sucks.

I see Uma waving from the other side of this giant bar-dance room, and I quickly turn around. I walk into some kind of library type room with a huge, very unnecessary fireplace. I lean against some bookshelves and text Nicci: '*Sorry, this isn't going to work with Uma. Get rid of her.*'

I snap my phone shut, then open it up again. My sister—Aerie. Shit.

I text: "Hi, Aer. How ya doing?"

I want to add a sorry for not contacting her sooner, for not giving condolences that the only parent who's ever home has lost his shit again, but what's the point? I'm an asshole. Son of two assholes. No point making excuses.

Speaking of assholes… I check the phone for a missed call from mom, and then I double-check my text box, but nope. Mom knows about Dad—my contact at Promises told me they'd reached her—but she won't check up on me, or Aerie. Never has, never will. If she treats us like her kids, she might feel the urge to be a mom, and who has time for that?

I slide the phone into my pocket, and when a crowd of guys my age walks in, hauling several handles of vodka and leading several hot girls, I try to slip out. Fail. The girls stare like they've just seen Bigfoot. One of the guys holds his hand up. It takes me a second to realize he wants a high five. Another second before he pulls his hand down.

"Dude, I love your movies!"

"Me too," says the brunette on his arm. She loosens her grip on him and shifts her weight in my direction, and that's my cue to go.

"Thanks, guys." I try the cool nod thing, try to step away, but the guy in the gray v-neck follows me.

"Hey, you wanna hang with us in here?"

I frown. The invitation is delivered in a tone that suggests maybe I've just been sitting here waiting for this.

I shake my head. School my expression so the irritation I feel isn't obvious. "No thanks, but I appreciate it, dude."

"Okay, man. No worries," he says. He gets all awkward and stutter-y, still shadowing me as I go through the door and back into the hall.

I should get back to my *Mistress* now.

I'm so tired now, like I should go to sleep, and shit, I don't know what I expected because the powdery stuff does this to me every time. I am not a coke head.

It occurs to me, as I make my way down the hall and back toward the large, glass bar-dance floor-room that runs along the back of the house, that I must have a real shit tolerance. Or maybe not. All I know is, I'm not doing this again anytime soon.

If I can keep my eyes open long enough, I'll drive the Lambo to the docks and get the yacht slipped tomorrow morning. Go back home. I've got three weeks before filming starts on the indie film Divining Rod, in Alabama.

I step into the glass room, and I'm feeling kind of sick. If I can keep my head down, try to dodge people, I think I'm gonna grab a ginger ale before I go. Every step I take, I can feel people's stares on me. I stand at the bar and or a ginger ale from a girl with huge tits. A few seconds later, Guy materializes from nowhere.

"Hey, dude. Been looking for ya." He slaps my back and gives me a look that says he knows something is wrong. We went to day school together—motherfucker knows me.

"What's up?" he asks.

I rub my head. "Probably gonna go in a few."

"How come?"

I get onto one of the bar stools and shrug as he stands beside me. "Just tired."

"And?"

"Bored."

"And?"

"This Uma thing is over."

He arches an eyebrow. "And?"

I might as well tell him. He'll find out soon, because my father loves to leak his fictionalized version of events to the paps. "Dad."

"Fuck, what now?"

"H," I mutter.

His eyes widen. "Shit, dude. He okay?"

"Promises," I tell him. "Probably pissed the fuck off, not that I care." I take a swig of my ginger ale, hiding behind the glass like a fucking pussy.

"Damn, dude. I'm sorry."

I shrug. "Thanks. I feel bad for Aerie."

I must sound as miserable as I'm suddenly feeling, because he asks me, "You coming down hard?"

I nod. "Guess so."

"Brody and I will catch a ride. You leaving Uma here? We'll give her one, too, if you want."

"That'd be pimp."

He slaps my back one more time, and I see him eyeing a small, black-haired girl across the room. Miss Morocco. Right. The reason we're here.

I wish I could find a lay like that. Except, do I? Maybe I don't give a shit. I'm just so tired. Of everything.

I'm rubbing my eyes, just about to get my wallet out and tip the bartender, when I spot the first thing with two legs and a pussy that's penetrated my haze tonight.

She's tall—even taller than Uma—with the prettiest skin I've ever seen, and mile-long legs, and a dark-colored dress that hugs her squeezable ass. I can't tell much else, because the shadows flicker over her as she moves. But every step she takes, my dick gets a little harder.

Maybe pussy *is* what I need.

It's not. I know. What's the fucking point? It's all the same. But damn…

I turn around and slide a twenty across the bar. Big Tits offers me her number, and I try to nicely reject her. When I turn around to head outside, the girl with the pretty skin is standing right in front of me.

CHAPTER 3

Ricardo

WELL, FUCK.

I look into her eyes, despite how badly I want another look at that tight body.

I'm surprised to see a softness there. Not like some women, who think they own me because they're willing to spread their legs and offer me their cunt. She looks at me like she's trying to read my mind. And carefully. So it doesn't hurt.

Her eyes are big and brown, and right away, they make me warm.

I tell myself it's just the comedown. Then she licks her lips, my temperature rises a few degrees, and I let my breath out.

"Cal Hammond?" She's got a sweet voice.

"The one and only," I say. I slide off the stool and stand right there, inches away from her.

She tilts her head up at me, giving me a nice view of her smooth neck. "You're taller than I thought."

"You're short."

She raises her hand to her face and laughs behind it. "Oh, wow. You're like…a real person."

"Yes, it's true." I press my lips together. "I replaced the last of my mechanical limbs with a biomechanical one just last week."

She gives me a smile that looks a little like a smirk, then blossoms into a full-on grin. "You're funny." She says it like it pleases her, and I'm shocked to find I feel a little kick of gladness.

"Does that surprise you?"

She shrugs. "Robert Allman was funny. Ted Bose was funny. But that doesn't mean *you*, Ricardo Condor, are funny. Except you are."

I look down at her—really look. She looks young as hell, with those sweet brown eyes and that delicious little mouth. I wonder how many dicks it's been around, then tell myself it's of no consequence to me. Who cares if she called me my real name? That probably means she's one of the crazy ones.

She cuts her eyes left, then right, as if she's looking for someone, or someone is watching her. She sways a little in her sandals, making it hard to keep my eyes off her amazing tits. I drag my eyes up to her face.

I need to walk around her; out the door.

I'm tired of fucking random fangirls. Tired of feeling like I'm leaving behind a wake of victims.

She looks back up at me, and there it is again: that uncomfortable warmth on my chest and neck. This is ridiculous. If I can't get my own feet moving, I've got to make her go. I wipe everything off my face, calling forth an expression I use when directors want me to look cruel or apathetic. I match my voice to the face and look into her eyes.

"Look, honey. You're making a mistake. I might have my funny moments, but I'm not nice, or sensitive, or available. I'm not Corey from *The Supers* or Hawk from *Sonic Waste* or even Ted Bose from *Florence Adams*. I'm just a dude who's high at a house party and ready to go home."

Her eyes widen. She drops her gaze to the floor between us and gives a slow nod before looking back up at me. She's got her lip between her teeth. She releases it and licks her lips. When she speaks again, her voice is softer. "I know you're not those characters. But you're my favorite movie star."

"Do you know why I'm a movie star?"

She shakes her head.

"Because my father was a movie star. You know why he was a movie star?"

"Because his Dad was Lambert Hammond?"

I nod, holding my 'apathetic' face. Whoever this girl is, she knows her Cal Hammond trivia. "We're no different than you or your dad, except we do a lot more blow. Come here." She steps a little closer, and I pull her to my chest. Her breasts press into my pecs, making my dick throb. "You feel my shirt? It's wet. I'm hot and tired, and high. I'm not your guy tonight. I'll never be your guy." I give her a grave look, and she pulls away from me.

Good girl.

"I—I was going to leave. Just not talk to you." Her voice lilts up on 'you,' as if she's asking me a question. It makes her sound even younger than she looks.

So why didn't you? Instead, I ask, "How old are you?"

She blinks. "Twenty-one."

"Now I know you're lying."

Her face falls. Dear God, this girl is obvious. She could be an actress, for all the emotion on her face. She lets her breath out. My eyes fall for a millisecond to her breasts, then flicker back to hers.

"I am," she says. "I just turned nineteen."

"You should leave, nineteen."

She glances over her shoulder. "Can you kiss me? Please? Then I'll go. I promise."

I squeeze my eyes shut. I've got a thing for voices, and hers is positively silken. I blink at her, and find myself reaching out to stroke her neck with the pad of my thumb.

I'm going to tell her no.

She puts her hand over mine. Slowly, her gaze never leaving mine, she drags my hand down toward her breast. Her skin is soft. So warm. And then I'm there. I'm cupping her breast with my hand. My hand is big. Her breast is bigger.

My cock is hard. It's instantaneous.

Annabelle

Oh. My. God.

Oh. My God.

Omigod.

In and out.

Breathe in and out.

Cal Hammond.

’s hand.

Is on my boob.

It’s heavy, his hand.

It’s big.

And he’s attached to it.

All six-foot-four inches of him.

His chest.

His neck.

His face.

His arm.

He smells so male.

His hair, the way it’s lying on his forehead.

His eyes look tired.

He said he’s high.

Oh God. I inhale deeply, and he moves his hand. I almost faint. Somewhere behind me, I hear Carolina squeeing.

But all I can see is his eyes. Cal Hammond’s eyes. Cool, condemning, curious.

“What is this? A dare?”

I shake my head. “Well…kind of. I’m a virgin.” They’re whispered—those words. I don’t say them. They fall off my lips. As if he’s a priest, and being in his presence is enough to elicit a confession from my body.

“Oh.” He blinks. His face goes shrewd. “You want to fuck me.”

I nod. Then shake my head. “I thought I did.”

His brows draw together. Is that irritation? Yes. Holy crap. He’s annoyed at me. “Did I disappoint you, Miss…?”

“Hammond,” I say. My cheeks are burning, but I can’t seem to stop myself. I reach into my bag and hold my ID out.

He laughs, and I can see his magic from the movies. His face is transformed. Lighthearted again, as if this—my obsession with him; our strange little encounter—is all a big joke.

“Annabelle Hammond. Ah, my young wife.” He takes my hands in his and looks into my eyes.

And as he does, his face changes again. His mouth hardens. His cheekbones look more prominent. His eyes look almost brown. And when he speaks, his voice is velvet. "You don't want to fuck me? Are you sure?"

I shake my head.

His hands tighten around mine, and then I'm being pulled through a sea of bodies, between elbows, past shaking shoulders, beside smiling faces, through an invisible veil of scents and an unknowable soup of emotions. Then we're walking under an archway, down a dark, narrow hall.

He picks up his pace, pulling me beside him, until we turn a corner. Then he takes my shoulders in his hands and presses me against the wall. His eyes, on mine, are so compelling. I would sell my soul to him.

His hand strokes my neck and shoulder. "What do you want, Mrs. Hammond? Do you want to have a story for your friends? Where are your limits? Do you have them?"

I shake my head. "I'm not sure. When it's with you…"

"Do you know how many one night stands I've had?"

I shake my head, robotic.

"Too many to count. Do you know where their limits were?"

I shake my head.

"Nowhere, Mrs. Hammond. Most people have no limits when it comes to getting what they want. You do. Is it fear?"

I lift my shoulders. Try to.

He strokes my throat. "You can talk to me."

I blink up at him, and instead of doing something suave and sexy, I say the stupidest thing I possibly can. "Your breath smells like cookies."

To my surprise, he laughs. He tucks my hair behind my ear. "It's ginger, Miss Nineteen."

"Were you drinking ginger ale?"

"I was."

I manage to get my breath. His body is pressed against mine in places. He's so warm. So *real*. I can't seem to get my balance. I look up at him, relaxed a little by a feeling of extreme surreality. "Did you have a stomach ache?" I ask.

"Let's stay on point. Why don't you want to fuck me?"

I can feel a heaviness between my legs, an energy gathering. Impatient. I want him. Of course I do.

"I just…I don't think I'm ready." My voice shakes as I say this.

"How old are you, truly?"

"Eighteen," I whisper. I can't seem to speak at full volume.

His hands come up to frame my face. His eyes on me are burning. "Sweet eighteen." One hand reaches between us. I feel the weight of it between my thighs. It wriggles between them, reaches up, and then his palm is covering my pussy.

"Oh…"

He curls his fingers. I can feel one of them pressing right over…my… "You're panting," he says slowly. "You do want me."

"For a long time," I confess. My legs tremble as his fingertip presses through my dress, my panties. Oh my God, it's pushing into my…entrance.

My eyes slide shut.

My breaths grow ragged.

"Little eighteen. I won't fuck you. You should wait. Someone you know. Someone who cares." He slides his hand away, leaving the core of me screaming with lust, and my eyes open—just in time to see the look of satisfaction on his face as he slides underneath my dress and pushes past my panties.

One smooth motion and he's parting my lips. He's gliding a finger between them, sliding easily inside. His finger goes in deep. I groan.

I can feel his other arm around me, pressing me against him, holding me up.

"Do you like me inside you? Does it make you feel full?"

I nod. I push against his hand, try to lift my hips.

"I think you want to come."

I'm so lust-drunk, I can only moan.

"Come with me."

And, because my body is motionless, gone numb except for where I feel his finger buried deep inside me—Ricardo Condor scoops me up and carries me.

His finger stays inside. He pumps it in and drags it out, as his other arm holds me to his chest. Air quivers in and out of my mouth, like one time I hyperventilated in a school play. The inside of my thighs press against his hard forearm. I moan as he pushes in a little deeper. I clench as he glides out. Then in.

I think there's stairs.

I know there is his face. His concentrating face.

Then a door swings open, I see yellow walls, I feel something soft beneath my back. And then he's there on the bed, kneeling between my knees. He's Cal Hammond. Ricardo Condor. He's leaning down, his face over my hips, his eyes on mine.

"I'm going to do something I think you'll enjoy." His hand strokes up my thigh. "But you'll have to trust me."

His finger, in my pussy, has gone still. I have to stop myself from clenching greedily around it.

"Do you trust me, Eighteen?"

I drag air into my lungs and hear myself say, "Yes."

He grins, looking like the cat who ate the canary. Then he leans down and licks me, cunt to clit.

CHAPTER 4

Ricardo

I'VE NEVER SEEN A GIRL like this. Maybe in porn, but never in reality. Every time I touch her with my tongue, she slams her hips into my face. Her hands are in my hair. When I circle the tip of my tongue around her clit, she pulls so hard it hurts.

I like it.

"Cal, Cal, Cal! Ricardo! Cal!"

I lick around the base of my two fingers, shoved deep inside this virgin girl. I can tell she isn't lying because she's tight around me, stretched. If she wasn't so turned on, it might hurt. As it is, she's sopping wet.

"Keep it coming, baby. I like to hear my name."

The next time I lick her little clit, she jerks her legs into the air. Her cheeks are cherry red, her pussy tight. I go gentle on her clit, flatten the tip of my tongue and drag it slowly down her slit, toward her cunt. She's moaning. Lost. Perfect. One more flick over her clit, and…

She screams, boxing my head with her knees, yanking on my hair like an animal in heat.

I swallow back a smug chuckle.

I know I'm good, but damn.

She's rolling over on her side, drawing her knees up to her chest.

Shit.

I lean back on my heels.

"You okay?"

I might fuck 'em and chuck 'em, but I aim to please.

I hear the first choke of a sob and shift so I'm leaning over her. "Hey…" I sink my hands into her hair. "What did I do? Does something hurt?"

She lifts her face up, and I'm shocked to see her laugh. "That felt incredible! Oh my God—incredible!" She sits up, and her curly hair is sticking up everywhere. Her dress is hanging off her shoulders, and her breasts are heaving with each punch of laughter.

"I was scared of that?" She grins, then shocks me by throwing her arms around my neck and kissing my mouth. Her lips are warm and soft. I glide my tongue into her mouth, and she fumblingly deepens the kiss.

I pull her closer. I'm so hard I'm aching. I'm wondering how it would feel to be inside her when she pulls back, beaming and totally oblivious to my brutal boner. "Thank you!"

I smile back, despite my aching dick. As if I don't want to throw her on the bed and shove inside her. As if this isn't my nine thousand seventy-fifth time giving cunnalingus. As if she's the very first.

I tug one of her dark curls. "The pleasure was mine." And I'm surprised to find it really was.

Her eyes roll down me.

I watch her face transform, giddy pleasure, then desire, intention. She leans over and slowly reaches out, flattening her palm against me. Holding me through my pants. She smiles, soft and knowing. "What about you?"

I'm loving her palm on my bulge. I'm also trying to decide what to do. It doesn't seem fair to let her suck my cock. Like always, I have the advantage in this situation, which is why I often go for older women. Women who seem more capable of choosing. Girls like her, they're just following their pussies. I'm Cal Hammond, media-made model cock and balls. The ones my own age can't help wanting me.

I look at her bright-eyed face and swallow back the part where I ask her to get down on her knees and suck my cock.

"I can take care of this."

"But I don't want you to." Her voice has gone all young and soft, which only makes me want her more.

I reach out and thumb one of her nipples, standing at attention through the fabric of her dress. "What do you want to do, baby?"

She smiles, pressing her lips together shyly.

"Say it." If she can't even say it without blushing three shades of red, I'll have to go jerk off in one of the bathrooms. That, or find another woman.

Inhale. Exhale. She looks nervous. Disappointment drags at me. "I want to suck your dick." Her eyes pop wide. "Is that dirty enough for you?" She laughs again, and my cock pulses.

I slide an arm around her waist and tug her closer. Lie down on the bed, and she moves in between my legs.

I already feel good, and she isn't even touching my cock yet.

Annabelle

I shove my hair out of my face and take him in my mouth. I'm able to start off with confidence, because my friend Alexia told me if the head of it tastes salty, the guy's already pretty turned on—and that's the case with Hal.

He's hard and warm, so thick and big, except the skin there feels so *smooth*. And underneath—the balls. I used to think that balls were weird, but I'm finding that, on him, I like them. I like cupping my hand around them. Most of all, I just like the rapt look on his face.

I suck and suck, and his hands clutch the bedding. I lick around the head of him, all up and down his shaft. Like every other part of him, he's perfect here. So big. I work up the nerve to lick his balls, and he moans. It's a really awesome sound. His knees are up now, the muscles of his thighs are tight. His face is slack, his eyes squeezed tight. His hands keep running up and down my arms.

He groans. He grunts.

"That's right. Oh yeah." He rubs my hair. He pulls my hair. And then, when my jaw is getting tired, he shoves my shoulders lightly, pulls out of my mouth, and spurts all over the bedding.

For a long second, as I lick my lips, he just lies there on his side, his mouth open a little, his eyes sort of fluttering.

When he opens his eyes, I smile a little, feeling nervous again. "Was that okay?"

"Hell yes, that was better than okay."

He gets up off the bed and walks out of the room, and for a sick second, I think he's gone for good. That's it. Then he returns with a handful of tissue. He wipes the mess off the bed, and says, "Lie back and spread your legs."

He cleans me off, then cleans himself.

His gaze catches mine and holds. There's so much in it. He looks gentle, smug, amused, endeared. I can't believe it's real.

"There's a story for your friends." He winks.

He helps me up, and my arms are already reaching out for him. I'm addicted. I just want to touch him. I grab onto his shoulder, and he strokes my cheek. "See ya, eighteen. Take care, okay?"

"Okay," I whisper.

He arches his brows, and just like that, he's going through the door.

I'm sitting here, shivering, wondering about the next time I can see him. I look up at the ceiling. *Please God, let me see him soon.*

Ricardo

For the rest of the night, I think about her. Uma finds me as I try to leave. She takes my hand and tugs me onto the dance floor beside the bar, and someone snaps a picture, so I stay and play my role. When we're finished bumping and grinding on each other, and have walked to a dark corner of the room, she shoves me. "Asshole."

And I guess I kind of am.

It's funny. Funny how many people are inside someone. For Uma, I'm the asshole. For that girl from earlier tonight, I bet I'm not.

I'm still halfway thinking of her, still halfway hard, too, as we leave the party a little after two a.m.

Guy has done some more blow, I think, because he can't stop talking about his Moroccan girl. Brody looks tired, so I assume, like me, he's coming down. Or is down. Uma sits beside me in the front seat with her arms folded over her chest.

"Take me home first," she says. "I'm tired."

Guy starts into a story about how some girl his girlfriend knows swindled millions from a casino.

I zone out and watch the road. I'm in that drifty stage of comedown. It's not terrible, but it's a definite contrast to the morning after smoking a few bowls.

We make it onto Highway 101, and I flick my eyes over at Uma. She's got her hands folded over her stomach, like usual. For a moment, I feel bad for her. I think she throws up everything she eats.

"You still staying with your grandmother out near Beaumont?" I ask.

She nods, but doesn't speak to me.

Okay.

Time smears. I keep seeing Eighteen's inner thighs. So creamy. Flawless. And, between them. God, what a pussy. My dick gets hard just thinking of being inside it.

Brody and Guy are arguing about something NFL-related. I don't really keep track of pro-football, so my mind continues drifting. My thoughts are interrupted only by occasional glances at Uma. I almost regret my message to Nicci. Almost.

We're on Highway 60 now. As we get further from Los Angeles, the land grows flat and dark. I can see a sprinkling of stars through the windshield. I'm driving too fast to make out any constellation, but I know they're there. I'm working so much these last two years, sometimes I forget about anything that's out of sight. I'm kind of glad Uma's grandmother lives way the fuck out here.

I drop our speed a little, almost hoping to draw this out. A couple seconds later, Guy leans up between the two front seats. "Hey man, how fast can you get this thing?"

"One eighty-three last time I tried, but I wasn't really pushing it."

"Try now."

I shake my head. "Too tired."

"Do it," Uma urges. It's the first word she's spoken in twenty minutes. Her eyes look shiny. High. "I want to feel like I'm flying."

I look in the rear-view. Last time I tried to max the Lambo out, my sister was in the back seat. It scared her so bad she slapped me afterward.

"Brody?" I say. "You got a vote?"

"I'm down for anything," he says, "but after that, I want to smoke a joint. You care if I light up in here?"

"Nah. I guess not."

I look, again, into the rear view. Nothing behind me, nothing in front of me. Nothing but a lonely desert road.

Uma's rolling her window down. Her red hair whips all around her face, as if she's in a wind machine. I look back at my boys. Brody's already twirling his joint around his fingers. Guy's looking out the windshield, as if he's planning to work the brakes while I hold the wheel. Guy is a serious chrome fucker.

"Three, two, one, blast off," Brody says drolly, and I press the pedal to the floor. I've got an Escalade you can't do that with, but in the Lambo, shit is fine. In half a second, we've gone from 93 to 115, a half a second later, 130.

Uma waves her thin arm out the window.

160.

180.

190.

Guy whoops.

I hear Brody say, "Hot damn."

I never lift my gaze off the road, but seconds later, as I max around 220, I'm aware of blue lights—somewhere. Blue lights in the rear view.

FUCK!

I hit the brakes.

Uma slaps my arm and shrieks, "GO!"

I don't even look at her. I've already been cuffed and hauled into the station twice this year—once for possession of a brick of marijuana another "girlfriend" left in my car, another time for driving home from a New Year's party baked and drunk. I've been talked to by the heads of studios, cussed out by my agent. I'm done with that shit.

It takes me a few seconds to slow down safely, and in those seconds, the cop speeds up, thinking I'm running. He doesn't back off even as we pull off the asphalt, into a sea of little desert rocks.

I'm rolling up the window as I skid off the road, because Uma is screeching and hissing like a pissed off cat. "Fuck you, Cal! I've got a bunch of blow in my purse!" She grabs my arm. "Hal, please, drive! Drive!"

"Hell no. You think they wouldn't catch us?"

"Then we've got to do this coke!" She sticks her face into an almost-full baggie and starts taking deep, fast breaths. I'm looking into my mirrors as she starts to sob. She whirls in her chair and tosses it to Guy. "Finish it off! Please, Guy! Please!"

He holds the baggie up. "There's too much of it."

Brody grabs the bag from Guy and stashes it between his legs. "I don't give a damn about a drug charge. It'll help me." His band is Southern rock, despite him being a second-generation Californian.

I look in the side mirror again and try to slow my heartbeat. Put on my apathetic face. Uma is still screeching about the coke.

"They're not gonna search us for drugs," Brody is saying.

"When you've got a car like this, it's normal to drive it fast. No drugs needed," Guy adds.

Fucking Uma.

I look up at the sky. I can see the stars better now. I suddenly wish I was alone—or with a girl I like. Someone sweet for once. I could use a little sweet.

Like always, the cop takes fucking forever. His flashlight streams ahead of him. Only when he reaches my window, I'm surprised to see that he's a she. She's got shoulder-length blonde hair, a nice enough face, and that's all I know, because a second later, her flashlight that goes straight into my eyes.

"Mr. Condor. I've run your plates and am having your records pulled. I'll need license and registration, please."

It's kind of weird that she found out who I was before I handed over my ID, but I guess she ran the plate. Not everybody has a Lamborghini after all. She probably wanted to find out what kind of rich prick she was dealing with. I dig for my registration in the glove box, then slide my license out of my wallet.

A few more seconds with that fucking light in my face, and finally, she steps back. "I've got a K-9 unit coming, so stay put."

I roll up my window, and Uma sinks her nails into my arm. "Oh my God! I'll lose my contracts! Mom will kill me!"

"I thought she was in rehab," Guy says.

"That's the point!"

"Snort! Snort! Snort!" Brody chants. He sounds like he's joking, but I can't tell.

He and Guy pass the bag back and forth a time or two, then Uma snatches it away. She's panting as she tries to snort it.

"Be careful," Guy says. "You're spilling it and dogs can smell that shit."

"I don't see why…Cal can't…drive away," she says between snorting. Her voice sounds weak, like she's trying not to cry. Her eyes, peering at me over the bag, are huge in her thin face. I think of that sick way my heart pounds when I've had too much, and I picture her throwing up ten times a day. Her face red, her eyes streaming.

Shit.

I snatch the bag away.

"Thank you!" she cries. "Do it fast!"

I snort a little right out of the bag, the way the other three have been, before realizing maybe I can eat it. If I'm remember right, it won't make me that high. After the first few snorts, I'm feeling pretty fucking edgy. Edgy enough that eating it sounds like a fine idea. I prop one end of the baggie in my open mouth and dump it in. I choke a little, and my guys in the back seat start chanting something. My head's spinning a little, so I'm not sure what.

When I hear a door shut and I know she's walking back up to my car, I struggle to get a breath.

"Fuck, man. Are you okay?"

I shove the bag under the seat, and Uma throws her arms around me.

The next still shot I see is the cop leaning into my window. No memory of how the window got rolled back down.

Her voice is tinny, surreal, as she says, "No outstanding warrants. I know your faces, kids. I don't want you out this way. Drug unit's still headed out this way, but if you want to go—straight home—I'll handle that. But no more driving anywhere near that fast." Her eyes, skimming the entire car, shift to mine. "You're going to get somebody killed," she tells me. Then she smiles. "I loved you in *Fair Bachelor*."

I nod.

I chew the inside of my cheeks and rub my hands hard against the wheel as she walks back to her car, then, a minute or two later, drives away.

Before her tail lights are even out of sight, Uma starts screeching, "Go! Go, go! Turn around and go back toward town and exit somewhere! We've got to get away from that drug cop!"

"Juice her up," Guy seconds. "Just fly. Get us out of here."

I'm feeling kind of weird, but he's right. We need to get out of here before the other cop shows up.

CHAPTER 5

Annabelle

SOME PEOPLE MIGHT THINK it's dumb to drive alone from La Placita out toward Yucca Valley this late at night, but I don't care. Tonight was crazy perfect, and I want to relive it in total privacy.

I drop my friends off and zoom down the lonely desert road between Mom's apartment and Dad's log cabin. That way, if I happen to run into some creeper or something, there will be a safety net at each end of the road.

I spend a few minutes, just after dropping Alexia off, thinking how I wish Mom and the man I know as Dad had stayed married. Holt was Mom's second and last marriage, and since they divorced when I was three, he's been my only Dad. I don't care if we're blood relatives. He's more than earned the title.

I turn the radio up—"Crazy" by Gnarls Barkley—and tap my bright green fingernails on my steering wheel as I pass through Sunnyslope, then Moreno Valley. As the duo sings, I groove my shoulders and swing my hair.

I feel…buoyant.

Stunned.

So fortunate.

And yet…hungry.

I'm not sure I'll ever rest again, knowing Ricardo is out there and his mouth is not somewhere on my body. Everything

I thought he was—everything I wanted him to be— Those thoughts are gone, punched out by who he really is.

I spend some time just grinning as I fly down Highway 60. Somewhere ahead, I see blue lights, and hit the brakes a little as a reflex. If the lights don't go away in another mile or so, I'm turning around. But they do. The night is dark, my car is quiet, and I can hear his voice inside my head.

"Why don't you want to fuck me?"

Oh, my.

I'm clenching my thighs together, thinking of his face between them, when a yellow car flies past me, headed back toward Los Angeles. It's gone in a millisecond, which means it's moving fast—like, really fast. For some reason, yellow cars always remind me of drug dealers, on account of my junior high friend Gabby having an older brother who dealt drugs and drove a yellow Mustang. For some reason, thinking of Gabby's crack head brother makes me nervous.

I'm out here all by myself. I probably don't even have cell phone service. Why was that car going so fast? Probably just speeding for fun, but I'm overtaken by a primal nervousness. As if the yellow car were running away from something. I'm headed toward whatever it was. Headed in the direction of the blue lights.

I think of lying in my bed, reaching under the covers, imagining my hands are his, and I'm sold. I turn around a second later, and I pick up my speed just a little.

I'm watching the horizon line, barely visible in the faraway glow of Los Angeles lights. I'm thinking about Mom and Bobby, whether they'll be up. Whether they would believe me if I told them I kissed Cal Friggin' Hammond tonight.

I'm deep in the land of daydreams and intangible possibilities when I see a spark of light ahead. It starts small, but in milliseconds blooms into an orange fireball. Fear cuts through me, and for a breath of time, I'm unaware of myself—my arms, my legs. During that time…I don't know. I guess I lose my grip on the wheel.

The next heartbeat, I'm tumbling like blue jeans in a clothes dryer. I open my eyes in time to see the road go upside down. And right-side up. And upside down.

I hear a crunching sound as the passenger's side hits something, and my head slams into the driver's side window as the car rocks, then settles upright. Smoke pours from the vents. Thick and black—it's choking me.

I can't move.

Can't breathe.

My brain spins, trying and failing to comprehend how I went from driving down a deserted highway to wrecking my new car. I look down at my hands. I can't see them. That's because the airbag came out.

My adrenaline rush begins to fade, and I worry I'm going to be sick.

I fumble with the seatbelt, and I start to cry because there's smoke everywhere, and my upholstery is fabric. It's ruined now. Baby Blue is ruined.

The yellow car! For some reason, my brain chooses this moment to synthesize: the yellow car must have wrecked and caused the fireball.

Oh, God.

I don't know how I get my door open, but I do. I get the driver's side door open and half-fall out. When I get my feet planted on the tilting ground, I realize the dampness on my forehead is blood.

I look on down the flat, straight road, and all the air leaves my lungs. The yellow car is upside down, no longer a car at all but just a burning shell. A bunch of stuff litters the road around it.

Oh my God, that stuff is PEOPLE.

People and pieces of the car.

As if the sound has just been switched on, I can suddenly hear groaning. Screaming.

I look around, hoping for—what? Help? It's just the night and me, so I start running. Like in a nightmare, I can't move fast enough. My legs aren't working right. I come upon the first body, and I can't tell if it's a girl or boy. There's blood all in the face, and the head…

Long hair. Girl. I drop down to my knees. My hands hover over her, because I'm not sure what to do. She's making a horrible gurgling sound. Oh God. Shit. Fuck. Do I pick her up and try to help her?

I need to call 9-1-1!

I run back to my car, and it's hard to move because I'm so, so cold. The sky is so big all around me, so dark. It's cold. I'm shivering. I look in cup holders, in the floor, for my phone and call 9-1-1, even though I'm not sure if that works on cell phones.

Someone answers!

"Oh my God, there's been a really bad wreck on highway 60 west—I mean east—of Moreno Valley! Send someone now! It's *really* bad!"

"Try to stay calm. Are you hurt?"

"I'm fine! It's the people in the other car!"

"Were you involved in a wreck? Stay on the line with me."

"We're on Highway 60. We need a helicopter! Now!"

My voice echoes in my head as I drop my phone and run back toward the girl. I can tell before I get up close to her that it's not good. She's gone completely silent. I can't see her chest rising and falling, so I move on numb legs toward the next body on the road. It's long, sprawled face-down. The face is pale, but that's all I can tell because he has a badly bleeding head. "Can you hear me?" I sink into a crouch and reach for his arm, but after a second staring, I can tell for sure: This chest is not moving. At all.

"Oh no! Oh God! Oh God!"

I dash down the road, past the car and the debris, and a few dozen yards later, lying in the rocks, I find another large, male body. Pale hair, bloody chest and legs. This one is shaking violently, so still alive.

I drop to my knees beside him. My arms go out to touch him, but I'm not sure what would hurt and what would help. "Help is on its way," I say in a high-pitched voice. "It's okay, they'll be here soon!"

He stares up at the sky, eyes never sliding over to me.

I look frantically around. Is this everyone? How many people could fit into a car like that?

I touch his arm. "You're not alone. I'm here." Still, he doesn't look at me. I think he can't. Something about that scares me almost more than the bodies of his friends.

Should I check the car?

I should check it.

I hope up, run over to the twisted pile of glass and metal that is the car. I look around it, sandals crunching on glass. Almost every window is broken. There's a door missing.

I peer inside, and as I do, I hear a groan.

"Oh my God!" It's coming from the car!

I rush around to the other side of the car, and that's when I realize: the other side is mostly gone. The person groaning is just kind of hanging from his seat-belt. Half of his chair is burned away.

He's curled down on himself, chin to chest, shoulders hunched, so I can't tell anything except he's got dark hair and dark pants. His arms hang limply at his sides. His face looks very, very pale.

Icy cold seeps through me. "Don't be dead! Please don't be dead!"

I drop down to my knees in the dirt, and he lifts his chin a fraction of an inch.

His lips move for a few seconds before I hear a hoarse sound. He makes the sound again and lifts his head a little more. Long lashes flutter. "Maria," he rasps.

That's the name of Cal Hammond's childhood nanny. What a stupid thought that is right now.

He writhes, his shoulders lifting, head moving a little. "Maria," he moans. His face is so bloody, I can't make out much of him. I can't tell where the blood is coming from. It streams down his neck and chest, coating his waist and jeans.

I'm scared to touch him, but my hand can't seem to help itself. I touch his right knee, feather light. "Hey, can you hear me?"

"Maria… Please help!" His hand juts out, grabbing my arm. His grip is weak, his fingers sticky with his blood. His eyes, on mine, are wild and—

No.

No, no. Fuck no.

I go very still inside.

My voice cracks. "Cal?"

His gaze grapples with mine, and my heart stops.

It's him. It's definitely him.

Cal Hammond.

"Oh my God. Oh fuck. Oh shit. Cal." It can't be him. It makes no sense. But every line of his face, every curve of bulky muscle tells me that it is. He's wearing black jeans and a pink t-shirt, like Cal was at the party.

I drop to my knees and touch his hair, just a tremble of my palm over his warm, damp head. It seems to bring him back into the moment. His hand catches my wrist, his face twists. He isn't focusing enough to recognize me. I'm ashamed that I notice that.

His chest rises and falls, like it's a struggle just to draw a breath. "My…shoulder," he moans.

I look at both his shoulders, but he's so limp, I can't tell which one's hurt. "What do I do?"

He lets his breath out. "Left…one. Push…on it. Push…up."

I notice belatedly that his left arm is tucked up, and his right one is cradling his left one. "I can't do that! I don't know how!"

He shakes his head a little, wincing. "Just…push!"

When my fingers close around his shoulder, heat spreads through me. I'm hesitant at first, but he growls, *"Now."* I push hard. He gasps.

The gasp is followed by shallow panting. Followed by a peek of his dark eyes. "Fuck me, angel. You're an evil one."

I grit my teeth. "I'm sorry!" My voice shakes. I think I'm crying.

I touch his back. His eyes squeeze shut. His breaths are hisses. I swear to the Virgin, I can feel his pain in my own bones.

He starts shaking so abruptly, at first I think I'm imagining it. But no. The tremors rip through him, and a second later he starts panting.

I come around in front of him. Kneel down, and look into his eyes. "Are you okay?"

"Hold onto me."

I hesitate.

"Hold onto me." His head snaps up. "One…hand. Just…hold on! I can't move." He looks frantically left and right, like he's just realized he wrecked his car and he's strapped into the charred driver's seat. "Please—help me move!"

"I'm scared I'll hurt you!"

"Tug…on my shoulder."

He curls over a little, letting out these awful little half-grunt, half-groans, and I wrap my hand around the bicep of the arm I just popped back into place.

"Harder," he gasps. "Make it…*hurt.*"

Horrified, I squeeze him harder.

"Use your nails."

I dig into his arm.

"Harder…or…I'll pass out." His voice is sounding garbled, like he's drunk.

That seems like it would be bad, so I squeeze him harder, hating that I'm hurting him.

"Where's…Guy?" His eyes find mine. "Where's…"

"He's here," I interrupt. "Your friends are here."

He must have just remembered them. I whirl around, gazing down the road where they lay. Which one is Guy? Guy Jacobsen. Blond. "He's still alive!" Last time I checked, he was still alive. I cover my face and start to cry.

"Come…hold onto my back."

I step quickly to him, feeling guilty for my crying; feeling frenzied for the ambulance. Where is it? Cal is still buckled, and I'm scared to unbuckle him, so I reach my hand between the tattered seat and his back.

"Up," he murmurs. "Don' wanna go up. Push me down. Please." The last word is barely breathed.

"What's the matter?" It's such a stupid question. I'm so stupid. I'm so scared.

He keeps shaking—unable, in his pain, to answer.

His shirt is torn, so I can feel his skin under my palm. It's cool and clammy. Wet in some places.

"Harder." He grits, "Nails."

"I don't want to hurt you," I whimper.

"Harder." He lifts his head a little more. I can feel his eyes roll over me. His mouth slackens, and his teeth begin to chatter. "A-are you an angel?"

Tears quiver in my eyes, blurring his face. I shake my head, and they spill down my cheeks.

"I saw your car. I called the cops." With my hand still on his back, I move, in a crouch, around in front of him. I want to hug him, so, so much, but I'm too scared.

His eyes are more focused now, ardent on my face. "Are you…sure…you're not an angel?"

I nod.

He tilts his head back, his mouth moving like he wants to say more, but can't. He grips the chair he's still strapped into with both hands and makes a low, pained sound. And that's the first time I notice, blood is dripping down the ruined leather seat.

"Oh shit, I think you should be still."

He shakes his head. "Belt."

When I don't move, he reaches out and grabs me. He pulls a little, and I'm so close, on the right side of him, my knee is touching his leg.

"My belt," he grates.

He wraps his hands around his thigh, which gleams in the moonlight. He must have been cut badly there, right through his jeans.

"Eighteen… Please! The belt…around…my leg."

My hands flutter over him, unsure where to start, terrified of hurting him.

"*Please*. I hate the smell of blood!"

"Okay, baby. It's okay. Hang on a minute."

I lean down and unbuckle his black leather belt, then slide it off. He raises his unhurt arm over his face and makes an awful moaning, half-sobbed sound.

"I'm sorry! I'm so sorry!"

I get the belt around his thigh, just above his knee, and slide it up to crotch level. Then I pull it tight."

His hand grips my shoulder, his fingers tightening as I tighten the belt around his thigh.

"Oh," he gasps.

"I'm sorry!"

I get it tight, and take his hand. I can feel his body struggling. Feel him shaking.

His eyes are shut.

I look him over.

He doesn't look like he's bleeding anywhere else except his nose and mouth. His face is starting to look swollen, though.

When he mutters, "Fuck," his face seems stiff, and the word sounds like it's being said around a retainer.

Inside my mind, I'm screaming, sobbing. Telling him he's doing great, asking him to just hang on a little longer. But I'm under a blanket of terror. I can't move. Can't say any of my wild feelings.

I can barely even stroke his hand.

"Can you stay by yourself for just a second? I need to check on your friends."

"Guy," he hisses.

"Yes. Just hang on, Ricardo. Hang on—I'll be right back to you."

I run back to where the other bodies are, reaching first the one who I now can tell is Brody Royce. He's dead. He's dead. The angle of his head—I cover my mouth. I start to cry again, but I can't let that slow me down. I dash to the girl. Uma. Cal's friend Uma Thornton. She's so still, so quiet, so thin. No breaths.

My legs seize up. I stumble to the third one. Blond. Guy. He's lying on his back, his legs sprawled out, arms resting limply on the road as if he just decided to lie down there. His face is plastic, wide eyes still staring at the black sky. Still breathing.

"It's okay," I tell him. "Help will be here soon!"

I look up at the stars, as if they can help me, then I hear a noise from Cal's direction and sprint back to him.

I find him unbuckled from his seat and on the rocky ground just under the car, which I notice is still burning slightly in the back. He's lying on his side, pushed up on one arm. His eyes are wide. Unfocused. Except when they land on my face.

"Angel," he whispers.

He lowers his torso down to the ground. His throat works, and for a second, we just stare into each other's eyes. Words tumble from his mouth, as if they're being forced out. "Eigh'teen. Can you…hold onto me? I'm…floating."

I sit down beside him, then stretch out behind him. His back seems okay, so I wrap my arms around him gently.

"Tighter."

I squeeze.

"Don't let go."

"I won't. I swear."

A cold breeze blows over the flat land all around us. I'm shivering now—or is it him?

His teeth chatter. I push my face into his back.

"Do you…believe in fate?" His breaths are fast. I'm scared.

I try to keep the fear out of my voice. To keep my arms around him snug and gentle. "I'm not sure. Do you?"

He doesn't answer.

Minutes later, long after I fear he's passed out or died, he mumbles, "I…believe in…punishment. And…*you*."

It's a long time before I learn the prescience of his last coherent words.

CHAPTER 6

Annabelle
September 2014
Seven years, eleven months later

"IF YOU DON'T SIT DOWN right now and stop touching the TV, I'm going to turn *Dora* off, Adrian."

"But Anna—"

"*Sit* down."

I hold my hand in front of the little TV/DVD player on the dresser inside Adrian's small bedroom: a silent threat.

She sinks down into her bean bag chair and blows her bangs out of her face.

I straighten my skirt and catch her big brown eyes angled my way. "When are you coming back, Anna?"

I exhale slowly and try to free myself from the sharp claws of my anxiety. "I don't know yet, Ad. But it shouldn't be more than four or five hours."

She points to her little digital clock, sitting beside a *Beauty and The Beast* lamp on the dresser. "You'll be back at five o'clock?"

"Yep." I tug at my skirt. "Something like that. Would you like some pizza tonight?"

She nods. "Absolutely!"

I don't even try to hide my smile at her enthusiasm. Since the August morning Mom gave birth to Adrian four years ago, I've been completely and totally in love. Since Mom got sick a year and a half ago, Adrian's been mine. She's all I have. She's all I want. I transferred from UCLA's main campus to a branch to finish my psychology doctorate, and when it became clear that Mom's brain cancer wasn't going to be cured, I switched into the master's program so I could find a good job and support them.

Unfortunately, that part of my plan hasn't been going so well.

That's the reason for my errand.

"What sort of pizza would you like tonight?" I ask as I step across the small hallway to my room, so I can get my blouse. I step back into Adrian's princess paradise. "Pepperoni, ham and pineapple…?"

She shoots up from her seat. "I want the supreme!"

"Are you sure?"

"Yes. I like onions!"

I laugh. "You like to breathe on me with onion breath."

I pull my blouse over my head, and from the inside of the soft, red fabric, I hear her soft voice say, "Does Mom have breath?"

I push my head through the collar and try to guess at what she's asking, even as my insides go a little cold.

"Mom's in her bedroom, with Nurse Casey. Remember?"

She shakes her head. "Does she have *breath*?"

It's a battle to keep my face neutral and my tone pleasant. "You mean, like onion breath?"

She nods quickly, like she's been thinking this over, and she's worried about it.

"No, honey. Mom doesn't have onion breath. She doesn't like onions."

"How do you know that?" Adrian whispers.

"Because she told me."

"When?" She scratches her neck.

"When you were a little baby." That isn't exactly true, of course, but I want her to know that at one point when she was alive, Mom wasn't like she is now.

I step over to her, pick her up, and sit on the edge of her bed to cuddle her in my lap.

"Sometimes it's sad when Mom is sleeping a lot, isn't it?"

She nods, and buries her face in my neck. I stroke her hair. "I'm sorry, honey. Mommy loves you so much, and so do I."

I rub her back for a few minutes, hating that this is all I can do. All I can say. I'm so much older than Adrian—I'm her stand-in Mommy—and still, I have no answers. As I hold her, she gets the hiccups, and somehow we start singing "The Ants Go Marching," to get rid of them. We're on eleven by eleven when Holly arrives.

Holly lives in the condo complex next door. She's only seventeen, but she's great with Adrian, and besides, the two of them are never alone. Mom and one of the nurses are always here.

When Adrian and Holly are settled, playing with dolls, I slip into my room and stand in front of the full-length mirror to assess myself. Shoulder-length hair, curly as always. Brown eyes. Small nose. Full lips, with red lipstick. I'm five-foot-seven, and I look it in my black skirt and red blouse. I'm wearing some cute black heels I got on sale a few weeks back. I look okay I guess.

Not that it matters.

It really doesn't matter, Annabelle.

I check out with Nurse Casey, who's reading a paperback while Mom dozes in her railed bed.

"Be back around five," I say. "See you soon, Mom."

She doesn't lift her head, and it's been so long now, I'm not surprised. I don't feel anything about the state of things with Mom. Nothing but a snake of fear coiled in my gut.

My heels clink on the brick walkway as I walk to the stairs, then down to my red Honda Accord. Like most things in my life, right down to the money for childcare and nurses, the Accord was a gift from Dad.

I sink slowly into the driver's seat and take my time pulling out of the lot, because the truth is, I don't want to do what I'm about to do. The thing is, I don't have a choice. I've been job-hunting for four months, and I've found nothing in driving distance of Mom's house that will pay more than the cost of daycare for Adrian.

Dad has been more than generous. He doesn't care that Adrian isn't his any more than he cares that I'm not his biological daughter. He cares about Adrian because I do, and he must be making bank as Warden, because the well never seems to run dry.

Which makes it strange that I haven't been able to get in touch with him lately. We keep playing phone tag, and last time I text'd him about a counseling job at La Rosa, he didn't even text me back. That was almost two weeks ago.

As I drive, I fret over whether he'll even be there. What if he got fired? But surely not. He's worked at the prison as long as I can remember. I don't go there often, but he talks about me so much that when I do, all the staff know my name.

The drive from our place in La Placita is a little over an hour if you drive like I do: fast. And on the way, I pass the spot.

That spot.

It's not the first time. Not the second, third, or fourth, or fifth. But every time, it gets me like a steak knife in the sternum.

I know exactly where the wreck happened, because part of the therapy I sought out in college involved placing an "In Memorial" sign on the side of the road.

Three lives were lost that night. Four, if you count Ricardo's. And I do. I definitely do.

The last half of the drive, I'm consumed with memories of that night.

For the years I saw Miranda, my therapist at the UCLA student mental health center, we talked about odds. The odds that I would plan to lose my virginity to Cal Hammond—a crazy plan any way you slice it. The odds that I would actually encounter him at the party. The odds that things would go the way they did. And then the odds that I would take the drive I took, when he and his friends were taking Uma Thornton home.

What did it mean, I used to ask.

Why do such things happen? The universe conspires… And why? I see no greater purpose to our strange night than maybe my own outcome: I decided to go into psychology because of the PTSD sessions I had with Miranda. So what? I'll help people? Will I? Maybe with a PhD, but I don't have that, do I? Like for most of my life so far, I'm just drifting. Wondering what my purpose is, other than loving Adrian.

I roll some chap stick over my lips and then refresh my lipstick. I pass a sign, letting me know there's a prison ahead, and I shouldn't pick up hitchhikers.

I hate coming here.

Not because of the prisoners.

Because of him.

Ricardo. Cal.

I rode with him to the hospital that night, using my ID to pose as his cousin, and I was there when the police officers arrived. I listened from a bench in the hall as they whispered about toxicology reports and manslaughter.

I avoided testifying in court with Miranda's help, but I wrote a statement that was read before the judge. How Ricardo was concerned about his friends. How it was clearly just an accident.

He realized in the helicopter that only Guy was being airlifted, and Guy was D.O.A. I leaned there helplessly against the railing of his bed as he put his arm over his face and cried.

I'm not sure what was harder on my heart: leaving him there at the hospital that night, knowing he was going into surgery and I'd probably never see him again, or witnessing the deaths of his friends.

Miranda thinks my leaving him there was harder on me.

I was obsessed. Love-struck and obsessed and shocked and hurt. I was awakened that night. In every way.

Miranda used to say a discussion of the odds was irrelevant.

"What happened, happened, and you'll never know why."

But things aren't so cut and dry, to me.

Over the years, every time I visit La Rosa, my chest tightens. My scalp prickles. If the universe threw us together once before, what's next?

Ricardo

"Why did you do it?"

I walk a circle around Holt's office chair, where he sits backwards, his squat legs spread around the rolling chair, his fat stomach pressed against the chair's padded back. His short arms are handcuffed behind him.

Never in the seven years that I've been doing business here have I had a problem with the warden. In the early years, I paid him to look the other way as I…reworked the system. Once I started turning a decent profit, I pulled him in, teaching him how to move discreetly through the internet's black market, teaching him the art of investing, and even allowing him to choose the timing of shipments to hub cities. If I'm this operation's king, Holt is my prime minister.

He leans his cheek against the scratchy, blue fabric of the chair and shuts his pale green eyes. When he opens them, they're red and wet. He heaves a big breath and tears start rolling down his cheeks.

"Tell me why, Holt." I drag the words out, as if I'm talking to an imbecile.

It's all for show. For closure. I already know it doesn't matter what he says. My lieutenants know of his betrayal. Everybody knows. My course of action is already set in stone.

Still, I stand in front of him and listen as he explains about his family. How his ex-wife has brain cancer and her daughter is only four years old. I allow myself to feel sympathy as he tells me how the little girl is under the care of her older sister, a wonderful young woman with a master's degree—but one who can't seem to find a good job within driving range of her mother's cancer clinic.

"It was stupid. So stupid. I needed money," he chokes.

"*More* money," I correct. In the past few years, during the time he's really been involved, I've made Holt a wealthy man.

He casts his eyes to the cement floor.

I step a little closer and catch his gaze. My eyes bore into his. Intimidating him. Not because there's any reason to, but because after eight years here, it's the role I play. "You needed money, so you stole from me."

"I didn't mean it." He strains against the cuffs, locking his jaw and jerking his chin up. "I was gonna pay you back!"

I drop into a crouch, so we're at eye level. "When?"

"When Annabelle finds a good job," he says in a scratchy voice.

"How long do you think it would take for Annabelle to make $800,000?"

He shakes his head. “I’m a fucking fool! I’m sorry, Ric!”

I stand up. “Don’t call me that. You’re not my friend. You’re not even my associate. Do you know what you are, Holt?”

His mouth trembles.

“You’re dead.”

He struggles against the cuffs, his torso flopping against the back of the chair, his face a mask of indignation, followed instantaneously by fear. “No! Forgive me, please! All these years, I’ve never betrayed you! Never once—”

“Until you did.” I look down into his small, green eyes. “You could have asked me for a loan. You could have trusted me to take care of you. But you didn’t. You decided it would be better to take what’s mine.”

His voice cracks. “I’ll make it up to you! I can get your sentence shortened! I can get you women! I can get you—”

“Things I already get myself?” I shake my head. “I don’t need anything from you. I don’t even need to kill you. If I had it my way, I’d cut you off and make you sell that big house you built. But it’s not my decision. There’s a system here, and you’ve left me no choice.”

“No, Ricardo. *Please*.” His voice cracks on the word, and I listen as it fades away to silence. And then the silence is overtaken by a roar.

I turn slowly, my palms already lifting up and out—a fighting stance from the martial arts I’ve learned here.

I walk to the door of the warden’s office, wondering which of my soldiers has failed me. I’ve got men all across this prison, and every one of them knows what I’m doing in this office right now.

I glance at Holt, then step into the narrow hallway with the faded blue floor. All along the walls, men’s hands protrude through bars. The roar is the sound of dozens of men chanting, “SNATCH!”

I squint into the sunlight streaming through the Plexiglas doors at the end of the hallway. A shadowed figure, tall and slender, glides over the powder blue tile. Two steps, stop; three steps, turn around. She brings her hands up to her face, and the chanting grows louder.

“JULIO! JULIO!”

So she's Hispanic.

What Juarez would do if he got his hands on her… The Mexican gang in La Rosa is especially brutal. I glance up at the cameras, and Nose, one of my lieutenants in the cam room, speaks into the Bluetooth in my ear.

"Checked with Lisa—" the woman at the check-through point— "and she's Holt's daughter. Annabelle Mitchell."

For a long moment, my muscles clench.

Annabelle Mitchell.

A common name, I'm sure.

I inhale deeply. Exhale.

I watch as the men reach their foul hands toward her. She shrinks in the middle of the hallway, looking like an angel in a bath of light.

I watch another moment, aroused by her silhouette—long legs and a generous bust—before I put two fingers in my mouth and whistle.

Silence sweeps the hall.

I walk down it slowly, my gaze on her. I don't waste my energy checking to be sure every pair of eyes remains downturned. I have men for that. Soldiers on the floor. They tell me when I'm disrespected; they take care of it.

I approach the woman slowly, knowing that, despite my Downy-fresh, black jumpsuit—a color no one here wears, except for me—I'll probably scare her. Thanks to my daily gym regimen, I'm bigger than I ever was outside, and eight years inside have left me scarred and calloused. I know that, even though I don't particularly feel it.

She's wearing a black skirt and a red sweater. The skin of her hands and throat is lovely cappuccino. Her hair is brown, and tightly coiled. I'm hungry for her face, but she's turned sideways, giving me a view of mostly hair.

Her hair…

She's facing David Baynes' cell, and I know what that sick fuck is doing before I step close enough to see. He's waving his cock at her. I see her eyes widen before she raises a hand to her face and spins around toward me.

The air leaves my lungs.

I can feel the moment recognition becomes mutual. Her shoulders tighten. The hand over her forehead slides down over her mouth, and that flawless swan throat stretches as she lifts her head.

Her hand more falls from her mouth than is lowered by her own design. It flops against her skin-tight skirt, and the men around us shift their weight. They dare not speak.

Her face is wide open, so innocent I want to laugh or cry. Her face is flawless, finest porcelain. Her face is fake. At least I think it's fake.

I'm imagining things.

I'm losing my mind.

Except her lips tremble and tug down. Her eyes, they drink me up. And I see nothing but that night.

It's her.

My angel.

My heart speeds up, as if her presence triggers an interruption in its electrical impulses. My throat goes dry, because I know she's here for me. I can feel it.

The thick scar on my thigh burns.

My dick stiffens.

I close the distance between us with one step and lock my hand around her arm. I drop my head down near hers and murmur, "Quiet and still."

I look up and down each row of steel bars—at the jockers, the punks, the vikings, the tecatos. I drag my dead gaze over all of them, letting them see deep down into me, where I keep the shadows of my sins.

And in a deep, resounding voice, I say, "She's mine."

It echoes off the walls and I can feel the men freeze as the words sink in.

Now that I've marked her, they won't touch her. I've made her safe from murderers, rapists, and serial killers with two words.

I have to speak to her. I need to touch her. I press my fingertips against the small of her back and try to keep my face a blank canvas as her elbow brushes my abdomen. The hall is silent as a tomb, pierced by the staccato of my angel's heels. All I can think about is getting to my cement bungalow. Pulling her sweater over her head. Ripping her bra off.

This woman is *her*. Annabelle Mitchell. And I've grown used to taking what I want.

We're passing the warden's office, our long legs moving perfectly in sync, when I hear a groan. Holt. Fuck!

If I leave him cuffed in here, there's no face to serve as greeter if someone from the state stops by. If I leave him cuffed in there, Annabelle will know.

She's about to find out.

What do I care?

I can make her see my side.

That's ludicrous!

I lead her into the office, feeling a surprising wash of relief as she moves through the doorway. I own this place, but for the first time in years, I'm reminded of how tenuous my hold is. I'm out of here next year if the parole board is sympathetic, and there are a couple of lifers already sharpening their shanks.

I flatten my hand against her back, wanting nothing more than to get her behind this door and lock it.

As if in disagreement, Holt cries out. The woman in front of me dashes to him and cries, "Daddy?"

"Annabelle!" He's made it out of the chair and is lying on the floor, his arms stretched over his head, his brown collared shirt pushed up, revealing his fat, pale belly. "Annabelle!" His face twists as he looks up at her. "What are you doing here?"

I step between the two of them, looking first at Holt and then at her. She's stunning—just as I remember her. For a moment, my words get hung up in my throat, but then I look at Holt and my feelings are muddied. "This is your stepdaughter?"

Holt cranes his neck up, his sweaty face looking pale and older than I've ever seen him. "Annabelle, what are you doing here?" There is frenzy in his voice. Of course there is.

"Dad?" Her voice is raspy, a veil of smoke over decadent darkness. She looks from me to Holt, to me again, to Holt. Her thin, dark eyebrows pinch together. "Dad, what's going on?"

I look her over once more, heels to breasts, and finally, after a moment's hesitation, I allow myself to look into her face again. She looks at me, too. Her eyes blaze. Curiosity or more?

"Annabelle, you need to go." Holt struggles to get into a crawling position, as if he'll be able to get up and help her. He looks ridiculous, a felled hippopotamus. I snort, and he cries, "Please! Don't hurt her! She's innocent!"

Disappointment flits across her face, heeled by skepticism. Her eyes admonish. "What the hell is going on here?"

"Your father stole some money from me. Almost a million dollars. He says he did it for you. You and your mother, and your little sister."

Her mouth falls open.

Holt is curled up in a ball, his face behind his forearm.

"Dad, why? We're doing fine!"

He looks up at her. Presses his lips together. Sobs, "I'm sorry."

"Your father owes me, Annabelle. He owes a debt too large to pay. He's going to die for that."

Her beautiful face pales. She looks from me to him, and back to me. Then steps away from me. "Dad, please tell me you're joking!"

"It's not a joke."

I lean down over Holt and uncuff his hands. I pull him to his feet, drag him to the closet behind his desk, open the door, and lean him against the shelves. With the door half shut behind me, I let my fist have at his face, aiming for the vulnerable places that will bleed a lot without necessarily doing lasting damage. I pound out my frustration, my anxiety, my fear, until Angel is screaming, Holt is crying like a bitch, and finally, her hands are on me. Grabbing at me. Making my cock hungry.

When Holt looks half dead and his shirt is bathed in blood, I grab him by the shoulders, haul him across the room, and shove him out the door.

"Consider the debt paid."

Annabelle

"Oh my God! What the fuck is wrong with you? You almost killed him!"

He stands there, at his full height, in front of Dad's desk. His fisted hands drip blood.

My stomach roils.

He steps around the desk to some metal file cabinets and grabs a bottle of hand sanitizer. He uses tissues and the alcohol-based gel to clean his hands, and I just stand there, watching. My heart beats so hard it hurts.

Even still, he's beautiful. A beautiful monster. Time has been good to his face and heavy on his soul. I can feel the difference in him.

He walks to the door, flips the lock, and turns to me. He's big. My God, he's ripped. His killer's physique is draped in black—black shirt, black pants—which makes his eyes seem darker. His dark hair is cut short, brutally so. His lips—beautiful and lush, always remarked upon by the Hollywood press—are cruel and hard. His throat is thick and strong, his forearms bulging. After a moment's hesitation, I can't keep my eyes from sliding down his body. They're drawn to his thigh, to that twenty-inch gash I watched the nurses staple shut on that awful night—but that's not what holds their attention.

His dick is hard.

And huge. My God, I can see every line of it in those tight pants, and it's as flawless as my recollection: a high-priced dildo, sized XL.

Heat spreads through me, starting in my cheeks and neck and spreading south, fast.

I back away. I don't mean to, but he's that commanding. Sharing air with him intimidates me. Frightens me. Angers me.

"You really hurt Holt. Who the fuck do you think you are? Do you have any morals? Any shame?"

The words are out before I have the chance to bridle them. My eyes pop open. "Sorry. No, I'm not."

His eyes bore into mine. For a halting breath, it feels as if they're reaching into me.

He remembers…

But the softness quickly gives to steel.

He moves quickly, like the superhero he was a lifetime ago, in movies. He catches me around my waist and tosses me against the wall. He moves like a ninja, all sparse utility and lethal grace. I brace myself for the impact of bumping into brick, but his arm behind me shields as it restrains.

He pushes his hips into mine, his chest against my breasts, till the air leaves my lungs and my unease dies in my mind. I'm panting as I look into his face. The cunning eyes; the tiger's hard bone structure.

He sinks his hand into my hair and stands stock still. Only two fingers move, rubbing the curl he's captured.

"I could kill him," he whispers.

"No!"

"Or I could allow you to pay his debt."

I'm so close, I can see his teeth. They're brilliant white, the canines sharp.

"What do I have to do?" My voice trembles, making me feel like the young girl I was when we met.

"You will give yourself to me. Body and soul." His thumb strokes my cheek, so calloused it almost scrapes. "You will be here every day. Ready to give me what I want. Ready to please me." His breath catches. "I'll please you, too, Angel."

His hand reaches between my legs, pushing my thighs apart so he can cup his palm over my pussy. I wonder if he can feel the heat there.

His gaze, directed downward, flickers up to mine. I'm looking for the guy I met that night. Twenty-one and famous, a renowned actor who'd just killed his three best friends in a horrifying car wreck. There is nothing left of him. These eyes are hard and cold. If they're a window to his soul, I don't want to get anywhere near him.

It's as if he can hear my thoughts. He stills, just staring at me.

I can't breathe.

A second later, he reaches up my skirt and pushes his hand under the elastic of my thong. His fingertips brush my warm lips, then curl, jerking up so he's ripped my panties clean in half.

"Let me stroke this hot cunt of yours. I can smell it. Sweet as honey. Are you willing to give it to me? I'll be good to it. So good," he murmurs. He glides a finger lazily between my lips, making me gasp. I grind against the wall. "But that won't change what this is. You'll be my whore, Belle. You'll be a killer's slut. Are you willing to do that?"

He finds my clit and traces lazy circles around it. I can't think, can only look into his stunning face. "You'd…really kill him?" I can't comprehend.

He nods. "Tonight. I've already given the order."

"Sick," I hiss.

"There are rules. He knew them, Angel."

"I'm not your Angel."

He pushes a finger inside me, then another. I whimper. Close my eyes. What's wrong with me? What does it say about me that I'm letting him do this? "I don't…want you. You're *sick*." I clench around his fingers, wanting more. I open my eyes and am stunned anew by who I'm looking at. Cal Hammond—prisoner. Without thinking, I reach up and grab his shoulder. "You don't look like a prisoner."

He takes my hand and pushes it off him, not harsh but not gentle. "I'm not. I'm a don. I run things here. All the business, all the gangs. I'm going to run you, too."

He flicks the fingers inside my pussy and I sag against the wall. As my knees go soft, I sink down on him, pushing his fingers deeper into me.

"Ricardo," I murmur.

"Not my name."

"What is?"

He kneels down, so I can feel his breath on my cunt. "Beast."

I writhe my ass against the wall, trying to get away from him. He holds onto my thighs and shakes his head.

"Are you sure you want to do this? Reject my offer? If you do…"

I slap his face. It's not a decision. I just…react. He pulls his fingers out of me, leaving me cold and hollow. I can barely stand on my own legs. I look into his face. I'm so confused.

"Who are you? What is *wrong* with you?"

His face hardens. "Will you accept my arrangement, Annabelle? Yes or no?"

My heart thuds hard. "Why do you call me Angel?" *Please remember. Please remember me.*

He stands up, capturing my wrist as he moves. He's so close, I can feel his breath on my forehead. He strokes my cheek. "You look like an angel."

So he doesn't remember. Or if he does, he won't say it.

"What arrangement?" I whisper.

"Your body. That's my price."

The tingling starts in my inner thighs and climbs, up to my cunt, into my belly, where it crawls deep down inside and goes nuclear. I'm so wet, practically dripping. So off-kilter. Dumb, blind, lost.

"What if I don't do it?" I whisper. "What if I say 'no'?"

"We discussed this. I'll have to punish your stepfather in the only way I can."

"You have a choice!" My voice echoes, then dies off.

"*He* had a choice, and he chose wrong. Do you think I pity him? Do you think I pity any man who chooses something reckless?"

I look at him, and all I can think is, *You were reckless.*

I step a little closer to him. "I don't understand. How can you expect forgiveness if you can't extend it? Everyone deserves compassion, Ric— *Beast.*"

He shakes his head, and I'm stunned to see the anger fall away. He looks desolate. So cold.

"No one deserves compassion. Not a man like Holt, and not a man like me." He takes a long stride back, widening the gap between us. He folds his arms over his chest, and I can feel my legs begin to shake because I know I have to choose.

"What will it be, Angel? You're out of time."

I shake my head. "Do you remember me?" If he doesn't, I don't know how I'll do this.

He frowns, and it's clear he has no idea what I'm talking about. "If we'd met before, I would remember you."

I put my hand over my chest. It hurts a little. More than it should, probably.

"Ricardo, I don't know if I can—"

"*Not* Ricardo." His long legs close the distance between us. Strong fingers clutch my shoulder, press me into the wall. *How can you not remember?*

His hand pushes up my skirt again. He parts my lips with two deft fingers and shoves three fingers into me. I'm so wet, it doesn't hurt. I simply *ache*.

"Never call me Ricardo." His face, so close to mine. "Never call me anything but Beast."

"It's not a name," I pant.

"It's my name." His hazel eyes burn mine.

"If I do this—"

He shakes his head. "It's best you learn now. Never ask for anything from me. I'll never give it to you. You take me as I am, Angel. Only as I am."

"I don't know who you are," I whisper.

And that's when he scoops me into his arms. My heart soars. Until he lays me on the ground and sinks down between my legs. He leans down, and for a moment I think he's going to kiss my pussy. Like that very first time. Make me see stars.

Instead, he spreads my legs wider and takes his pants down. His cock springs free, and it's so hard it's pointing straight up, the head of him furious red, his balls drawn tight and impatient.

"Let me show you who I am."

With one hand, he holds both of mine over my head. He looks into my eyes. His are screaming: what? He thumbs my slick folds, parting them, then plunges in—hard! So very hard.

"I—" he thrusts— "am no one—" he thrusts— "that you know. I never will be. I will hurt you—" he thrusts— "for my pleasure—" he thrusts— "I will make you pay—" thrust— "Every day you fuck me, I will make you pay."

He thrusts brutally hard, so hard the carpet burns my ass. So hard I can feel him buried deeper than anyone before.

I moan.

"Your call, Angel. Your choice."

His eyes, when I look up at him, are redolent. His eyes—they beg me to say "no."

But I'm hungry. Foolish. Daring. Reckless. I'm dancing in the eye of the storm. Drowning in a fairy tale. Living in a dream. I can't say no. Not even if I lived to be a thousand.

BEAST

Volume 2

CHAPTER 1

Annabelle

THERE'S A WINDOW UNIT humming in the office, and that's all the sound in the world as I try to straighten out my clothes. My shirt is pushed almost over my head, and my bra is shoved above my breasts, pushing them down and out, as if they're on display for him. My skirt is jacked up past my belly button. I tug it down to my hips and put my bra and blouse to rights. My panties lie on the cement floor, a slip of red silk he just…annihilated.

My hands shake as I bend to pick it up.

He's leaning on the desk, just watching me. My jaw tenses and I can feel pressure build behind my eyes when I remember that night, so long ago, at the house party. The way he brought me a cloth.

I move to tuck the thong into my bra, and he steps to me, snatching it away before I even pull the neckline of my blouse down.

"Mine," he says flatly.

I think I may hate this—the way my eyes widen, the way I swallow whatever I might normally say and just let him have it. It isn't that I want to submit to him so much as I just can't seem to form coherent thoughts here in this little room. He fills it way too thoroughly.

Up and down, my gaze flits over him. I'm like a computer program trained to map this man's body. I note a thick scar on the back of his right hand, a fresh, pink lightning-bolt-shaped scar just underneath his jaw. His face is different. Well, of course. I can see every change, because it's been years since he's appeared in a magazine or on TV.

By any account, he's gotten even more handsome. Harsher, yes, but also more filled out: his cheekbones higher, lips more rapt, his eyes darker, more cunning. His hair is shorter now, nothing to tug.

In his black pants and shirt, he looks like the grim reaper. Not the Hollywood kind. Everything about him has turned *realer*. I can feel it.

I press my lips together and try my best to turn off my feelings. If I don't, I'm afraid I'll cry.

"I don't know if I can do this." Why? Because despite the way he man-handled me, my body is still craving his. Part of me wants to push my skirt up again, lie down on the cold floor, and let him fuck me until I can't see straight. But the other part of me—the emotional part? That part wants to run.

"You just did," he says. "You bought him a reprieve of one day."

I lose my battle with my tears. They fill my eyes and threaten to streak down my cheeks. *How did you get like this?* I want to ask, but it's a stupid question. Prison: that's how.

He blinks, and I can't stand how beautiful he is, how wrong he is in this setting. How wrong it is that he just hurt Holt. Maybe Holt did cheat him. As I've grown older, I've learned Holt isn't the perfect "Dad" I used to think he was. But that doesn't erase the wrongness of what Cal—Ricardo—*Beast* did to him just now.

"I really don't know you at all, do I?"

"Of course you don't. Why would you?"

I swallow and avert my eyes. Just because that night was pivotal for me doesn't mean he should remember me.

I manage to blink away my tears. I wrap my arms around myself and get the nerve to look at him again. "What are the terms of this?" My voice is soft. My gaze on him is ginger. Because he kind of hurts my eyes.

"Whatever I say they are. Every day, for three hours."

I shake my head. "I can't." I have such an easy, safe way out. "I have to find a job."

"This is your job."

"No, I mean I really have to get a job. I have…bills."

He turns around and plucks a pen and a sticky note from the desk. He props the pad of yellow Post-Its in one big palm and looks up at me. "What's your bank account number?"

I laugh—just a little bit, despite myself. "You think I know that?"

He arches one dark brow. "No?"

"Not right off." I move my arm to dig into my purse, then realize I didn't bring it with me. I turn a slow circle. There's my brown leather clutch, on the floor by the door. I scoop it up and pull out the business card that has my bank account number written on the back.

I cup it in my hand and look back up at him. "What are you going to do with it? I mean…exactly?"

"I'm going to put money in it, Angel."

I bite my lip and try to think of how to get my point across without coming out and saying that I'm broke. "I need to be sure it's enough. For me to…do this. And not find another job where I'll be treated better." I can feel my cheeks heat a little, and it makes me feel ridiculous. Why does he affect me this way? If I feel this way every time I come here, I'm going to get broken.

"I'm not a hooker, you know. I care about my dad, but I'm not having sex any time you ask me to. I'm not that kind of person."

He closes the distance between us with supernatural-seeming speed. His hands are on my face, bringing my eyes level with his. And his are blazing.

"What kind of person aren't you, Angel? The kind of person who fucks without a thought? Who spends half of the day flat on her back, being pounded to oblivion? Or is it me? You're not the kind of person who fucks someone like me?"

I blink, and his hands, on the sides of my face, gentle a little. "It's not you," I murmur. "I'm just…not a whore."

"You're not a whore. You're *my* whore. If I want to pay you for your time, it's because I take care of what is mine."

He releases my face, and I stare up at him, searching his Cal Hammond face and finding no trace of the man that was.

"I'm not yours," I whisper.

"You are mine. You're about to sell yourself to me."

"Because I have to. Because…"

"Because you want to. You want this. Why can't you just admit it, Angel?"

My mouth wants to open—to admit he's right—but my battered pride prevents it. He's just so…arrogant.

I hand him the card and fold my arms over my chest, watching as he steps back, leans the backs of his thighs against the desk, and starts jotting down my account number. Now's the time to say more. When he's not looking at me, crossing the wires inside my brain.

"What you did to Holt was unacceptable. It was horrible. I don't care if you are in prison. If you've turned into someone…violent. That doesn't make it right. I can't handle that."

He blinks coolly. "I'll decide what you can handle. Incidentally, I'm not in the habit of hurting those who work with me. Of course," he says drolly, "I'm not in the habit of being swindled out of just shy of a million dollars, either. Holt is special that way."

I want to tell him, *He was doing it for us*. For Mom and Adrian and me. Instead, I nod and look away.

A second later, he hands me back my card. I slip it back into my clutch, and gasp as he wraps his arms around my waist and lifts me off the floor. Heat spears through me, making my entire body tingle as he hoists me over his shoulder and steps toward the door.

"What are you doing?" I cry.

"Getting you out of here," he says as he twists the doorknob. "I've got a riot to handle, Angel."

And, to my astonishment, that seems to be true. The hallway he whisks me down is absolutely silent—it's almost weird; the men won't even look at him; the guards just nod us past—but from somewhere not so far away, I hear the roar of many male voices.

I open my mouth to ask him if everything will be okay. I'm worried about Holt. Worried about him, even—just a little. But

I can tell I shouldn't speak while we're in this hall. Everything about the atmosphere is reverent.

I hold onto his shoulders as his long strides eat up the distance between the hallway and the prison's main entrance. I'm stunned when the woman at the security check point waves us through, and he carries me past two more guards, through two more sets of doors—all the way out of the building.

He sits me on my feet, and I'm double-stunned to see my car pull up in front of us. A trustee wearing orange steps out, and the ignition cuts off, as if by magic.

I feel his hand pressed against the small of my back for just a breath of time. "Get out of here. A car will come for you tomorrow."

I swear, as I get into my seat and he lords over me, I hear him say "Eighteen."

This is the weirdest thing that's ever happened to me. Hands down. I never thought I'd be raising a child at my age, so that's weird, too. But this is weirder.

All night, I dream of Beast. The dreams are strange. He's shirtless, lying on the desk in Holt's office with his big, hard, pretty dick out. I can see his hand stroke up and down it. I can feel my pussy getting wet.

Every muscle on his shoulders, chest, and abs stands out: pure male perfection. I'm standing above him, and he's reaching up, stroking my neck. Stroking my hair. Pulling me on top of him and kissing my breasts. He's banging his fingers into my cunt. He's whispering my name. His fingers plunge in. Slide out. His hand, on my shoulder, is caressing me.

And then he pushes me off of him. My feet hit the floor with a gentle smack, and his eyes harden as he tells me to go.

It's not because he doesn't want me. It's because he cares for me.

That's how, when I'm tangled in my covers, drifting somewhere in between my dreamland and the pre-dawn light, I know I'm only dreaming.

I check my bank account after I shower, and it's still dismal. We're down to eleven hundred dollars, which is pretty much five dollars when you have the medical bills we do. I spend the morning in a state of flux, wondering what I'll do if this doesn't come through. Maybe I should give in and file for unemployment. What other options do I have?

One of my friends from UCLA keeps joking about how I should sell my used panties on some pervy web site. How many pairs of panties would it take to pay the bills?

I set my phone down on the bathroom counter. Lean toward the mirror and press my palms against my tight curls. So I'm broke. This is a problem I understand well enough. If the car never comes, I'll figure out something. I always do.

But what if he *does* put some money into my account? What if a car really does arrive, as promised?

I haven't called Holt, even to check on him, and I guess it's because, deep down, I don't want to know what's going on. I don't want to know how probable it is that this is happening. That my spending three hours per day with Cal—with *Beast*—is the only thing keeping Holt from being killed for his embezzling.

Aside from the general insanity of Beast's proposal, I'm also having trouble wrapping my mind around the fact that I encountered him again at all. And in such a way…

I rub balm over my lips and try to shut my brain off for a few minutes, but it's not happening. I see his face on the cover of the magazines I used to hide under my covers. I hear his voice in Holt's office.

"I am no one that you know. I will hurt you for my pleasure. I will make you pay. Every day you fuck me, I will make you pay."

Does he mean that?

Yesterday, it didn't take him very long to come. I came just a second or so later. Which shocked me.

He pulled out and spilled on the floor, and wiped it up with tissues from Holt's desk. And I felt shame. And elation. And, more than anything else, confusion.

How does someone change that much?

I keep feeling like yesterday wasn't real—but it was. If the car shows up, what will I really do?

Would he really hurt Holt if I refuse him?

He said three hours a day, but he didn't say three hours of sex per day. What would we do if we didn't have sex? And if we did… I feel warm between my legs and shift my stance a little.

I re-tuck the towel that's sliding down my still-damp breasts and dab some moisturizer underneath my eyes and on my throat.

I must be even more messed up than I thought. That I didn't refuse him outright when he made his screwed up offer. That I didn't ask more questions about how he has so much control. How does a prisoner have that much control? It doesn't make sense. He said he runs the gangs, so there's that, but that doesn't explain how he was able to walk outside the prison doors.

How is it possible that a former celebrity—a rich boy, sent to prison for a fatal car wreck—was able to turn into…well, Beast?

I look into my brown eyes in the mirror and try to imagine the guy from the house party. It's been a long time, but I have flickering memories of that night that changed my worldview in a moment. Sometimes when I dream, I can still smell the tang of his blood. Hear the helicopter blades coming to save him. But those images have been painted over by the vivid, ultra-ripped, dirty-talking monster from prison.

I think I could hate him.

I think I could save him.

Stupid girl. So dangerous…

I finish my lotion and am stepping into my bedroom to get dressed when my phone rings. I jump, and my poorly tucked towel falls right to the floor, leaving my body as naked as I feel.

I snatch the towel up, wrap it back around myself, and check the name on my phone: Holt.

I let it ring one more time while I debate answering. Then I take a big breath. "Hi."

"Annabelle. I'm glad you answered."

"Yeah?"

There's a pause—not much of one, but a pause during which I can almost see his lips tuck down into a frown. "Annabelle, honey. I'm sorry. Really sorry about yesterday. Makes this old man feel a long ways away from proud. Know what I mean?"

I nod.

"I would tell you I did it for you, for you and Mom and Adrian, but that would be a lie, and I don't lie to you. I've been greedy. Got caught up in the money and I—"

"Dad, *what* money?" I don't understand what kind of business deal my dad could have with Cal Hammond.

Silence spreads across the line, and when my Dad speaks next, I can hear the dark tones of evasion in his voice. "Details aren't important, dear. I did some things that were wrong, and I got what was coming to me. The important thing… The thing I want you to know—that is, I'm not a victim. I don't know what you said to him—I don't even really remember how I ended up in the hall, and you shut up in the office with him. But I know one thing…" His voice cracks. "That's not the way things should have been. I failed you."

I shake my head. The ice around my heart begins to drip a little. "Dad, you didn't fail me. It sounds like you failed *you.* You almost got killed! How can he do that, anyway? You're the warden."

"You're probably scared to death," he says, evading my question. "And—I'm going to be sexist here—I've thought on it, and it would be better if you never come back here. The men here… After you left…" More silence. Followed by a gruff: "You're safe. That's all that matters."

"What are you talking about? What happened after I left?" Is he referencing the riot Beast mentioned? How did Beast even know there was a riot? He mentioned it before we left Holt's office yesterday.

"Prison politics are none of your concern. You've got other burdens. And—well, that brings me to the one piece of good news I have for you, Annabelle, honey. I've got a way for you to focus on family." A pause, during which I can tell he's smiling. "I've found a job for you. Beast—er, Ricardo—he and I have made amends, and he had an idea that's good. You're going to be hired to organize a prison library. You'll solicit donated books, and Ricky will finance e-reading devices. Those newfangled things—"

"I know what an e-reader is, Dad."

"Good. So you'll set it all up. I know it's not in your chosen profession, but it's something at least. I've got all the paperwork ready, and I've emailed it the application, which will get approved without hassle. There's no nepotism concerns because you're not my biological daughter. The pay's not much, but it's something. Fifteen dollars an hour."

My heart beats hard. He just said he thinks I shouldn't go back to La Rosa. So…"I'm doing this from home? Not at the prison?"

"That's right," he says proudly.

I sink down onto the edge of my bed and try to get my breath.

"It wasn't me," he says. "It was Ricardo's idea. And speaking of that, he told me that you met before. Is that what happened, when he locked you in that room with him? He cut the cameras off. I don't like that, but he said the two of you were just getting reacquainted."

I feel a blast of heat between my legs.

My throat tightens. "Dad… I don't like Ricardo all that much. Can we just not talk about him anymore?"

"I'm sorry again," he says remorsefully. "I hope he didn't treat you badly."

My cheeks burn. *He fucked me like an animal—and I came.* I press my lips together. "No. He didn't."

"I'm glad to hear that. Annabelle, I've gotta go now. I'm leaving for a business trip in two hours. Something urgent down in Honduras."

"What? *Honduras?*"

"Don't worry about me. Only lasts ten days. Ricky has forgiven me and all is well. I love you, Annabelle."

When I hang up, I'm more confused than ever. I slip into my powder blue robe and walk into the hallway. I can hear Adrian and Holly through the door to Adrian's room, talking about Cinderella's hair. I booked Holly every day this week, all day, because I didn't know when the car might come for me, and I thought I had the money.

Tears fill my eyes, then spill down my cheeks—because I'm stupid. So stupid. Why do I want him? He's right. I don't know him. Not at all. And what I know—what I know of him recently—is terrible.

He treated me with no regard. No care. And I'm so pathetic, I actually got off. *Because you're obsessed with him. Because your life is so empty.*

I step back into my room and try to let my feelings ebb. I should be happy I don't have to go back to the prison. Obviously, he was just threatening me. Toying with me. Maybe that's why I feel so foolish. So…used.

He wasn't going to kill Holt. There's no way. Despite how Holt sounded on the phone with all his 'Beast has forgiven me' babblings, it doesn't make sense that a prisoner would hold any sway over a warden.

I guess I'm the sucker here.

I walk into my room and shut the door. Sit down on my bed and put my head in my hands. I ask myself what on earth is wrong with me. When did I get so lonely? So desperate?

I tell myself I'm glad his proposal turned out to be some perverse bluff.

That's the moment that the doorbell rings.

CHAPTER 2

Beast

I LEAN AGAINST THE WALL, in the low-ceilinged basement hallway where eleven cells are devoted to solitary confinement.

The knuckles of my hand—the one that holds the phone—still drip blood. Franklin Maloney: a woman killer and one of the highest ranking Black Guerrillas here. He's the one who started the riot over Annabelle. He's the one who'll get daily beatings until he can't disrespect her anymore. Then the guards will spread the word that he's been cowed into submission by me, and I can let him back into the general population.

"Is Holt still in the dark?" asks the voice on the other end of the line. "Does he know the plans you have for her?"

"Yes, and no, of course he doesn't. My proclivities are none of his damn business."

"She's his daughter," he says.

"She's my plaything. Now quit prying."

"Who do you think is in charge here?" he asks me.

"In this way, I am. Moving on."

He chuckles. "How are things going on the Juarez Cartel? Any new intel? Progress on the accounts?"

"Still haven't gotten into the Swiss one. The second one, rather. First one's still like I told you last time."

"Keep trying."

"Planning on it," I say.

"And the riot?" he asks.

"I've got Maloney nearly subdued."

Again, his lazy chuckle. "The mighty Beast. I assume your cover is still intact?"

I snicker. "What do you think, dumbass?"

"You always were a compelling actor."

"Guilty as charged. Till next time." I toss my prepaid phone onto the brick floor, stomp it until it's unequivocally broken, toss the pieces in a garbage can, and walk back upstairs.

Along the way, I stop and shoot the shit with a few of the guards. Give an update on when my next deposits will hit their accounts, and listen to their wish lists. The money keeps them compliant, and doing them occasional, pseudo-political favors here makes them feel as if we're friends.

I use one of the guards' codes to gain entry to a few personnel passageways that will shorten my walk, and point myself toward the middle of the hexagonal prison. Toward the kitchen, where I wash my hands, and then to the back segment of the main building, toward the unfinished add-on that will, some months from now, become the prison's library, thanks to a generous donation from the Hammond Trust.

I enter the guard's pass code into another keypad and the door clicks open. I step into the wide, tall space—shaped like a beehive, with windows punched into the conical ceilings. It's all just plywood now. Plywood reinforced with steel on the exterior, and triple-paned bullet-proof windows that turn the sun's light slightly amber.

I look around the room, where built-in shelves, benches, and even window seats are already taking shape. The grant from my family's foundation pays for the books and any non-prison workforce, but the interior construction is being done by us, almost exclusively.

Near the back of the geodesic building, there's a little computer lab, partitioned off from the rest of the space. Already, men are constructing desks. Inside a drawer on one of them, I keep my tools. Things to spice up the conjugal visits I schedule once or twice a month, when my needs grow too great to manage.

I tuck the little cedar box under my arm and walk back into the main room—empty at this hour, while most of the men are doing rec.

I stand at a pile of plywood balanced on a desk and start measuring off sheets for various projects. In between measuring and leaving penciled notches on the boards, I watch the little steel door out in front of me.

Annabelle

The man ringing my doorbell looks a little like a young Bill Cosby.

He's wearing a deep blue, canvas jacket over a brown guard's uniform he's paired with black boots, and when I answer the door, he surprises me by looking not at my bust, but right into my eyes, and holding out his hand.

"Clinton," he says, perhaps a little cheerfully.

I shake his hand, then take a half step back. "May I help you?"

"You're Annabelle?"

I nod.

"I'm here to get you."

I think I know where he means to take me, but still, I'm having a little trouble believing it. "Where will we go?" I try—just to hear his answer.

One eyebrow quirks. "La Rosa. Beast told me you knew the score."

Knew the score? I frown. "I'm not so sure I do."

"You're helping with the library? That right?"

Huh. I thought that was only from a distance.

"He wants to show you the layout I think. Talk planning." The man smirks. "Probably fuck that tight ass."

I gape at him.

"Sorry, ma'am. I got a prison mouth."

"Yeah. I guess you do." I look him over again, then say, "Hold on, please. I'll be back in a minute."

I close the door in his face and stand on the interior side of it with my hand over my chest. I can't really go with him! The insane girl buried several layers behind the usual, rational, boring Annabelle tries to argue *yes, you can*, but when I sift through my memories for something comforting to cling to—a thought that will make me feel like I can do this—absolutely nothing comes to mind. It's true: I don't know Cal/Ricardo/Beast. I don't even know his name. And what I know of him is scary. *Admit it, Annabelle. You don't know what he'll do to you.*

He wouldn't hurt you.

He could, though.

Not physically.

Is that all that matters?

I don't know!

I walk down the narrow, faux hardwood hallway. I stop outside Mom's room and listen to the gentle puff and pull of her oxygen machine. I could step inside, sit down, read a book to her. If I'm very lucky—or very unlucky, depending on my tolerance for pain—she might open her eyes and train her gaze in the general direction of my face.

I could go into Adrian's bedroom and help her braid a baby doll's hair. Tell Holly she can take off early.

I linger outside Ad's door for a few minutes, listening to her postulate on the mysteries of how her doll will learn to walk with fabric feet.

My heart is beating so hard, I feel ill.

How will I feel if I don't go? What will happen to Holt if I don't go? Was he lying when he told me they'd worked things out? I shut my eyes. I can still see Hal— *Beast's* fist swinging in between the door frame and the half-shut closet door. Can still see little drops of Holt's blood flying through the air.

If I go with the man at my front door, I won't be dumb about it. I can't harbor any illusions about why this is happening. He doesn't remember me. He isn't obsessed with me—*the way you are with him.* He's an opportunistic…predator.

If I go, I will probably regret it.

If I don't…?

I take a few steps in the direction of the front door, then turn and look back down the hallway.

I feel the turning of wheels inside my head, and it's decided by some deep, executive part of me: I'm going. I know I'll regret it, but I'm going anyway.

Because I want to know what happens.

Because, despite the abject stupidity of it, I want to feel his body over mine again.

Not 'want to'.

Need to.

I walk quickly back down the hallway and say goodbye to Holly. I kiss Adrian and check in with Mom's nurse. Mom is sleeping: very normal. Then I pull a black sweater over the white tank top I'm wearing with jeans and boots, and step out onto the walkway.

Clinton is still there, looking totally neutral, as if I didn't just make him wait ten minutes while I wandered around my house trying not to pass out from the stress of my decision.

He walks a half a step in front of me as we traverse the railed, cement walkway, moving toward the stairwell that will take us from my family's third-floor unit to the parking lot.

"How is it," I ask as we walk down the stairs, "that you're coming to get me on Beast's orders, when you're an employee and he's a prisoner?"

He laughs affably. "That's a good question," he says.

"How did he get that way? Where he has so much authority?"

Clinton shrugs. "It happened gradually. He's good with managing people. He throws in some perks, too."

"You mean he pays you off? He pays off all the guards to let him do whatever he wants?"

Clinton nods, a lighthearted bob of his head. "To do what he asks. It's not bad for any of us."

"But this is a federal prison! There should be…rules."

He gives me a look that says *yeah, right, honey. Keep on dreaming*. "Crazier shit goes on in the prison every day. There're always gangs, always somebody in charge. Gang leaders running the streets on the outside from behind their bars. That's just the way things are. Rules—they don't matter at La Rosa."

I nod, although I really don't understand what he's describing, and we start walking through the parking lot. "How long did it take him to become the Beast?"

He laughs as we approach a black Ford Explorer with a state tag. "He ain't 'the Beast.'" He opens my door for me. "Just Beast. And it didn't take him long. After he killed Rupert Warren, it was fast."

He walks around to the driver's seat as my gaze swoops over the car's interior. I zero in on a red cigarette lighter in one of the cup holders, and a La Rosa staff badge on the dash.

"Buckle up," he tells me in his Southern drawl.

I do, and he backs out.

"Rupert Warren? I've never heard that name." If Ricardo killed someone in prison, wouldn't it make the news?

"Well he got beat the shit up by your Beast, broken nose. Went to his head and killed him." He turns onto the street that will lead us to the highway that will lead us to La Rosa.

"Went to his head?" I frown.

"Nose right up into the brain," he says as he steers us toward the desert.

I nod slowly. "Oh."

"He's made the best of himself, Beast. Don't let him fool you. He's not like some of them others."

Geez. I pick at my jeans. I'm not sure I want to imagine what the others must be like.

"He's not a moral man, but he understands morality. He's off the compass, you know?" I nod a little bit, even though I don't. "He's not *on* the moral compass, but he knows there is one. That's a good thing.

Hmm. That makes a bit more sense.

"So he really runs the…gangs or whatever?"

Clinton's eyes meet mine. "Or whatever. Prison's gotten better since he got here. He got the men in line. Put some structure into place."

"My Dad—Holt—he didn't do that?"

He scoffs. "Holt's the worst warden we've had in years. Doesn't know his left foot from a hole in the ground."

"What does that mean?"

"Mean's he's an idiot. No offense, ma'am."

"None taken?" I rub the bridge of my nose. "Holt doesn't know you're here, does he?"

He shakes his head. "He's gone."

"Where?" I ask. I want to see if he tells me the same thing Holt did.

"Family vacation. Shouldn't you know that?"

I chew my lip. "Guess it's his new wife. Bea. I'm not a big fan of her." Maybe that's why he said he was going out of the country for business. Because he didn't want to tell me he went on a family vacation with Bea and her 17-year-old son, Luke.

I picture that for a few minutes while we drive in silence. Short, round, fair-skinned, red-haired Holt, holding hands with tall, blonde Bea, while sulky Luke stands behind them, throwing rocks overboard. In my imagining, they're on a cruise ship. No puffs from the oxygen machine in the background—that's for sure. I scold myself for being bitter and look at the road.

After a while, Clinton turns the radio up: some station playing a lot of old-school Brittney Spears. "Kinda music that makes you feel upbeat," he explains, and I almost laugh.

We're nearing the prison now. He presses the brakes, tugs his jacket off and tosses it in the back seat. He clips his badge onto his shirt and touches the plastic tag hanging from the rear view mirror, as if he needs the physical confirmation that it's there.

We pass the huge, cement sign: LA ROSA PRISON – STATE OF CALIFORNIA. The road goes from old asphalt to dirt, and the Explorer bounces over it.

The moment we sight the first tall, barbed-wire fence, my stomach does a back flip. I've been here at least a dozen times in my life, but today is different. Today, I'm here because I've made a questionable decision.

I turn over the why of it in my head as Clinton slows the SUV beside a metallic-looking tower bearing several key pads.

Why? I fold it up and hold it. Squeeze it like a dirty tissue. Toss it over my shoulder, because the truth is—I don't have the slightest idea what's behind this particular unwise choice. You could put it down to pure obsession.

Clinton rolls his window down, reaches out, and punches in a code. On the other side of the barbed-wire fence, I see a flash of green light: acknowledgement that Clinton got the code right. The fence—which, evidently, has wheels—rolls slowly open, just wide enough for a car's passage, and Clinton gasses it.

A second later and we're through, and the person at a small kiosk topped with red and green, police-style lights strolls out. It's a tall man wearing the same outfit as Clinton's, only blue.

He walks over to the Explorer, leans inside, and looks right at me for a long, assessing moment. My throat tightens.

Then his pale blue gaze drags over Clinton's face. "This your cargo, Clint?"

Clinton nods, and the guard rolls his eyes. "Looks 'special' to me."

Clinton shrugs. "I'm not one to judge, sir. Special cargo is special cargo."

The man in blue steps back, waves his arm, and a second later, when he disappears inside the kiosk, another fence rolls open: this one shorter and less prison-y, but still topped with barbed wire.

I want to ask on whose order Clinton went to fetch 'special cargo,' but I think I already know: Beast's. He really does call the shots here.

Clinton repeats the code-punching at one more keypad—this one attached to a very ineffective-seeming mechanical arm that bars our path—and then we're in the clear. Sort of. The prison parking lot is smooth, black asphalt. It's basically a circle that runs all around the hexagonal facility. Every however many feet, near the outside of the lot, there's a tower that holds an armed guard, looking down on come and go traffic.

"That make you uncomfortable?" Clinton asks me as he navigates the spottily filled lot.

I shrug. "Not my first time here."

He chuckles and gives me a smirk. "I don't think it'll be your last."

My face reddens, more out of indignity than embarrassment. "Does everybody know I'm coming here?"

Why did I do this?!

Holt said everything was okay!

LIAR. SUCH A LIAR. Even lying to myself. I'm here because I want to be.

Foolish.

Masochistic.

Fed up.

Trapped.

Maybe I need to have something go horribly wrong. So the fact that my mom is dying in our apartment while Adrian plays IV-fluids Barbie isn't the worst thing in my life. Maybe just one time, I want to pick my own poison.

Clinton parks the car and leads me through the raggedy grass that fringes the building. I feel like a lamb being led to slaughter. Except my face is red. Heat brews somewhere deep down in my belly, suspiciously close to my girly bits. My eyes water. Adrenaline, I tell myself. I've got way too much adrenaline going through my veins right now.

"You heard me, didn't you?" Clinton asks, pausing on our trek to wherever.

"Umm? Maybe not?" I raise my eyebrows.

"I said nobody knows. You're a big secret. Only Memphis, back there at the gate, myself, and some of Beast's one-to-ones."

"What's a one-to-one?"

"You know, some of his right-hand men." Clinton laughs. "Nobody is gonna know, girl. Last time you came, you caused a riot."

"I did?"

He nods. We're walking right beside the building, following its every hexagonal turn. He gestures me to stop, and I notice we've walked from the front of it to the back. Just out in front of us, connected to the back of the hexagon by a tunnel-like hallway, is a big, plywood structure shaped a little like a bullet.

"What is this?"

"This," he says with a dramatic wave, "is the library we're building."

"Back up a minute, though. Why was there a riot?" I want to know the answer to this question before I go inside.

Clinton shrugs. “Someone got his sights set on you. Tried to make a move to…you know, get you. Snatch you up and get a taste of that Julio pussy.”

My eyes widen. “Julio?”

“Hispanic. Latina. You’re not white, are you?”

“Does it matter?”

“Here it does.”

“Julio is La Rosa slang for Hispanic. Anyway, this guy, the one who started the uprising—he’s got some supporters. Trying to be the number one of his people’s clan. A little emotion got out of control and you’ve got a riot. People flexing their muscle, trying to look like they own this place.”

“But they don’t? Because Beast does?” He nods. “By clan, do you mean the other prisoners of that same race?”

He nods. “That’s how we do it here in prison.” He nods ahead, at the spot where the closed walkway leads from the hexagon to the bullet—I mean, library. “There’s a door. I’ve got a key. I oversee construction here. I’m one of the guards that does that. I can let you in. Patricia and Fred—they’re the checkpoint supervisors for guests—both of them already know. Beast is there today. Most of the other men, they’re working on special projects in another area of the unit.”

I nod, and we start walking toward this door on the other side of the tunnel. “Do you always do what he asks?”

“There are junior wardens,” he says. “Three of them. Perkins, Lully, and Perez. I’m under Perkins. Perkins told me to do this, I do it. Perkins and Beast, they on good terms.”

“And Perkins does what Beast wants?” I bite my lip as a breeze whips my hair, and little raindrops start to fall, cold on my scalp. “What happens if he gets in trouble? Beast, I mean.”

“He’s a model prisoner.”

“Are you serious?”

“Of course.” His face is a mask. I can’t tell if he’s serious or sarcastic.

We bridge the dirt-patched grass in silence, side by side, and then he leads me around the back of the library building. On the other side of the tunnel that connects prison to library, there’s a small, steel door.

“Fire exit,” he tells me with a wink.

He waves his badge over a little rubbery-looking square beside the handle, and it clicks and flashes green.

He nods at the door, and I wrap my hand around the handle.

My palm tingles. My brain tingles. My breaths grow shallow.

"Good luck," he says, and tips an imaginary hat.

I think I hear him chuckle as he walks away, but I'm too busy peering into the building to know for sure.

It's shadowy inside, as if the only light is the sunlight streaming through windows in that high, dome-like ceiling.

I step inside, and am reminded, strangely, of a cathedral. Everything is bare wood: raw, unsanded. Wooden ceilings, wooden floors, and walls, with scaffolding here and there. Square windows punch into the walls. Round ones dot the ceiling. Shelves line every wall, and little window-seat alcoves break up the semi-circle walls. It's as if my eyes know just where he is before I actually set my gaze on him—because I can't bring myself to look dead at the center of the room until I've checked out every other detail.

When I do, I feel the air whoosh out of my lungs.

He leans on a ladder, arms folded, looking enormously bulky in just jeans, which hang loose around his *holy fuck yes* hips. In the dim gray light streaming through the windows, I can see his body is covered with a sheen of sweat.

As I step toward him, he leans down and sets a sheet of plywood on the floor. His eyes never leave mine.

They're doing something to me. Making me feel…almost high. I stand there, with my sweater tugged around myself, staring at him as if I've just beheld the sun.

CHAPTER 3

Annabelle

"HOW DO YOU LIKE my library?" he asks.

There's fifteen or so feet between us, but his low, resonant voice is loud in my ear.

"It's yours?"

His gaze rolls up and down me. "I'm financing it."

My eyes flicker up and down him, around the room, then back to him. "How are you allowed to be here with no guards?"

"I've got certain…privileges."

I tug my sweater more tightly around myself, and he takes a few strides toward me. "How?" I hear my voice ask. "Do you pay everybody off?"

A few more strides. He's looking right at me. Moving slow, almost as if he's stalking me. My God, he's tall—so tall. So tall and ripped and handsome. He looks pissed. "Does that notion offend you?"

I shrug. "It's not how things are supposed to be."

"Why's that?"

"It circumvents the system. How it's supposed to work."

Another two steps, and he's close enough to touch. He holds his hand out. "Give me your phone."

"Why?" I whisper.

"Because I asked you to."

And because he asks me to, I do it. I hand him my phone, and study the fresh scar underneath his chin as he punches something in. A second later, he hands it back to me with my bank's home page open.

"Put in your information."

"Why?"

"Because I said so." His hand cups my cheek, and his mouth tugs into a grim-seeming half-smile. "Oh, Angel," he says softly. "I see we've got a lot of work to do."

I can't look at him. My body's gone white hot. I keep my eyes on my phone's screen and try to remember to breathe. My fingers type my sign-in information. The page flickers, then loads.

AVAILABLE BALANCE: $51,110.03

My eyes fly to his. "Why? Holt told me the two of you made nice."

He closes the remaining two-inch gap of space between us. His hips against my stomach. His abs against my breasts. One hand comes up to caress my hair. "I'm doing it," he says slowly, "because I want you. And what I want, I take."

I wonder who else's he's wanted since he's been here. Do women line up on conjugal day to fuck him? If they do, does he meet them here, in this empty library?

"Who's the warden when Holt is gone?" I ask instead.

"Name is Perkins."

I'm lost in his eyes. Now I understand that phrase from books: I've fallen into them. I blink. Still in. "He lets you do what you want?" I can't tell if I'm whispering, or if my voice sounds small because the roaring in my head is so loud.

His fingers comb through the coils of my hair. "He and I have an understanding."

"Not just him," I say. "Everyone seems to do whatever you want."

"You want to know how much power I have. Why? Because you need to know before you fuck me again?" He drags his thumb over my lip. I have the urge to part my lips, but don't obey it.

"Last time," I manage. His eyes are rapt on mine. "I wanted it," I hear myself explain. "But…"

I want to tell him that it frightened me. How utterly I surrendered. The way I lay there, letting him have his way with me. He flung me down and pushed inside, and I— I what?

I let him.

I shake my head. "If that keeps happening…"

Already happening.

I'm drifting like space dust, no longer corporeal. All my atoms are vibrating in sync with his. My feet work on their own. I take a small step back.

"You look nervous," he says. His hand, still in my hair, turns to my cheek. It's warm. Calloused. "Come sit down."

He takes my hand and leads me to a window seat. A built-in bench, pressed up against a wall of glass. He wraps his hands around my waist and lifts me up. My eyes scan the patchy, dirt-strewn yard outside. The way the raindrops make the puddles ripple. The sky is white. Stark white.

"Just a minute," he says.

I turn back around to see him reach onto some shelves along the wall and grab an armful of navy blue blankets. Painters' blankets, I realize. He sets them on the bench beside me. Smoothes one out. Lifts me up and sits me on it. Then he tucks another one behind me.

"Thank you," I murmur. Despite the blankets' tattered appearance, they seem soft enough. There's no paint on them, and they don't smell like it. Another one unfolded by his big hands, tucked around me.

"You got wet. Warm up a minute."

I sit there because my brain is broken and my heart feels puffed up like a balloon. I sit there, watching him. The last thing I expect is him, climbing up behind me. He leans his torso against my back, spreads his legs around my butt and thighs. Gentle fingers stroke my hair off my back, over my shoulders. Strong hands begin to knead.

"Don't be nervous, Angel. I'll take care of you."

Beast

I've brought many women here. Conjugal sessions are every Tuesday and Thursday, on a small hallway with hard cots and no heat. But I bend the rules to suit me. Holt and the others let me get away with it. I'm a bad habit, one none of them understand how to shove back into a box. Which is a good thing. Which was the plan.

I'm special. A special prisoner.

Special privileges, special obligations.

Like tonight…

I got the phone call today. The go-ahead. The confirmation.

Tonight will be…trying, but today is Angel.

She's got tight shoulders. Tiny shoulders. My hands fit around them so thoroughly, I'm scared I'll break her.

Maybe she's scared, too, because as I massage, her muscles tremble.

"How can I not be scared," she says. "Considering where I am…"

Her voice is so soft. Trailing off. My hand are overtaking her.

I lean down close enough to smell her hair. Something soft and warm, like flowers in the sun.

"No one will ever hurt you while I'm here, Angel."

"What about a riot?" she almost slurs.

I'm so glad I did this. My thumbs rub a line on either side of her spine, and she leans over even further. "There won't be another riot while you're here. If something comes up, we'll reschedule. I won't put my needs above your safety."

"The other day," she says, "your needs were… You were rough with me."

I sit up straighter. Dig my fingers in a little harder. Remember how to find air with my lungs.

"The other day was a fuck up," I murmur. Shame spreads through my head like so many cobwebs—and at the same time, I'm getting hard remembering. "The other day I was an animal. *You* were an animal. I was angry and my mind was somewhere else—where it was all—more straightforward." In that place I go where consequences melt away, at least for some amount of time. Where I'm what I became that night she held me. Where nothing matters. I close my eyes and inhale slowly.

"Annabelle. Do you know what these things are like in prison?" I lean down, touching my forehead to her soft hair.

"You should never know, Angel. Tell me—why did you come back here?"

My fingers, now pressing all around her shoulder blades, stop.

Horror strikes me. "Were you…hurt before?"

"Hurt?" she says.

"Is that why you liked it rough? What I did?"

She's still for a long moment while my soul riots. Then she shakes her head. "I don't think that's why."

"Holt was right. I wanted him to tell you things were mended. That coming back here wasn't a necessity. It is a necessity," I correct, "it is a necessity that I touch you, but I wanted you to have a chance to back out."

"I did," she whispers.

"And you didn't take it." My voice is a growl now. I'm becoming animal again. This is what she does to me. "Why didn't you take your out, Angel?"

She bows her head. I want to bite the back of her neck. I cup her shoulders. Rub…

I'm not breathing.

Why did you come back for this? Why did you come back for me?

I remember her hair and her eyes and the stars flung up above us and the smell of blood. It could be blood from *them.* It could be the blood I wash off my hands after tonight. If there is any justice in this world, it will be my own blood sometime soon. Karma will catch up with me, and I'll pay for all my crimes.

I can't sit still like this. I stop rubbing. Get down, so I'm standing beside her. I frame her flawless angel face with my hands.

"I'm going to kiss you now, Angel. My tongue against yours. My mouth over your mouth. My lips bruising your lips." I flick my eyes at the door. "I'll give you one last chance to go. If you stay, I'll fuck you hard."

Annabelle

"I want to stay."

I look at him and I feel down in my bones that I'm making the wrong move. Not because I'm afraid of him. Because of where we are. Because of where we've been. He may not remember that night, but I'll never forget it. In fairy tales and myths, sometimes there are people meant to spin around each other, their cycles intertwined. Pleasure and pain, pain and pleasure. I know he's about to give me pleasure, so when the pain?

That's all the time I have to wonder.

He hoists himself back up on the window seat with me. He snatches me against him, and his mouth comes down on mine. Our kiss is hard—painful. But it's not all him this time. My heart is beating hard, my blood singing for his. I give as hard as I get. I grip his neck and cup his jaw and lock his mouth on mine.

A few frantic kisses, and he's in control again. He pushes me back against the blankets and crouches over me like a predator. His hands press my shoulders down as he kisses down my neck. His hands cup my breasts. His fingers tweak my nipples. His tongue dances with mine. I throb between my legs.

"Oh—" gasp— "God…" He rubs his cock against my thigh, and I can feel a gush of heat and moisture in between my legs.

His fingers work my jeans open and stroke my mound. I buck my hips. "More," I moan into his mouth.

Down and around, his fingertips feeling. Parting me. Pushing in. One finger, two.

I'm panting.

"Spread your legs wider, Angel. I want to bury myself in you. Feel you clench around me."

I obey without a word, and with his free hand, he yanks my jeans down. His mouth is on my neck. Is on my throat. My purple and white striped panties are being pushed aside.

"Oh GOD."

He's gliding in. So slick. I'm so slick. Filled up by his fingers. Rocking up, against him.

And then it's like my brain snaps back to life. My hands, grasping gently at his abs, jet to his jeans button. Work it open. He helps me take the zipper down. My hands fly inside and find he's wearing boxer-briefs. Soft cotton over that big bulge. I'm panting: little gasps.

I work my way under the elastic of his briefs and find his hard, flat belly like warm velvet. Warm and hair-dusted. The head of him juts up. I wrap my hand around it. So soft. And damp.

Holy fuck, he's oozing. Ready for me.

Beast wants me.

I want him.

His fingers push inside me till they're buried to the knuckle. He spreads them out a little, making me feel oh so full. Then he curls them back, toward my spine. His fingertip brushes my g-spot and I grunt and thrust against him.

My hand tugs on his dick. Up and down… I'm stroking: wrist flick, wrist flick. My hand shaking.

"That's it," he grunts. He grabs my elbows. "Put your arms above your head."

I'm flat on my back on the library window seat. As he grinds himself against my leg, his fingers move a little deeper.

Then, moving sure and quick as a sexual superhero, he flips me over on my stomach.

I hear a tearing sound—a condom wrapper being opened—and have the brief, terrifying thought that maybe he plans to fuck me up the ass, the way they say it's done in prison. I'm gasping in advance as he jerks my hips up off the seat, grinds his length against my butt, spreads my legs, and positions his head at the pool of moisture right there at my entrance.

"Hope you're ready," he says.

He punches in and starts out slow. Push and slow drag out. Punch and slow drag out. Punch and out and *punch*—"oh God!"— and PUNCH!

"RICARDO!"

His hand curls around my shoulder, comes over my throat, pressing just enough to scare me. "Beast. Beast. Beast."

"Beast," I repeat.

"You like my cock inside you?"

"Yes!"

He thrusts.

"You need my cock inside you?"

"Yes." The word shudders from my mouth. "My pussy is so full!"

Another thrust. Pull out. Thrust in. I'm pressed against the glass of the window. Eyes shut. His cock is gliding in and out of me. I clench around him.

"Picture my mouth on your clit," he breathes into my ear. "After this, I'm going to suck your clit."

It *throbs*.

With one strong thrust, he buries his cock a little deeper. I'm *filled*. Filled so thoroughly I scoot on my knees so I can spread my legs a little more. Take more of him.

"Imagine my mouth on your nipples—sucking. That's where they're gonna be, Angel. Me, sucking your tits. My tongue rolling all over you." He rocks against me, drawing himself out a little before pushing back in.

"Feel me," he says. "All of me."

And I can feel him—every inch. His head, his shaft, even his balls, a gentle weight bouncing on my taint as he thrusts.

I groan.

He groans.

He picks up speed. His hand comes around my hips, then down; his fingertips parting my lips. He drags one finger through my moisture, glides back up, over my clit. I'm shaking with his impact, poundPOUNDpound.

His dick in my cunt, slick finger on my clit, and then he parts my ass cheeks and he presses a knuckle gently at my back door.

That's the end of me. I shatter.

CHAPTER 4

Annabelle

"TELL ME ABOUT YOURSELF, Angel. I want to know about your family."

"What about them?"

"Your mother is sick?"

I nod. "She has a brain tumor."

"I'm sorry to hear that."

"I'm sorry that it's true," I murmur.

"And you have a sister, too?"

"She's mine. My baby. Adrian."

His palm cups my forehead, holding my head up as I lean forward, mostly limp. His fingers get to know each pressure point along my neck and shoulders. "You're tight. Take a few deep breaths. That's right, Angel."

"This feels amazing."

"Good. You deserve amazing."

"So…nice of you," I whisper.

"My pleasure," he says. "In fact, it's my demand."

His voice, hanging in the air behind me, asks, "How long were you looking for a job?"

"Long time," I mumble.

"What kind?"

"Counseling."

His fingers, on my forehead, press in a few spots, and I feel a floating sensation. "You like helping people, Angel?"

I can't nod, so I say, "Yeah. When I can."

There's a pause, and I can feel the tension in it. "That's not what this is about, is it? Pity?"

I'm so relaxed I'm drooling, but I manage to laugh. "No. Of course not."

He takes my shoulders in his hands and turns me over, so I'm lying on my back.

"I don't need your pity. You know that—yes?" As he speaks, he's peeling my clothes off.

I'm so limp and zoned out, I can barely nod.

"It doesn't surprise me," he says as he tugs my jeans off, "that you like helping people." He pulls my shirt over my head and deftly rids me of my bra. My breasts spring out, round and heavy, and his lips cover my nipple.

"Oh!" I arch. I grab his neck.

He jerks my panties down, one-handed, and I feel the slap of cool air on my pussy. He runs his tongue along my slit. A few lazy circles around my clit and I'm clawing his face.

He parts my lips a little more and licks my sopping entrance. I arch up. "Inside. I need you…inside," I pant.

"That's too bad." It takes me a few seconds to comprehend the words, and by then I'm being rolled onto my stomach once again.

I feel him leave the window seat for a second, hear him dig around for something. Another condom?

A minute later and he's back, kissing my neck, behind my ear; tickling my ass cheeks. He pushes a finger in between my ass cheeks, stroking in a way I almost like. And then before I know what hit me, there's pressure back there. Not just pressure. I cry out as he shoves something inside.

Is it his dick?

It's not his dick…

I shake my ass.

"What is this?" I moan.

"It's a buttplug." I can hear the smile in his voice. "Do you know what a buttplug does?" he asks.

I clench around it, and on cue, it starts to vibrate.

I moan, because the pleasure-pain I feel back there seems to have a direct connection to my cunt. I move my hips and clench my ass and feel my pussy pulse inside—as if it knows my ass is filled and envies it.

He chuckles.

He presses his hand against the buttplug. I guess part of it is sticking out?

He pushes it in a little more, sending pleasure through me. It vibrates through my inner walls, rings through my cunt, sends mini shock-waves to my clit.

"How's that?" he rumbles.

He rolls me back over and spreads my legs wide, drags his finger through the wetness of my pussy lips.

I moan. It echoes through the room, but I don't care. I lift my ass up off the window seat, hungry for his fingers inside me. His cock inside me.

"Oh God!" I'm about to come.

And then he withdraws his fingers and leaves the bench.

My eyes peek open as my hips continue surging. I'm stunned to see him standing several feet away.

"I'm going to go make some measurements for shelves. You stay here."

I'm in a thick daze, rolling my hips and craving cock. "I can't! Don't leave!"

"I want to know more about you," he says with a satisfied little grin, as he walks to a stack of plywood a dozen feet away. "Tell me about something illuminating. Let's try…high school."

I'm panting. I've got my hand over my cunt, and only pride is stopping me from rubbing myself off.

I shift my lower body, clenching around the plug, my cunt squeezing tight in anticipation of what it wants inside. "High school," I say hoarsely. "That's when I had…a major crush on you."

"Oh yeah?"

"You…should remember me." I writhe.

"In college, were you over that crush?"

I press my legs together. Deep inside my ass, the vibrations feel incredible. My cunt is a creaming bliss bucket. My clit is swollen. Hot. Needy.

What did he ask me? About college? "You were…here," I pant. "But…no."

Something passes over his face. Just a flicker through his cheeks and brows, but I'm too strung out to name it.

He holds up another board and begins making notches on it with a pencil. Damn, those biceps… I look at his fingers. Down to his crotch. I can see his erection, outlined by the fabric of his jeans.

Inside me… Get inside me…

"I want to hear about the first time you had sex," he tells me.

"Come closer."

The hand between my legs has lost restraint. I'm playing with my pussy, my fingertips skating over my slick clit.

He smirks a little—or is that a smile—and closes the distance between us with his long legs. He peers down over me. Folds his hand over mine.

"Annabelle," he purrs. "So desperate. Tell me… What should I do for you?"

"Lick me," I gasp. I reach out and grab his other arm. "Fuck me! I just…need you. Either one!"

He props the board he's been holding up against the wall, climbs onto the window seat atop me, and parts my knees with his big hands. He leans down over me, and my heart goes crashing back in time.

"Lick you?" he says. "Where?"

I rock my cunt up to his face, and he drops down on me. His mouth and tongue are hot silk. Magic. Parting my swollen pussy lips, flicking up and down. He rolls the tip of his tongue around my clit as two fingers slip inside my cunt and his pinkie puts some pressure on the plug.

I feel so teased, so full, so drunk.

He lifts his mouth off me and looks into my eyes. "Come now," he says, and when his warm, wet lips touch back down on me, that's exactly what I do.

I come with a shriek, feeling like I've been thrown into the air. I sink back down. Peek my eyes open.

Beast is sitting with one leg pulled up on the bench. The other dangles down. My eyes gravitate toward his cock. It's hard and thick inside his jeans. Already, I want him again. I push myself up onto my elbows, feeling shaky. Raw.

"I want to hear…about you too," I murmur.

He smiles. "Time is up, Angel."

From somewhere behind him, he produces a clean, wet rag and spreads my lips apart to gently wipe me down.

When the rough texture of the cloth skates over my clit, I start to pant again.

"You dirty Angel," he says. Then his jeans are down, his cock is in his hand. His head is at my entrance. He's stuffing himself inside me, and we're riding…riding…riding away.

I cling to his shoulders. His hands lift my ass up off the ground as he thrusts. Somewhere in the space between my legs, his huge cock and the buttplug send spirals of pressure bouncing off each other, lighting me up thoroughly inside.

I come with a gasp. He pulls out, his seed straining against a white condom I didn't even see him roll on.

"Let's try this again." He smirks, and wipes me gently as I shriek and writhe.

When he's finished, he turns to dispose of the condom and pull his jeans back up.

I struggle to get mine back on as well.

He helps me off the window seat and is buttoning my jeans before I realize—

"Omigod, the buttplug! It's still in me!"

"Take it home." He grins.

My face heats so much my eyes water. "I can't wear a buttplug home! And ride in the car with that guard—"

"Oh, you won't." With a smack of my ass—it sends so much pleasure through me, my legs almost fold—he takes my elbow and leads me to the door. I'm still unsteady—still panting. He wraps an arm around my back, punches some numbers into a keypad I'm too lust-drunk to even see. "I've got another car for you—for this very reason."

When he pushes the door open, there's a black limousine idling in the wet grass.

I wrap my arms around him, feeling weak-kneed and faint. The plug is still vibrating. "Can you walk me out?"

He shakes his head, and moves his leg. It takes me a moment to see that there's a metal band there.

"Just take it slow. Think of baseball."

I smirk.

He grins. "Bye, Angel." He bends down to plant a hard kiss on my lips. "Tomorrow. Clinton again."

"But I never got to ask you any questions."

He laughs—dry and self-deprecating. "It's been an unproductive few years."

Something about the easy way he says it makes me very sad. So it's all the weirder when I get into the limousine and almost fail to hold my orgasm back while the limo bumps over the dirt road.

When I get out at my apartment complex, my knees are so weak, my body so shaky, I can barely make it up the stairs.

I go straight to my bathroom and start the shower, prepared to pull the buttplug out.

Instead I wind up on my back in the bathtub, my legs propped against the shower wall, my knees spread wide, so the water spewing from the faucet hits me exactly where I need it to.

I emerge, clean and stretched and tired and finally plug-free, two hours later, feeling like I tumbled into Wonderland.

CHAPTER 5

Beast

BLAINE MCGUIRE IS HEAD of the Aryan Force at La Rosa, and despite our obvious aesthetic differences, I consider him a friend of sorts.

After the first two years of my ruse, once I killed a few man and let the surviving gang leaders see I had control of this place, I started offering them freedoms. Freedoms only I could give, because only I work under someone high-enough-up to grant me the power to hand them out for the purposes of winning gang leaders over.

I started offering them freedoms, protection from uprising—until I got an order to end their lives, anyway—and what you might call financial planning. Three of them—McGuire's predecessor, Tommy Smith; T-Dog Bosman, head of the Guerrillas; and Juan Juarez—were still running gangs outside the walls. Over the next year and a half, I worked hard to get them in my pocket, helping them strategize and helping them invest their illicit monies in accounts whose information could later be given to my bosses.

I benefit, too, in some ways. I can wear jeans, for instance. I've got a swanky cell. But in other ways, this is hellish. I have enough guilt over the way I got in here, and that was before I started ending lives on the inside.

Smith, I killed in on the basketball court with a well-placed elbow to the temple. My superiors let T-Dog die at the hands one of one of his underlings, an ambitious thug named Bently Kennard, who turned out to be much easier to manipulate than was T-Dog. And Juan Juarez is still in play. Still head of the Julio gang here at La Rosa.

Of all the point guys, he's the one I know the best. Although I know the world would be better off without him at the helm of a large terrorist organization, I'm kind of glad it's not him I'm doing in tonight. Fucker is funny and we share an appreciation for Marlon Brando's acting.

Like me, McGuire is segregated from the general population. He stays in a two-story cement penthouse at the end of the Aryan hallway. It's a decent enough space, and it comes with a private shower. Unlike me, McGuire hates his private shower. He's never been so direct with me, but my impression is he was raped in the shower as a kid. So unbeknownst to almost everyone, he showers in the Aryan communal room around three o'clock in the morning, when a white power guard named Tom lets him out of his cell and escorts him to the 'stalls.'

This means that by two a.m. tonight, I need to be in Fred Burns' cell, smacking tape over his mouth, tying rope around his ankles and wrists, and hauling him off to my own cell, where he'll wait under Clinton's watchful eye until I've finished off his boss. There, he'll be in the ideal position for indoctrination—indeed, for ordination—by yours truly.

Tasks like this are few and far between, but lately, my superiors are beginning to seem antsy. I haven't figured out exactly why, but I don't like it.

I've got a ritual I do before something like this. Showering and meditating and reading from the Bible. I know it's fucked up, but since I've been here and started reading as much as I do, I fucking love the Good Book. Poetry of War, they might have called the Old Testament.

When that's done, I communicate via Bluetooth with the guards on staff tonight. Almost everyone at La Rosa is in my pocket, but there're a few who aren't. I can't control them all, even with an outlandish amount of support from Holt and his junior wardens.

So I have two of the ones I can control send the one I can't out to grab some grub from a burger joint a few towns down.

The signal I give them is: "I'm using my juice card."

In prison-speak, that means I've got something to take care of, but I'm not going to tell them what. The guards may not know who I'm working for, but Holt's immediate subordinate, Perkins, is tight with me, so instructions to support me trickle down.

I nab Burns without incident, lock him in my cell, and make another call, this time only to Perkins, the interim warden who knows my secrets. Perkins doesn't know my real situation, but he knows I'm in charge here. Doesn't hurt that I pay his mortgage and bought his mistress a Mercedes.

"Back door parole for McGuire," I tell him. "Hold the bugs."

After a brief hesitation, he says, "You got it, Beast."

As I leave my room, I think how sick it is. The way people just…bend to me. Because I pay them, or do them favors. I shouldn't be allowed to do what I'm about to do. Not without more trouble. It seems somehow doubly unjust.

I find McGuire in the showers. He's hunched over, like he's washing his legs. He knows something is wrong when he sees my face, and immediately straightens up. He takes a few steps back, inching closer to a soap dish where I imagine he keeps a shank or other weapon.

It's pretty obvious he's reaching behind himself, but still, he casts his eyes down as a sign of respect for me, as if everything is normal. I close the gap between us quickly. I step into the cool spray and clamp a hand on his shoulder.

"Get down on your knees, McGuire."

They call this going Prison Wolf, and it's not something I get off on. But I've done it a time or two, and I'll do it again now, because if I can get his lips around my cock, I can stab him in the base of his head, and he'll go fast and painless.

Unfortunately, my guess seems to've been correct about his history with bathing. Rather than suck my dick in a shower, McGuire goes for his own shank. He's juiced up on adrenaline and moving fast. Still, I could evade him. I just…don't.

I let him get me in the ribs, just under my pec, and then I drive my longer, heavier shank into his back.

It's not a clean kill.

We wrestle in a spray of water droplets and a haze of steam, rolling in a sea of blood so thick I'm glad I know McGuire tested negative at his physical a week ago.

I drive my shank into his muscular neck, and the smell of blood fills my head. Oh. Because it's spraying all over me.

He's fallen down on his back beside the drain. His eyes are slits, but his body is still twitching, still trying to buck although he doesn't even have the strength to jeopardize my balance as I straddle him, preparing to get him once more in the jugular.

"W-why?" he coughs. Blood gurgles in his throat. The smell is so overpowering, it takes everything I have not to get up and stumble out of the shower room.

I'm feeling head-fucked, so I end things quickly, burying my shank in his jugular then climbing off his body fast.

I think, after I rinse myself off and walk back toward my room in my wet clothes, how I could have answered: "For those kids you were picked up with that time in '03."

Motherfucker might have been raped, but he turned into a rapist, too. That's not why he was in—McGuire headed up an MC, where he killed anyone he didn't like—but he was a diaper sniper, too. I'm probably the only one around here who knows it.

I shake my head. Hold out my arm and run my pruned-up fingertips along the cement wall. I'm feeling light and airy, like a helium balloon.

I barely make it to my door without tripping or passing out. As soon as I'm inside, I puke in the sink, then use one of the many prepaids I have to let my boss know it's been done.

"Burns has been instructed to lead the group in the way that I described? With focus on cocaine and heroin?"

"Coming up," I tell him.

I pull on a jacket and step into my closet, where I shake off all vestiges of pain and weakness and spend two hours getting Burns hyped up about his new position. When I've guaranteed his loyalty to me and proposed a few lucrative-seeming business deals, promising to use some of the Hammond fortune to funnel into his group's illicit accounts—thereby getting my bosses the account numbers—and suggesting there is good money right now in cocaine and heroin, if his guys can get it from this supplier I know down in Colombia—I cut him loose and peel the jacket off.

Lots of blood.

My blood.

Fuck.

I stumble toward the shower, but my head is spinning. Reroute to my bed and reach my shaking hand under the pillow. The creases around my fingernails are still lined with blood, but I'm too tired to get up and wash again. I know I'm contaminating the screen of this outdated iPhone, but I don't care. I just want to see her face: Angel in Technicolor.

So many pictures... Paid someone to get them. Lots of years.

High school prom.

College...soccer.

Angel.

I call Clinton right before I pass the fuck out. The smell of blood... Her face. So many stars. "Go get her. I don't...care what time...it is."

Annabelle

Mom's night nurse wakes me a little after five a.m. with wide eyes. She whispers that there's someone at the door.

"Clinton, he says it is."

And that's the first of the alarm bells.

The second, really. His arrival at this early hour is the first. I pull a robe over my night clothes and hurry to living area. I swing the door open and check him out. He looks normal enough in his brown uniform and boots.

"Clinton. What's going on?"

"I came to get you," he says.

"Right now?"

He nods. "Yeah."

"Why? He asked for me?"

"That's why I come and get you, isn't it?"

"Yeah. Guess so. What's with the early hour?"

He shrugs.

I raise a skeptical eyebrow at him, then leave him waiting as I change out of my pajamas, call Holly over, and get an update on Mom, who seems to be fading even further, having not opened her eyes in almost four days now. I'm all too glad not to think about that as I grab my clutch, slip into sneakers, and pull the front door open. I stand there for a long moment, breathing in the dewy, pre-dawn air and assessing the guard for warning signs that I shouldn't go with him.

"Is something unusual going on?" I ask.

"Don't think so."

But I can tell. I can just tell he's hiding something. Normally, he's looser. Less…still. Tonight he seems subdued, almost frozen, as if he doesn't want to say or do something wrong.

Still standing in the doorway, I bite my lip and shake my head. "Clinton, I'm really sorry, but can I get you to call the prison and let me speak to your boss? Or maybe just him? Beast?"

He nods.

"Can you call him?" Clearly, Beast isn't foolproof in the trustworthiness department, but he was normal enough to me yesterday.

Clinton nods and slides his phone out of his pocket. "I can call him. If that's what it takes for you to come."

I roll my eyes and abruptly change my mind. "Whatever. Let's just go. Live dangerously and stuff. Going early today will help me be home in time to spend the day with my little sister, Adrian."

"That's good," he says, but he seems distracted.

By the time we roll through the last of the gates, I'm absolutely positive something is wrong.

Despite Clinton's repeated insistence that everything is fine—and his insistence that we listen to Mariah Carey's debut album on CD—I've got a creepy crawly feeling in my stomach.

I decide to go out on a limb as he slides into a parking spot just in front of the main entrance.

"Is this a test? A trap? Be honest with me, because right now, I'm kind of scared."

What if something happened to Beast and the others…I don't know…take me? The thought makes me want to lock the doors and stay inside the car.

Clinton's brown eyes rest on mine. "It's not a test. Or a trap. He just wanted to see you."

"Is something wrong?"

He puts the Explorer in park and turns off the ignition.

"So something *is* wrong!" I notice an ambulance parked over to the right and point accusingly at it. "Did he get hurt?"

"You're about to see him," he says, and gets out of the car. I know he's walking around to open my door, something I'm pretty sure is common in the Southern U.S., where Clinton's accent indicates he's from.

The center of my chest goes hot and melty at the thought of something happening to Beast, even as fear floods in behind concern. I shouldn't be here if something's wrong. I can't take care of myself here without the aid of someone much stronger.

Clinton opens my door, and when I get out, he gives me a reassuring smile. "I wouldn't let you do something dangerous. I'm a warden, not a prisoner, remember?"

I nod.

He's latched his arm companionably through mine, but when we go through the doorway, he takes his arm back and moves away from me.

"Go through the metal detector, Miss Mitchell," he tells me.

I walk through. It stays quiet, and as I'm standing still so a male guard can wave a wand over me, I notice a cluster of medical personnel standing about fifteen yards ahead, at the mouth of a hall. That must be why Clinton is acting distant.

Finally he and I are through security. He starts down a hall, but my sneakers are rooted to the floor.

He turns around.

"Is it bad?" I ask.

"Nothing to be scared of, ma'am."

He nods at a female guard posted at the mouth of the hall we're going down, and she nods back at us. I try to keep my gaze on him, but it wanders. I'm curious to see that sheets of metal have come down from the ceiling, covering the barred façade of every cell. The metal sheets leave a small hole for a few of the bars on each of the cells, so fresh air can circulate, I guess, but the cells are mostly covered.

I try to keep my footsteps quiet as I follow Clinton around two corners. Despite my bad sense of direction, I can feel us traveling through the prison's hexagonal arms. When we take an abrupt turn left, down a smaller hall, I have the feeling we're veering off into the middle of the hexagon.

There's a guard station, behind which a woman with short dread-locks is playing a crossword puzzle. She and Clinton exchange some kind of look—a nervous look?—and then we're walking past a few nondescript metal doors, down a small swatch of hallway. He stops abruptly at the last door on this little route.

He punches some numbers on a keypad to the left of the door, and it clicks open.

Cooler air flows from the inside of the room, and I just know that this is his cell. Beast's.

Clinton nods, and I hold my breath as I step into the room. Under my sneakers, a plush, burgundy rug sprawls over a white-washed cement floor about the size of mine and Adrian's combined bedrooms.

The walls are stark white, the ceiling low. In between a few disoriented blinks, I manage to glean that this room is some kind of prison suite; his flatscreen, in the corner, is bigger and nicer than ours at home; and that's a queen-sized bed ahead of me.

"Oh." *He's in it.*

He's sitting up, wearing a tight, white undershirt that clings to his big biceps and broad chest. Black pillows are propped behind him, as if in symbolic contrast to the pristine white of his shirt. Light, surrounded by darkness…

He's covered to his waist with a soft-looking, black duvet. Maybe it's the contrast of the bedding with his skin, but the first thought that I have is his face looks whiter than usual.

I see Clinton give a wave, and Beast nods in acknowledgment. Behind me, the door shuts.

Then his eyes hit mine.

My legs forget how to stand. I almost sink down to the floor. Instead, I step over to the bed and touch the edge of his black blankets with my hungry hands.

My gaze sweeps up and down him—a compulsion—but I can't see anything obvious: nothing but a faint bruise along his cheekbone.

He sits up a little straighter, then captures my wrist in his hand and looks up at me with cautious eyes and a tight jaw. "No questions, Angel. Take off your pants and sit on my face—or else you'll have to go."

"But—"

"No buts, Angel. Not today."

I search his face, but it's on lockdown. His eyes reveal nothing, just roll up and down my body like black lasers as I slowly strip off my red jeans, yellow t-shirt, and beige bra, and climb onto the bed.

As I'm climbing up, he scoots down, lying flat on his back. He leans his head back, but instead of straddling his face, I sink down atop his thighs and plant a kiss on his beautiful throat.

He grabs my wrist and shakes his head. "Sit on my face. I want to taste you. Now."

I start scooting up him, dragging my bare pussy over his body, through the blankets, and he grabs my hips, pulling me to him.

"I want this. Need this," he says, and then he's raising his head up off the pillow, pushing his face between my legs, and lapping at me. His tongue between my lips is exquisite. I howl—low and loud as I dare—and spread my legs a little wider for him. As he licks me up and down, he reaches around behind me and threads one powerful arm through my legs, so his fingers are positioned to plunge into my wet cunt from behind.

His other arm wraps around my waist, hand pressing against the small of my back so as he works me with his tongue, he's almost hugging me.

My eyes close as I gasp and pant and grind into his warm, wet mouth.

"Yes," I'm panting. "Yes, yes…"

"Yes what?" he breathes against me.

"Yes, Beast."

The tip of his tongue flicks my lips open again and traces up and down me, pausing to roll over my pulsing clit.

My hips jerk. "Oh God I'm close!"

The words burst out, and his mouth stops.

For half a second, our gazes meet, and his is dark. So raw and bare and desolate.

A heartbeat later, he rears up under me, lifts me by my hips, and tosses me down on my back atop his duvet. As he moves on his knees, between my legs, I catch a glimpse of something bright white beneath the t-shirt he's wearing.

I open my mouth to ask what happened, but like last time, he knows exactly what to do to head me off.

His hands go to the elastic of his boxer-briefs.

The boxer-briefs are tugged down, freeing an enormous, perfect cock I want to suck.

He grabs my thighs and scoots between them, moving tantalizingly closer to my core. He takes himself in hand, aims for my cunt, and, after a flicker of a glance up at my eyes, he slams into me, the force of it so strong I nearly fly right off the bed.

CHAPTER 6

Annabelle

HE FILLS ME COMPLETELY, obliterating all thought. Lighting up every nerve ending. I'm groaning like an animal. Clutching his forearms. Panting as he—"no!"—pulls slowly out.

His gaze bores into mine. "I need your body, Angel. Nothing more. Do you want to feel me inside you?"

I nod and claw his forearm. "Yes, please! Now!"

He punches into me again and groans. My eyes fly open. "That's gauze under your shirt. I don't want to hurt you."

He drags himself out, and I reach down between us, as if I'm going to—what? Keep that, big, hard, veiny cock out of me?

No.

I want him.

He's panting as he pushes back inside me. "Fuck me or leave." He looks desperate. Even a little haggard. I lift my hips and put more effort into thrusting. "Harder," he snaps. "Angle this way." He lifts my hips, positioning me at a slightly different angle, and his thick shaft rubs down my clit as we move together.

"That's right. Let me fill up that wet pussy."

"Ahhh!" He thrusts so hard, I see stars around his handsome face. He pulls out again, and I lift my lips, trying frenziedly to prevent it.

His lips curl. "You like it on your back. My cock stretching that sweet cunt." His hands stroke my shoulders, and I peer up at his pale, intense face. "Tell me how you like it, Angel."

"Hard," I whisper.

He gives it to me hard, and I grunt like an animal in heat.

"Again," I moan.

"Again." He thrusts, and I feel his balls slap at me.

"You're my whore," he says as he draws out. "I call, you come. You're here for me. Just me." He slams back in and groans roughly.

"You'll take all of me." He twists his hips, wedging himself still deeper. Till I feel nothing but his huge cock; I exist only to clench and pulse around it.

"Feel that? That's me owning you." Out and—"oh, fuck!"—in again.

I wrap my hands around his arms and throw my head back, allowing my legs to fall all the way open. My hips to lift exactly when my body wants them to.

I'm nothing but an orgasm barreling down the tracks, and he's barreling with me.

We come together—him panting, me screaming.

He pulls out and stretches out on his side, balancing on one elbow, and my eyes rove down the front of him, seeking out the scar on his thigh from the car crash. That's when I notice his shirt is red.

"Shit."

The second I reach for him, he rolls away from me. He lands agilely on the floor beside the bed and looks at me as if I've done something to hurt him. His eyes are dark. His face is tight.

"I don't need or want a lover, Angel. You're here because I like that pussy, and you want my money and my cock."

When he says it so bluntly, it sounds terrible. I draw my knees up to my chest and rest my cheek on them. Shit. So this is how he sees me. This is how he sees this twisted thing we're doing. I can't blame him I guess, but still… "That's not true for me."

I'm looking up at him, and I'm almost scared of his response. Scared because I care. It's pathetic. I know. But when his face twists in what looks almost like anger, my throat tightens. "What is?" he asks. "I told you that you would be my whore. We would fuck, and I would pay you. It's that simple, Angel. And the moment that it isn't, is the moment you don't need to come here anymore."

I don't want to face the real implications of what he said, so I bite my lip, then softly ask, "Is that how you treat every woman that you…see here in prison?"

He gives me a strange look, and when he speaks, his voice is quiet. "I don't need to pay them, Angel."

"Because they still think they're having sex with a movie star. I guess they are. You are still him. Technically, you're still Cal Hammond. But not really." I slide down off the bed as pressure mounts inside my chest. "I don't think you're that person anymore at all. Maybe you never were, but I *know* you're not now. You're so different now, and don't think it doesn't freak me out and scare me just a little. But you know what? I'm here anyway. Not because I want your money—that's not all at least. And not because of Holt. I'm here because I held you one night in the desert when I thought you were dying. You *were* dying. You were DOA at the hospital. I know because I called and said I was your sister, and some dumb nurse told me you had a heart attack in the helicopter and they had to bring you back."

His face is made of stone. He doesn't even blink.

"I don't get it! What's the point of saying that you don't remember me? Even if you don't remember the wreck, I was there at the party earlier that night."

"So were lots of women," he says flatly. "Do you think you're different? That we had a…what? Some kind of fucking connection?" He paces back and forth over the rug, giving me a good view of his shirt, where red is blooming slowly.

"You know what I remember about that night?" he says, his head still down. "The smell of blood. That's all it was for me." His eyes collide with mine. "I killed three people and I got sent here for it. I'm sorry if I'm not what you want me to be. You want me to tell you thank you? I'm not thankful." His lip curls up, he shakes his head, and quietly he says, "I should have fucking died."

I purse my lips to keep them from trembling and just…stare at him.

He sits on the edge of the bed and looks down at his thighs. They're bare, and very muscular. I can see the scar across the left one—the one from that night. It's thick and pinkish white and jagged. I can't even imagine how much it must have hurt.

He rests his elbows on his knees and props his face up with his fingers, looking at the rug—and then at me. "There are lots of reasons why the world would be a better place if I had died that night. If you knew what I did tonight—how I got this gash—" he plucks the fabric of his shirt between two fingers and pulls gently, lifting it up off his skin— "then you'd understand. If you knew anything about me. But you don't. And here's the thing, Angel: you don't want to."

I step a little closer to him. "I'm not fragile. Not at all. And I care about…knowing you. I— I want to." I look into his tired face and find the strength to put myself out there. One quick swallow and I'm diving in. "Let me get to know you beyond just 'Beast.' If something gets too much for me, I can say so myself. In the meantime, let me call you Ricardo. You're a man—not a beast. I'd like to find out what kind of man you are, even if you don't think I should."

He blinks out at me, reminding me for a moment of a sullen child. He slowly shakes his head. "I am a Beast. I'm not human—that's for sure."

"Don't say that. I don't believe it's true."

He drops his head into his hands, and his low voice fades down to a murmur. "I do things that would make you hate me if you knew."

"I don't think that I could ever hate you."

His eyes lock with mine. "Annabelle, my father is a sociopathic drug addict. I barely knew my mother. I'm on my eighth year in this place. My eighth year. If you knew anything about prison you would know what that means." He gives a little shake of his head, as if he can't believe how naïve I am. "I'm not the kind of guy you need to give a shit about."

"But I do," I whisper.

"Then you're stupid." He gets up off the bed, and I can feel the storm of his emotions swirl around him as he works to change the mood of things. As he works to push me away. Long strides; he's pacing. Looking down, because he can't look me in the eye when he says whatever's coming next. And then he does. It's fast and hard, and I know in a breath that whatever he says next, it's going to hurt. "You're a stupid girl, Annabelle, and it's time for you to go."

"You're trying to drive me away."

"Yes hell I am. I hope it's working." He waves at the door, and when I don't move, he steps over to me and takes me by the elbow. "I see now this was a mistake. I thought it could be sex, but you're showing me it can't be just that. You want…more than I do. You need to go now, Angel."

Tears blur my vision. Maybe he's right. I am stupid. To think…what did I think? That we might really hit it off? That the feelings I've been carrying around with me all these years could be unloaded? Updated? The truth is, I didn't think at all—I only felt. And from the moment I first saw his face on *Good Nebraska*, when he was a fourteen-year-old actor and I was just a little girl, I've simply…felt for him. I don't know why. There's no making sense of it. It's just a sort of magnetism.

One fat tear rolls down my cheek. I shake my head and dash a few more away with my fingertips.

"Angel," he groans.

"Don't say Angel to me." I duck my head. "From what you say, you don't even remember me. So you know what? Fuck you!"

Before I can say anything else—before I can stalk out, his hands are clasping me around my waist. He picks me up and tosses me on the bed. His arms are around me before I have a chance in hell of processing what just happened.

His face is buried in my neck. His lips move, soft and slow, behind my ear.

"Angel… My Angel. I remembered you. Of course I did."

I cling to his shoulders. "You did?"

"I kept track of you," he says into my hair. "High school. College. Like a goddamned stalker. You were just so fucking nice. That's goddamned weird where I come from."

I wrap my arms gently around his waist as my heart starts pounding—so hard I feel almost sick.

"I was obsessed with you," I whisper. "And then afterward…I would try not to think of you, because it drove me crazy. Knowing you were here… I hated it." I press my hand against his cheek. "You don't belong here."

His mouth finds my mouth, gently exploring, then tugging away. "Oh, Angel. You're wrong about that."

I run my fingers through his hair. My other hand finds his and strokes over his knuckles. I'm surprised to find his hand is shaking just a little.

"Adrenaline," he murmurs.

I kiss his palm. He winces. "Don't."

"It hurts?"

He shuts his eyes and shakes his head. "It's wrong, Angel. The only time these hands are kind is when they're on your skin."

"Then they should be on my skin more." I shove him gently off me and climb on top of him, and am surprised when he lets me. He's flat on his back, and I can see his thick erection straining against his boxer-briefs. "Don't give me any trouble. I want to fix where you're hurt, and then I want to fuck you."

His eyes widen, and I giggle. "You better turn on the TV so I'm not heard screaming."

He smirks, and I snap my fingers. "You think I'm kidding?"

"No. You wicked banshee." He leans over and grabs a remote from his nightstand. He points it at the TV. I see a news anchor's suit and return my attention to Beast.

I lift up his shirt, in awe of his beautiful body. It's perfectly conditioned…as beautiful as it was when he was starring in movies. Probably move. The gauze bandage is soaked red. I lift one corner of it, and my stomach twists. I'm staring at an angry-looking stab-wound, maybe three inches wide. I can tell it's deep because it splits open pretty wide. I rub my lips together, trying not to feel ill.

"How did this happen?" I whisper.

"I should tell you." Worry whispers over his face, and when he speaks again, his voice is very soft. "I should—but…I can't."

I nod slowly. "It's okay."

I kiss his neck, his mouth. I'm already wet and needy, and I can see his hard cock, so I know I need pull away for just a few more moments. I brush his hair off his forehead and caress his bruised cheek. "You have a First Aid kit?"

He tucks one arm behind his head and nods. "Below the bathroom sink. But I can get it."

"No." I press against his waist. "Stay here, you crazy man. I'll be right back."

I get it and am pleased to find him in the same position he was in when I left. I straddle his hips and tear open a Betadine swab. I bite my lip and look into his eyes, and he gives a little nod. His hand crawls up my hip, closes around my waist.

I rub the rust-colored swab over the wound.

He squeezes me.

I pause. "I hurt you?"

He shakes his head. "I just want to feel you. Make sure you're real."

I grin as warmth spills through me. "I'm real, and I'm here. And after this, I want to suck your dick. What do you think about that?"

His cock twitches, bumping against my ass, and I laugh.

I doctor his wound as best I can, using tape and going liberally on the antibiotic ointment. Then I seal a bandage over it.

"Thank you." His eyes, on mine, are dark and sensual. As if he's already shifted into *fuck* gear.

I tug his boxer-briefs down and watch his cock spring free.

I put my mouth around it, and his hands come down on my shoulders.

"Angel. Angel, Angel…"

He thrusts into my mouth. I moan, sending vibrations through his shaft.

I take him deep down in my throat and cup my hand over his balls. That's when he stiffens.

My eyes fly up to his. I'm expecting to see lust. Blind, beautiful, heady lust. Instead, he looks stricken. I follow his gaze to the flatscreen and move my mouth off of him.

"What's wrong?"

He holds up a hand, and I listen to the announcer as the blood drains from his face.

"…killed Blaine McGuire, leader of the Aryan Force at La Rosa. Police say Hammond will spend time in solitary confinement, and may well have his sentence extended."

It's like a movie, how the next few minutes unfold.

For the first thirty seconds or so after that, he just sits there, stone still. My heart races. That's what he did to get this stab wound? He killed someone? My heart aches. My stomach hurts. I'm not sure what to say. And maybe it doesn't even matter at the moment.

He's off the bed and across the room, yanking open drawers in his desk—ignoring me—when I hear footsteps in the hall. He flies to the bed and pulls me down off it, shoves me toward the bathroom. "Go in there, Angel. Stay quiet."

And so I see the whole thing happen through the vent at the bottom of the door. I see them burst through the bedroom door. Men in suits—one in a dress suit, and two others wearing black.

The one in the suit says something I can't hear, and Beast's voice booms. "You fuckers lied to me."

The man in the suit chuckles. I don't know who he is or what his role is here, but it's an evil sound.

One of the men wearing black pulls out what I think is a gun, and I almost shriek. He fires it, and a streak of what looks like blue lightning jumps from the gun to Beast's shoulder.

His knees hit the rug. He moans a little as his head lolls in between his shoulders. The men in black each grab one of his arms and hoist him up.

"Solitary," the suited man orders. "Dose him when you get him there. I want him docile as a kitten." He walks ahead of the men and pushes the door open. Then he turns around. "And when you're done, check this area for her. I don't trust him not to spill the beans, and if she knows, we'll have to deal with it."

I watch as the suited man holds the door open, and the other two lead Beast through it.

His room is quiet except the pounding of my heart.

BEAST

Volume 3

CHAPTER 1

Annabelle

EVERY TIME MY LUNGS expand to draw in air, it feels like too much movement. Too much noise.

Logically, I know I can't keep hiding indefinitely. If I stay here, someone will find me. But I'm not ruled by logic. I'm compelled by fear. So I crouch down on Beast's bathroom floor until my knee caps ache and my back knots, and my fingernails are sore from picking at the grout between the small, gray tiles.

They just...took him.

How could they just take him that way?

Did he really kill that guy? The Aryan?

Where is he now?

Too many questions banging around my head, so I stand up. Blood rushes into my legs, making them tingle, then ache.

I slide my phone out of my pocket and scroll to Holt's name. If only I could call him—but I don't have service in the prison.

Clinton. I turn toward the mirror mounted over the sink and inhale slowly. If I'm going to leave this bathroom, the first person I should look for is Clinton.

I can do that. Surely I can find Clinton before the men who took Beast find me, too.

But what if I don't?

I imagine myself in a small, empty room. Water dripping down the walls, leaving slimy mold trails. Rusted bars through which hazy sunlight floats. Nothing in the world but me and the dust particles drifting through the gross, stale air.

They couldn't do that to me, right? I'm not a prisoner.

Beast is.

Shit, I've got to help him. I won't leave here until I find out what the hell is going on.

I blink into the mirror one more time, then slide my phone back into my pocket. Step slowly into his room. His room. This is *his room.* That bed there—that rumpled bed, with its soft, black duvet—is where I lay with him and felt the hard warmth of his abs; his scratchy face; the softness of his lips pressed hard against mine. I sucked the head of his cock into my cheeks and tasted the slick saltiness of him. Just a little while ago, his tongue flicked between the swollen lips of my pussy.

He told me he remembered me.

He said he practically stalked me.

It's so hard to believe.

It's like a dream.

Like a fairy tale.

A twisted fairy tale, because my prince is stuck in prison and as soon as he told me he remembered me, I lost him.

Tears fill my eyes as I stand there in the bathroom doorway, and in the blur of them, I notice the bookshelf that runs along the wall out in front of me. Somehow—I guess because my eyes went straight to him—I didn't notice it when Clinton first brought me here.

I know I need to get the hell out of dodge, but I can't stop my renegade feet from carrying me over, or my eyes from skimming the spines of the books he chooses to keep here in his room with him.

Beloved. I Know Why the Caged Bird Sings. The Curious Incident of the Dog in the Night-Time. A Clockwork Orange. Fight Club. The Bible. The Koran. Peace is Every Step. The Diary of a Young Girl: Anne Frank.

I wonder if these books were donated. I pull out *The Diary of A Young Girl: Anne Frank* and skim through the pages. I only have to flip a few before I find highlighted text.

"It's really a wonder that I haven't dropped all my ideals, because they seem so absurd and impossible to carry out. Yet I keep them, because in spite of everything, I still believe that people are really good at heart."

My eyes widen. Okay, well I think that confirms it: These books were definitely donated.

I flip a few more pages and see boxy, all-caps handwriting. 'THE WEAK DIE OUT BUT THE STRONG SURVIVE.'

Well, hot damn. That's *his* writing. I'm almost sure I remember the tabloids reporting that he wrote in all caps. It was one of these mundane articles I remember only because I used to read so many of them in my star-struck, younger years.

I pull out *Peace is Every Step*, because I want to know what a man like Beast thinks is important about peace. After only a few pages, I start finding passages highlighted.

"When you love someone, the best thing you can offer is your presence."

"To be loved means to be recognized as existing." And out beside this, in the margin: MANAGE EXPECTATIONS.

What does that mean? He feels no one loves him, and therefore no one recognizes he exists? That can't be true.

I flip through more pages, and find another highlight.

"People have a hard time letting go of their suffering." And beside this: PAN—ATTAX?

I stare down at the handwriting, scrawled into the margin with a thick black pen.

Is that code for panic attacks?

Does Beast have panic attacks? It seems impossible to believe.

I let the breath out I've been holding and put the books back. Too many things about this man stir me up. Too much about him haunts me.

I walk to the door and stand there, with my over-hot cheeks and my racing pulse, and wonder what's the best way to find Clinton.

First, I need to get as far from Beast's quarters as possible. When I'm found, as I assume I will be pretty quickly, I'll tell whoever finds me that I'm here to see Clinton. They'll probably ask me how I got in, or maybe they won't. Probably whoever mans the cameras is in Beast's pocket like everyone else, and they'll remember letting me in on the sly.

But what if they're in the pocket of Beast's enemies now? My body goes a little cold. I don't know anything about prison. About the politics here. About how to take care of myself here.

Surely the people who work here will help me get to Clinton.

It's a civilized place. The employees are just regular people.

If I get caught, I'll say I'm here to see Clinton, and whoever finds me will take me to him. Right? He's not a prisoner. He's a guard. They can have guests; at least I think they can. I've always been able to visit Holt when I wanted. Maybe I have special privileges because I'm his daughter?

Regardless. I will find Clinton.

I need to woman up. Shake off my anxiety and get this done. I push through Beast's door and spirit myself out into the hall. I'm so anxious, I forget to look around. I just bolt to the right, hoping to get down the short hallway that houses Beast's quarters before someone sees me. That way they won't know I was visiting him, and the men who took him won't feel the need to "take care of it," or whatever it was they said they'd have to do if I was found.

I'm mid-stride, hurling my body toward the doorway that leads back to the main hall, when strong fingers close around my upper arm. I gasp and whirl.

For a second before my brain registers the face, I allow myself to hope it's him. Instead, when I blink and my mind clears, I find myself nose-to-nose with a hulking, blond guard. He's got freckles all across his nose and cheeks, and a wicked-looking scar on his forehead. His blue eyes are so cold, I glance up and down his body to confirm he's wearing a brown guard's uniform and not a prison jumpsuit.

He's a guard, but he looks mad enough to kill. "Let go of me!"

He clenches my arm a little tighter and rolls his gaze down me. His brows draw tightly together, as if he's never seen a woman before. In a thick, Southie accent, he says, "Who the fuck are you?"

"I'm…Belle. I'm looking for Clinton."

"In Beast's room?" He shakes his head vehemently. "You're looking to get banned from here because you're a fucking liar."

"You're right. I am." I open and shut my mouth convulsively, trying to get my brain to come on board. Honesty. Just be honest, Annabelle. "I was looking for him—for Beast—but he's not—"

"He's not there," the guard snaps.

I nod. "Right. But before I go, I really need to talk to—"

"Clinton's gone, too."

"He's gone? What do you mean?"

"Went home."

"His shift ended in the last hour? I thought he just got—"

"Doesn't matter why," he interrupts. "Clint's not here. You need to go. You don't belong here." He drags me down the hall, punches some keys into a keypad to open a thick, steel door, and puts his hands on my shoulders. He points me in a direction I think is the front of the prison. "Guard at the end of this hall's Germain. Tell him Larry sent you."

Before I can fully process what's going on, he says something into a Bluetooth. I hear mostly just grunts, and then an African-American man appears at the other end of the short hall.

I figure this new guy can't be as bad as Larry, so I take a few long, quick strides. Germain grabs my elbow and I fear I'm wrong. He starts to drag me past the rows of steel doors on each side of the hall. I jerk my arm away and dig my heels in.

"Stop it!" My voice rings through the empty hall, and Germain peers down at me. "I don't know who you people think I am, but—"

"I know exactly who you are, sweetheart. Come with Daddy. We've got some questions for you."

"Beast?" I say. Is he taking me to Beast?

"You're his bitch. That's why we're asking you the questions."

I'm about to tell him I'm also Holt's daughter when I feel his hand press down on my back, and I'm guided through an open doorway to my right.

And there I find all three of them: the amoral-looking bastard in the dress suit, and the two men in black jumpsuits and boots.

CHAPTER 2

Annabelle

THE MAN IN THE SUIT is sitting at a faux wood table, in the middle of a boxy room. Under the harsh fluorescent lights, I can see he has salt and pepper hair and thick frown brackets around his mouth. He's lean but well-worked-out. Maybe sixty? The other two, both closer to my age, sit on his left and right wearing apathetic frowns.

As soon as Suit sees me, his eyes widen. "Miss Mitchell." He sounds pleasantly surprised. After just a second, he locks his face down again, the frown lines reminding me a little of a Hollywood movie villain.

I stand up straighter and try to look tough, despite Germain's death grip on my forearm.

"You can let go of Miss Mitchell," Suit tells Germain.

He does, and then steps back behind me somewhere. I have to resist the urge to massage my arm.

I try to keep my face as neutral as possible while Suit stares at me. After a few seconds, my patience and anxiety get the best of me, and I speak first.

"How do you know my name?"

Suit smirks, and it's a handsome smirk. A smirk that makes him look like the embodiment of 'The Man.'

"You're Beast's new pastime," he says in his old Marlboro commercial voice. "Everybody at La Rosa knows he fucks you."

My eyes bug out. Did he really just say that to me?

"'Mine.'" His lips draw into a smug-looking pucker. "Isn't that right, Annabelle?"

If his goal is to throw me off, he's starting to succeed. I'm confused and self-conscious, wondering if I look just-fucked in my yellow shirt and red jeans. I run my fingers over my curls, and he drags his gaze up and down me, blatantly assessing. I can't tell what his judgment is. His face remains impassive. He waits another second before speaking, and I can tell this is his M.O. Whoever he is, and whatever he does, intimidation is not something he's new to.

"Why don't you sit down, Annabelle?"

I shake my head. "No thank you. I've gotta going home. I've got family waiting on me."

His eyes flicker past me, to Germain—a silent order. "I don't think so."

I fight the cold fear that washes through me. "I do. Do you know who my—"

"Your ex-step-father is?"

My mouth goes dry, my tongue sticking to the roof of my mouth as I say, "Yes. That's right. Mr. …what's your name?"

He stands up and extends his hand across the table. "Robert. Robert Ryan."

I lean over and shake it, because I'm moving on auto-pilot and I'm not sure what else to do. Why does that name sound so familiar?

"I'm the district attorney, Miss Mitchell. I'm here for a specific purpose, and I'm enlisting the help I need, in whatever form it may present itself. Prisoner. Not. It's all the same to me. Now why don't you have a seat and tell me what you know about Blaine McGuire."

I square my shoulders and do my best to look unflappable. "I don't know anything about Blaine McGuire. I've never even heard of him."

Something bumps the back of my knees: a chair. A glance over my shoulder has me looking into Germain's eyes.

"Sit down, Miss Mitchell," Robert Ryan says.

I shake my head. "I don't want to talk to you, and you can't keep me here. I'm not a prisoner. I didn't do anything wrong."

He arches a brow. "No?"

He pulls out an iPhone and presses something, then slides the thing across the table. I see a video start to flicker over the screen as he says, "Is this not you, entering through a rear door of the premises, an entrance at a federal prison not intended to receive visitors?"

I realize the moving figure on the screen is Clinton, showing me to the door of the library. And—shit—that's me. The footage ends as soon as I step inside, and I realize the camera must have been behind me somewhere. Pinned to a tree or something, I guess. The camera wasn't inside.

Whew.

Still, the fact that he has any footage of me breaking rules here is probably bad. I blink at the phone and try to decide what I should say about it. Pretty quickly, I decide nothing. What can I say? I'm not willing to throw Clinton or Beast under the bus, so I simply bite my tongue.

The DA's face hardens, and he looks at me like I'm a frustrating five year old. "I'm conducting an investigation into this prison, Miss Mitchell. An investigation that's about to be official. Into your ex-step father's activities as warden, and into activities endeavored by the man these people know as Beast. Cal Hammond." His jaw clenches. "That fuck. There's something here. And it involves bank accounts and politics and bribery and a very large number of misdeeds by your father and I will get to the bottom of it. So tell me, Annabelle. What do you know about the murder of Blaine McGuire? I think you'll find you like the outcome better if you tell me what he told you about what happened here last night. Your Beast, that is." His upper lip curls into a sneer.

I step back, and the chair I bump makes a screeching noise against the cement floor. "I'm not involved in this—at all—and I'm not about to let myself be talked into something I'm not comfortable with. Let me go, or my family will come looking for me."

He laughs. "Your dying mother? Or your little sister? What about the babysitter, Holly? She looks tough for such a skinny girl."

My heart stops. I swear, for a full second, every cell inside my body freezes. "How do you know that?" It's a whisper, because I can't seem to get my vocal cords to work.

"I've been investigating your 'Dad—'" the DA bends his fingers into air quotes— "for months. Ever since a little bird told me that a worthless, disgusting, *murdering PRISONER* was calling all the shots here! There's something illegal going on here, probably a very many somethings, and I intend to see them prosecuted. Before I'm finished, your father will be behind bars. Starting tomorrow, someone else is in charge here. And your Beast? Your murdering...*stud*? He's never getting out of solitary. Not as long as I'm alive and holding this office."

He locks his jaw so hard I can almost hear his teeth crack and folds his arms over his chest.

I want to yell, to argue with him, to defend Beast somehow, or intervene on his behalf, but I can't seem to move my mouth. At least not right away. When I can, the words just tumble out.

"It's not going to bring her back," I whisper.

He leans forward. "What did you say?"

"Uma." I clasp my hands together and speak softly. "I know that Uma is your granddaughter. I was there that night. I drove up on the wreck. I know how bad it was...and I know how much it hurts to lose someone you love." I have to stop and swallow, because the time is coming soon for Mom. I know it is. "But you're not going to get her back. Not by throwing Be— Cal Hammond into solitary. Not by doing anything."

He throws his head back and starts laughing. It sounds so much like a cough, I think if I had my eyes closed, I'd never know the difference. I fold my arms across my chest and watch until he shuts his mouth and the sound stops echoing through the little room. He straightens up and meets my eyes again. His are so cold. So filled with hate and bitterness. "You're not very bright, are you?"

I blink. I'm not going to dignify this asshole with an answer.

"Honey," he says, "I know I can't bring the dead back. But I can add to the count. You know what I mean?" His eye quivers. Or maybe that's him blinking. It looks like a seizure, but I think it's just pent up fury. After just a second of that horrible, freakish, unhinged look, he stands again and thrusts his hand out. He seals the deal on freakish by giving me a phony grin that looks like it must hurt.

"Good to see you, Miss Mitchell. Germain will see you out."

The guard grabs my arms and snatches them behind my back, and I jerk against him. "No! I want to know what's going on with Beast!"

"Germain," the DA says. His tone is a warning: *Get her out of here*.

"I'll tell Holt about this!" I cry as I'm dragged out of the room.

"That's the point, honey."

I'm escorted all the way to the security checkpoint by the guard named Germain. When we get there, he asks one of the female checkpoint guards to see me to my car.

By the time the guard and I are pushing through one of the glass doors that leads to the parking lot, my eyes sting with unshed tears and my chest feels uncomfortably heavy.

I step out of La Rosa, into the bright, pale day, and glance around the parking lot, not because I want to leave but because even my eyes aren't sure what to do next. It's then I remember: I don't have a car.

Shit.

From where I'm standing, at the top of the stairs to the main entrance, I can see two guard towers, but no one is nearby except the guard who brought me out.

I pull my phone out of my pocket and turn around to see if she'll leave me alone now so I can call a cab or even Holly if I need to.

Instead of leaving, she spits some fruit-scented chewing gum into a wrapper and puts a cigarette between her lips. It dangles there as I say, "I can't leave right away. I don't have a car here."

She ignores that and holds out a pack at me. "Want to bum one?"

I shake my head, but I'm surprised she asked. Maybe I've finally found La Rosa's one friendly employee. Besides Clinton, that is.

"Do you know Clinton?" I ask as she lights up.

Her thin, dark brows draw together. "You do?"

I nod.

Her gray eyes widen. "I remember you now. You're the riot girl! I recognize you from the cameras." She laughs. "If Clinton is your ride, you'll be waiting as long as the lifers. He just got escorted out like you."

"He did? Why?" I assume I know why—he's part of the housecleaning that's probably going to get rid of all Beast's posse—but I want to hear what she says.

She tosses her gaze left, then right, like she's trying to be sure no one is watching us talk. She steps closer to me as she blows smoke out the side of her mouth, toward the parking lot. "He's under investigation."

"Why?" I breathe.

"That's not something I can tell you, doll."

I bug my eyes out, as if to say what the hell, and she laughs a little. "Mostly 'cause I don't know."

"Where is the warden?" I try. "Is he still away?" I know the answer, of course, but I want to see what she says. See if I can figure out more about why the DA thinks he can come in and start messing with the system here. See if I can tell by her reaction to the question whether she knows I'm the warden's daughter.

"You mean your dad?"

I nod. Question answered.

"I'm surprised that you don't know. But yeah." She nods. "We've got an interim—Jenkins, one of the three wardens under your dad—but Jenkins got suspended, too. We had the DA come out. Fancy suit and all. He's all good and pissed off. Shaking things up." She drops her volume a notch. "Some people are saying it started with Cal Hammond. The DA thinks Beast killed his granddaughter."

"Huh?" I feign.

She nods solemnly.

"Do you mean the girl in the wreck that night? Uma Whatever Her Last Name Was?"

Her brows arch up. "You knew her?"

I shake my head. "I just remember her name. First name."

She shrugs, and takes another drag, then slowly blows it out. "I don't know much about the wreck, except some people died," she says, still blowing smoke. "I don't care, either. That man in there—" she jacks her thumb toward the doors— "is not Cal Hammond. They call him Beast. But then, I guess you know that…rict girl."

I swallow, trying to loosen my throat. It feels tight. Because my body knows, a second before my brain does, what I'm about to ask her.

"Did he kill that guy tonight? The Aryan?"

"You tell me," she says. "You were here for him, weren't you? Don't you lie to Maura. I can tell."

I nod slowly, and she smirks. "Conjugal visits at all hours, that big fucking cock. I heard his cell is swank as shit, too. How did it go down? When they came for him, you were sucking his dick?"

I bite my lip. I'm not sure if I should tell her anything—definitely not whether I was sucking his dick when he got taken—but I figure if I want more information from her, I might need to give a little. "They just came and…took him. Two guys dressed in black, and one in a suit."

"The DA," she says, nodding. "One of the other assistant wardens told me he had it in for Beast."

I grit my teeth. It's wrong. So wrong. I don't care if Uma was the DA's granddaughter; he shouldn't be allowed to pop up and start playing out his own vendetta. Not in a place like this, where Beast doesn't have any rights. It's abuse of power in the worst way.

"Don't look so upset," the guard scoffs. "He's killed a lot of men in here. If you ask me, he gets privileged treatment." She leans in a little, blowing a curtain of smoke into my face. "I fucked him a few times—privacy of the kitchen—" she smiles— "and he's got a big, pretty dick, but he's no warden. He roams the halls with no escort or nothing. Not that I don't like to see that pretty face, but it's fucked up, the way things are. Probably because he killed so many people. He's got respect from all the men. Even the gang leaders treat him like a…I dunno. Some kind of Mafioso. I heard he bribes the ranking guards with money."

"You're not a ranking guard?" I ask.

"I'm just a junior. New hire."

"Did you know the guy who…died?" I brave. "The…Aryan leader, or whoever he was?"

I'm nervous about asking, because she's white. I'm not sure how the guards and the prisoners get along. Maybe the white guards like the white prisoners, and mentioning the dead Aryan will make her angry.

I'm relieved when she takes another drag of her cigarette and shrugs. "I heard he got offed in a shower stall. Buck ass naked. Someone squealed to someone saying it was Beast and the media found out like that." She snaps her fingers to emphasize *fast*. "DA showed up and you know how that went down for Beast. People are saying your daddy's gonna go when he gets back from his vacay. His head is gonna roll. There's gonna be some changes around here. Everybody's just a normal prisoner, and the new person is running things."

"Who's the new person?"

She shrugs. "Someone on the DA's good list. He's supposed to get here in the morning." She looks me over and laughs, a little wryly. "Look at fucking me. I'm spilling all my fucking secrets." She looks around, then frowns as if she's straining to hear something.

Right about that time, I hear the rumble of a car's engine. I peer around her to see a yellow van bouncing down the dirt road. The gate begins to open. I wonder if whoever called the cab would mind if I rode with them.

"That's you, doll."

"It is?"

She nods. "Germain, he called about thirty minutes ago. Said you'd need a ride out. Asking me to get you one."

"How did he even know that?" I wonder aloud.

She shrugs. "Word here travels like a wildfire sometimes."

"Oh." It's hard to get the word out, because my throat feels thick. I can't believe this happened. I can't believe I'm leaving, with no idea what's going on. I start down the stairs, then turn to her and struggle to think of what to say. "Thanks for talking to me."

She blows more smoke out. "No problem, hunny."

I step down the first stair. Then I turn back toward her. "I've got a question." She arches a brow, and I let my breath out slowly as I try to wrangle up the nerve to ask it. The nerve to hear her answer to it. "Could you do me a favor?"

"What now?" She looks both annoyed and slightly amused.

"Can you let me know if you hear anything? About him—Beast?"

She throws her head back and laughs. "Honey, you're dreaming. He's never gonna keep in touch with you. You're just a lay. Even in the pit, he'll find some pussy. That's the way things are for a rich movie star like him. You won't ever hear from him again."

I nod slowly, discarding what she's saying and trying to think of how to endear her to me so she'll give me an update even if she thinks that I don't need one. "I know I probably won't hear from him or anything, but I want to know when he gets out of solitary. And how he's doing and stuff. Maybe it's dumb, but I don't care. If I give you my number, could you call? I could pay you or something…"

She presses her lips together, like she's considering the idea. "You got plastic?"

I nod.

She snickers a little, and pulls a phone out of her pocket. "You got it bad, girl. Got it bad for Beast." She slides her fingertip over the screen and flicks her gaze up to mine. "I make bows." She rubs her hair. "You know, for little girls? Got a shop on Etsy. Give me your number. Two hundred bucks will help me buy more ribbon. I'll give you a buzz tomorrow."

I can feel my shoulders loosen as a little of the tension leaves my body. "Tomorrow. Okay, that's perfect." I hold up my finger to tell the cabbie to hold on a minute and pull my card out of my pocket.

"Ready?" I look up at her.

She nods, and I rattle off my card number. My head throbs as she punches it in.

She turns the phone around to face me, revealing a nifty little screen with a line for my signature. "Use your finger," she says.

I rub the tip of my pointer finger over her screen, and am relieved when she shows it to me again.

PAYMENT ACCEPTED.

"Thank you. Thank you so much. I really mean it."

She chuckles. "Welcome, hun. Now get going."

I get into the van, clutching my phone like it's a bar of gold.

CHAPTER 3

Beast

NIGHTMARES ARE NOTHING NEW for me, but this one is fucked up.

I'm stuck in dreamland, and I keep blinking, because I'm looking at Guy in a body bag and I'd give anything to have my gaze somewhere else. The sides of the rubbery, black bag are zipped around all of him but his face.

And his face…

Unlike other nightmares, blinking doesn't send me to a different room in the house of horrors. I remain right here in this miserable dimension, where I can't look away from all the blood caked on him. It's black, crusted and dried onto his blow-white skin. Except his skin's not really white; it's slightly blue. And his lips are black; black like a bruise. His handsome face is sunken in some places and bloated in others, and I'm starting to feel sick as shit.

I don't want to see this.

I finally get my head to move so I can look the other way, but then there's Uma. And yeah, I'm in a different place now for fucking sure, because unlike very dead Guy, dead Uma's only a little dead. She's still in the road. She's sprawled out on her side, and her body is… Jesus. It's fucking twisted—like a pretzel.

I try to look away, but a sick sort of curiosity compels me. It's been a while since I had a dream this vivid. Years since I was confronted in the courtroom with the damage I did that night. So I blink and look at Uma's broken body. At her pretty face, which I can't see. Her head is blood. Nothing but fucking blood and gore.

I look the other way, and I wish I could get up and run from this nightmare I'm having, because I've got a decent guess what's next.

"Oh God…"

Royce. I try to open my eyes but it doesn't go away. I see Royce a hundred times. Like somebody took a bunch of Polaroids of his dead ass and taped them on a big, white wall.

It's a…fucking…I don't know. A fucking progression of death.

Royce is on the road and his skull is cracked open like a…

"Fuck."

I try to cover my mouth but my hands won't move. I can feel the vomit moving up my throat. Then I'm turning my head and it's going everywhere, and someone is laughing.

I should try to see who it is. I should try to get up. But I'm too fucking tired. I lie there panting, looking out or up or somewhere at Brody. Brody Royce. The inside of his bleeding head is white like bone or brains or both.

I clamp my jaw down, hissing breaths out of my nose, and I remember Brody's blunt that night. He wanted to smoke a blunt and I did this to him.

"Jesus," I gasp.

I don't want to see this!

I scrub my hands over my face, and I can feel the wetness on the heels of my palms. And I can feel the sticky cool blood on my face.

I'm dreaming I'm dead, too. That one's normal enough. Except in this dream, it hurts. My right cheek hurts like a fucking bitch, and that's how I realize: I'm awake.

Annabelle

In the middle of my sophomore year of college, I was diagnosed with endometrial cancer. *Mis*diagnosed.

Of course, I didn't know at first.

When the doctor at our campus clinic told me what she thought, I felt like I'd been punched in the face. The few days after that, I held onto my awful secret with both hands and learned what it was like to live in a state of perpetual terror. Inescapable dread.

Wanting to do something. Unable to do anything, because my campus doctor was contacting a specialist in Atlanta—but until that happened, I was just in limbo.

The few days after I leave La Rosa are just like that.

I want to know what's going on with Beast, but there's no one I can ask. Holt is still away. I've called his house and talked to his new wife, Bea, who tells me he is, indeed, in Honduras on a "business" trip.

"He's visiting a prison there," she says, almost defensively.

"When will he be back?"

"I'm not for sure. At least another week."

"Can you have him call me?"

"I can ask."

But she doesn't, or if she does, he decides he doesn't want to. Maybe he knows I'm wanting information about Beast. Maybe he knows nothing. That would make sense, if they're replacing him as warden.

Days roll by. Stifling days where I fake my smiles for Ad and sit in the bathtub every night until the water turns cold.

Days—and my friend Maura, the junior guard who stole my money, never calls.

The news networks report the same story over and over: Cal Hammond killed an Aryan gang leader. It's the first time he's been in the news in years, it seems, and "average Americans" are shocked at his violent deed.

"I think he's just playing a role," says a woman interviewed in New York City on a late night show.

I hear a National Public Radio analysis of "Cal" and his career as I drive Ad and I home from Wal-Mart the next afternoon. Some stupid expert says the same thing. Just a role. *Right.* Because eight years in prison is nothing but a feigned tough guy mentality. Because he goes home every night to his Hollywood castle and only wears a jumpsuit in the day. Because murdering someone is just part of his effing role.

Why is it so hard to accept that sometimes people change? Not for the better. For the worse. That night, my Mom slips into a coma, and I cry into my pillow—because sometimes people change. *Always*, people change. And so much of the time, it's for the worse.

When I fall into my tear-soaked dreams, I feel his mouth. His hands. His blood.

Exactly a week after the last time I visited the prison, they send a new hospice nurse to the apartment. She tells me, "We don't think your mother will wake up again."

I cry into my hands while Adrian eats a bowl of cereal behind me, peacefully oblivious, at least for now, and after that, we go for long rides in the "country." There, I roll the passenger's window down and let her lean out just a little. As her hair flaps around her rosy cheeks, we pass the spot where the wreck happened.

When we get home, Ad and I draw on the sidewalk outside our apartment door with colored chalk. The next day, when Mom's blood pressure goes lower than it's ever gone before, I teach Ad to ride the "Tangled" bike I bought her with Beast's money.

The day after that, I break down and call the prison, pretending to be a relative of Clinton's. I ask the operator for his phone number. The man on the other end of the line tells me he's gone.

"Gone?" I say.

"He doesn't work here anymore."

I call two days later, at a different time of day, hoping for a different staffer on a different shift. I get a female this time, and ask if women can sign a waiting list for conjugal visits with Cal Hammond. She laughs. "Don't you watch the news, honey? He's not taking any visitors."

Ten days drag by, and still no return call from Holt. Still no update from the guard I paid.

On the twelfth day, after hours hanging around Mom's bedside, waiting for it to be time to get Ad and Holly so we can say goodbye, something shifts inside me, and I just can't do it anymore. We haven't left the house in days, but I don't give a shit. I'm not standing here any longer, waiting for my mom to die.

I load Ad into the car and drive to Dad's house.

I'm surprised when, on the third ring of the doorbell, Holt appears, wearing jeans and a "Mrs. Doubtfire" apron and holding tongs.

"Honey," he says.

"Dad." I tighten my grip on Adrian's hand. "Why the heck haven't you returned my calls?"

"I just got home last night," he says, wide-eyed and innocent.

He smiles down at Ad.

My heart beats too fast. "Why did you never call me back?" I say. "I want to know what's going on with Beast."

"Who's Beast?" Ad looks up at me.

"I don't know," Dad says over her head. "I'm only in charge of managerial oversight now. Prisoner relations is being done by someone put in place by the DA."

"Is that even legal, that he can just come in and clean house this way? Is it the grudge he has over his granddaughter? Is that why he went after you and Beast?"

Dad waves us inside without looking me in the eye, then drops down and takes Ad's chin in his fingers. "How are you, sweetie? You look pretty in your pink shirt."

"Thank you, Holt." She beams, and I simmer as we follow Dad down the hardwood hall, into his large kitchen.

Bea, Holt's new wife, is there—of course. She's sitting on a bar stool, playing on her iPad. When she sees Adrian and me, her eyes go slightly wide, and her thin lips make a little 'o'.

I ignore her as I lift Ad up onto another of the stools, and Dad slides an oyster-shell-shaped plate of chips and dip across the granite counter to her.

"Have some, guys." He looks at Bea. "Bea, why don't you get Luke downstairs?"

I shake my head. "We won't be here for long. I just came here to ask about Beast." I huff and decide, why be fake about it? "I've tried to reach you for weeks now, Holt. You never even bothered to call me back." I glare at Bea. "Did she get calls from Honduras? I bet she did." I glance at Ad and swallow the rest of my anger. "I only want to know what's going on with Beast, and then I'll leave you to your life."

Now it's Holt's turn to go all wide-eyed.

"What? It's not like it's not true," I snap. "I'm not a priority for you. Financially, maybe, but that's all. I'm an obligation."

Holt glances at Adrian, as if to be sure my outburst of truth hasn't harmed her in some way.

"How is your mother?" he asks slowly. His gaze shifts from Adrian to me.

"That's not what this is about," I say. At the exact same time, Ad wails, "She's going to be dead *tomorrow*!"

"What?" I whirl around to her.

"Lucy said so. On the phone," Ad says in a tiny voice. Her eyes fill up with tears, and she bites down on her lip to keep them from falling.

"Oh baby." I scoop her off the stool and walk into Holt's den. I sit her down on his big, suede couch and put my arms around her. A few seconds later, I hear his footsteps and feel him kneel beside me.

"Why didn't you tell me?" he murmurs.

"I tried," I say out of the side of my mouth. Holt needs to leave me alone right now. Give me some space to straighten this out with Adrian. I ignore him and rub Ad's hair back from her forehead.

"Baby, that's not true. Lucy was just talking. The truth is, nobody knows when Mama might go to heaven. And if somebody did know, it would be me and you, not a nurse. Lucy shouldn't have said that. Even though she is a nurse who takes good care of Mama, I don't think she's very smart."

Adrian clamps her teeth down on her lower lip and nods, then slides her eyes to Holt, who's still crouched down in front of the couch beside me.

"Hey, Holt." She smiles a little. "Did you know I can spell triskaidekaphobia?"

He grins back at her. "No way. I'd like to hear that."

Holt and I spend the next half hour lavishing Adrian with attention. Then we return to the kitchen, where Bea's son, Luke, is asking if he can use "the Benz" to take his girlfriend out to get a milkshake.

The Benz.

Dear God.

I make a show of looking at my phone. "We should be going. Things to do at home," I tell Holt with my eyebrows raised. "Can you walk us to the car?"

He nods.

I buckle Ad into her booster seat, shut her door, and stand outside the driver's side with my hands on my hips.

"I know you've been avoiding me, Holt. So let me tell you this. It's true what Beast—Ricardo—told you. We did meet one time way back, and while you were gone and I was starting to help with the library? We got to be friends again. I like him, Dad. I want to know what's going on with him. Did he kill that guy like everyone says he did? Is he still in solitary? Because I was actually there when all this craziness went down, and the DA acted like he really had it in for Beast."

Holt looks into my eyes and nods. My stomach lurches.

"So he's still in solitary?"

Holt shakes his head and looks down at his feet. He shifts his weight a little while I hold my breath. Finally, he looks back up at me. "Honey, I'm sorry but…I lied to you. I wasn't demoted. I was fired. I don't know what's going on at La Rosa. I miss it like hell and it's killing me to be away. I made that place what it is."

Is that something to brag about? I wonder, but aloud I say, "God. That sucks. I'm sorry for you."

The truth is, I'm incapable at the moment of feeling anything but anger, but I know if it weren't for Mom and my continued wondering over what's happening with Beast, I *would* probably feel sorry for him. Maybe.

He shakes his head and presses his lips together. "You asked about Beast. You know the DA's granddaughter was that model who was killed. In the wreck a long time ago? The one that landed Beast in prison?"

I nod. "But I don't care. He shouldn't have that kind of power. He's not the warden."

"It's not that simple."

"What does that mean?"

"There are a lot of different things at play here—a lot of different…players, if you will. The DA is being opportunistic. And, unfortunately, Beast is taking all the fall."

"Taking all the fall? For what? For stuff he did with you? The way the two of you ran the prison? You did do illegal things, didn't you?"

He shakes his head. "There's no point in talking about that old stuff now."

"Look at me!" I snap my fingers. "Quit looking down. I think there is a point. I want to know what's going on."

"Not now." His eyes are sorry. No, not sorry. *Guilty*. "I can't talk about that stuff, and Annabelle? You should try to stop wondering."

I hop into the car and slam my door, then speed off so fast I leave rubber streaks on the drive.

CHAPTER 4

Beast

IN MY FREE TIME, I look up the man Beast supposedly killed, and decide, after just a few news stories, that Beast probably did the world a favor.

More days creep pass. Three. Four. Five.

Mom hangs on, barely. Ad and I paint her fingernails and toenails, rub lotion on her bony legs and arms. At night, when Ad's in bed and the nurse is reading quietly on her tablet, in the hallway, I spend hours talking to her. Telling her all kinds of things I've never told her before. The kinds of things I used to wish I could tell my mom, if we'd been BFFs, and she'd been…normal. Mom without the drugs or drinking. Mom without the men.

This is her, and even though it may be sad or sick, I find myself clinging to her.

Days fade into nights and nights bloom into days, and I hate the passage of them. It's been two weeks. Three weeks.

Mom's deep in her coma. I begin to think the hospice nurses are right: She's not waking up.

I call Holt again, begging him to give me Clinton's number. I think Clinton will know at least how Beast was treated when they took him, but Holt tells me there's no point.

"I talked to a friend. He's not being treated great, Annabelle. And his sentence has been extended. Four more years."

For some reason, the news is a crushing blow. I cry more that day about Beast than Mom.

And then suddenly, a few days later, TV news says it's been a month since he killed the gang leader. A month since he told me he remembered me. A month since I touched him. A month since I heard his voice.

I try to get a pass into the prison by calling and asking the director of outreach if I should continue trying to get donated paperback and hardback books for the library. Not that I ever really got that rolling, but I can now. I can do it easily if it means I might be able to get a glimpse of Beast.

I'm told by someone at the prison that the library project has been put on hold.

Depression sets in.

Ad starts sleeping in my bed. She cries at night, and so do I.

I never drift off before 3 or 4 a.m.

Until a Sunday night. The night of a day we were all sure Mom would breathe her last. The night of an exhausting day, one where I just can't hold my eyes open, so I fall asleep with Ad's arms around my neck.

My ringing phone wakes me from a fitful sleep. The area code is local, but the number is unknown.

I blink at the phone, held up over my head with the bright screen pointed away from Ad. Then I answer on a whim. "Hello?"

"Riot girl. Maura here." In the pause that follows, my heart beats so hard I feel like I might black out.

Finally, after a few breathless moments waiting for her to speak again, I cough out, "Yes."

"I've got some news for you."

I push up on my elbows. Swing my legs off the side of the bed. If she tells me something bad, I'm going to run into the bathroom. If I start to cry, Ad will think it's Mom.

"What is it?" I croak.

"It's your man. Your Beast. They told us he was transferred out, but I went downstairs with Tony—he's another guard, a senior one—and we heard him. Down there moaning in a solitary cell."

"Is he okay?"

"I don't know. I think…he's taking something. He was…different. But that's not why I called." Silence spreads out, cruel and thick. "Tomorrow, there's a hit on him."

I step into the bathroom in my cotton shorts and bra and whisper at my screen-lit reflection in the mirror. "What do you mean a hit?"

"Some people are gonna sneak down there and kill him. While he's not defending himself."

My blood runs cold. Ice cold. It takes me a minute to find my voice. "Is this a known thing? Can someone stop it?"

"You want to help?" Her voice sounds hopeful. "I can sell you my pass code."

"What's a pass code?"

"Like an employee ID code."

"And…? It gets me into places? Different areas of prison? You're just a junior guard, you said. I'd have access to the solitary units? I find that hard to believe."

"Well…it's not my pass code," she says. "It's Tony's."

I take a deep breath. Let it out. In the eerie light of my phone, with the reflection of the mirror transposing the part on the left side of my hair, I look strange and thin and sick. "You wouldn't cheat me, would you, Maura? I feel cheated from last time, because you never called. I don't like to be cheated."

"A pass code is a pass code," she tells me. "Ask Holt."

I straighten up to my full height, as if getting more vertical will help my head stop spinning. Help my chest stop aching.

"I need the money," she says. "My baby daddy doesn't have a job, and I pay child support. I'm running low. If I give the pass code to you, it needs to be today." She waits a beat, then tells me, "Seven hundred dollars. You have that much money?"

I take a deep breath and step back into the bedroom so I can find my card.

CHAPTER 5

Annabelle

I END UP NOT GIVING her my card number again. I realize as soon as I reach for my clutch, at the foot of the bed, that this is not a smart idea—no matter how desperate I am or how much money is still left from what Beast gave me.

"I'll pay you when I get there," I say firmly. "You'll have to meet me to let me in, anyway."

"The library," she says. "You been there before?"

I press my tongue into the roof of my mouth. My head pounds. "Have *you*?"

"No, but I heard it's a blind spot."

I exhale—relieved. "A what?"

"No cameras there. Not yet. Cause it's unfinished. No one goes there."

"There is one," I say. "Not on the inside, but outside."

"How do you know?"

"What does it matter? I just know. You'll have to find another way to let me in."

"Everybody knows your face. They know you're Holt's daughter. And the gangs that are gunning for Beast—they know you're his lady."

"I can assume this is a bad thing?"

"Oh yeah. Really bad." She's silent for a moment, then she says, "You need to cut your hair."

"I need to what?"

“Cut off that curly frizzy shit and wear a hat or something. Dress in…I dunno. Hell. Cover up that sexy body in some coveralls. Something plaid or…damn. A jumpsuit. I can get you prison orange if you want.”

“No. No way. I’ll find my own clothes. And I’ll fix my hair. I’ll be there. When?”

“Come now.”

“What do you think I can do to help him?”

“Help Beast?”

“Yeah.”

There’s an ugly little pause that tells me she doesn’t have an answer. She just wants to sell the pass code.

“That’s what I thought.”

“You still want it?” she asks.

I chew on my fingernails. I step back into the bathroom, where I look at myself in the mirror. I’m Adrian’s only guardian. If something happens to both Mom and me, Ad would have no one.

I shouldn’t go to the prison on some fool’s mission. I can’t see Cal Hammond—Ricardo—Beast in solitary.

I shake my head, but when I open my mouth, I hear myself say, “Yes.”

Maura knows the camera guy working tonight, and after some wheeling and dealing I don’t even want to know about, she gets him to disable the camera that monitors the back door to the library.

She recommends, in addition to all her other insane recommendations, that I rent a car and come in through the back fence, where the employee parking is.

I do everything she tells me, except with my hair. I’m not cutting my hair. My crazy, curly hair is totally my thing. I pull it up into an uncomfortably tight bun and stick a Lakers cap over it, then find the least fashionable outfit I own—which turns out to be a pair of baggy jeans that belonged to my college boyfriend, and a plaid button-up I sometimes wear when I'm styling my hair. I add a pair of paint-speckled boots and call the rental company to let them know I need a car, and that I need someone to pick me up.

I spend the next hour cutting up fruit for Adrian's breakfast, calling Holly over to our apartment, and saying "bye" to Mom, who is clinging to life with a stubbornness I have to admit is kind of surprising.

"I love you so much, and so does Adrian. I'll be back soon," I tell her. "Adrian is here, and so is Nurse Sarah."

I step back into the bedroom to kiss Ad and grab my purse, then go down to the parking lot to wait for the car rental guy to pick me up. I could always take my own car to the rental place, but Holly's '89 Accord is a piece of shit, and I want her and Ad to have mine if they need something.

I don't need to discuss what we'll do if Mom passes away while I'm gone. The plan has been in place for weeks. The prison is only about an hour and fifteen minutes away, so if something happens, I'll come home immediately, and Adrian won't be told until I'm there.

The guy who picks me up is lanky, with spiky, puke green hair and a lip piercing. Strangely, he has the radio station set to country music.

His weird taste in music reminds me of Clinton. I wonder, as I sign the paperwork for my rented van, what happened behind the scenes that led to the breakup of the Beast regime.

I wonder about the DA looking into my family. It's disgusting, that I'm feeling almost sick with worry, considering driving back home to check on Ad and Holly, just because that asshole is misusing his power. Maybe Holt and Beast did a lot of things wrong, but Holly didn't. Adrian didn't.

I call Holly, who assures me that Ad is fine—other than refusing her fruit and begging for waffles—so I end up driving on toward La Rosa.

An hour is too much time to think, these days.

I worry over whether I'm wasting my time and energy… What if Mom dies while I'm gone, and I can't get into the prison with the stolen pass code anyway? What if—God help me—Beast gets killed before I get there? What if it's some kind of set up? I can't really think of a reason why… but I feel generally nervous. Death is all that's on my mind. I feel its fingers tap, tap, tapping on me, reminding me it's only one wrong moment away—for everyone. I stop at a gas station, because the sun is finally starting to come up, and I need something basic for breakfast. There, I lament the way they have a thousand caffeine products—even gum—but no sedatives.

In the car, I do a few deep breathing exercises before I pull back onto the road.

I just need to calm down. Think positively.

I'll get there in time. I can…what? What can I do? God. How will I even help him once I'm there? What if Ad is left with no one? Mom and I both die.

The scariness of thinking that thought again, not in the darkness of my bathroom safe at home, but here in the car, on the way to La Rosa, has me considering turning the car around.

I don't. Because I'm an idiot. The same idiot who tried to get her V-card punched by a celebrity. The same idiot who agreed to Beast's initial deal—three hours a day. The same idiot who fucked him after he beat up Holt.

It's true, I've done a pretty good job at life for the most part, but when it comes to this man, I'm an IDIOT.

I laugh a little as I turn off the highway and onto the long dirt road that I'm pretty sure will lead me to the employee parking lot.

I've got my big purse with me this time…and part of the reason is because I've tucked my Mace inside. I've also got a can of that awful new age spray sunscreen, which hurts like a bitch if you get it in your eye. These are my weapons. This is how I'll help him if someone tries to come and kill him while I'm visiting.

I roll up to the gate and try the pass code Maura gave me; this one's hers. She refuses to give me Tony's until I pay her. She said if I didn't pay her when I got inside the prison gates, she'd "go prisoner" on me. I told her if the pass code for the gate didn't work, and I drove all the way out here without even getting in, I'd report her.

Luckily, or maybe very unluckily…her pass code works.

The gate wobbles open on its big wheels, and I roll through. I park between a Subaru and a Toyota Prius and get out of the car slowly. There's a guard stand looming over the asphalt lot, and for a moment, as I glance up, I feel ill. I'm wearing plaid, not the brown guards' uniform. But no one jumps out to grab me as I walk around the building, toward the library.

I find Maura sitting in front of the door, opening and closing her palm like a greedy monkey.

I pull a wad of hundreds from my purse and wave it in her face.

"I want to get inside first. I want to see that it will open the door to the solitary area." Thinking of what I'm about to do makes me feel off-balance. Kind of dizzy.

Maura stands up and dusts off the butt of her uniform. "You drive a hard bargain, woman. If you get caught, don't say you got this from Maura. Blame Tony."

"Why?"

"That guy's an ass," she tells me. She uses what I assume is her own punch code to get into the library. I follow her inside and look around, remembering the way Beast made me feel last time we were here. Remembering the feel of him inside me. Good God, that man knows how to please a woman.

I look over at Maura as we pass through the area, headed toward the hall. "So what do you know about him? Is he really bad off?"

She lifts one shoulder, but I notice that she tries not to look at me. "See yourself. Down this hall and down some stairs, then it's solitary."

I stop walking as a wave of anxiety prickles through me. "How will I even see him? I'll get caught in a second."

She shakes her head.

"No?"

Maura smirks. "We've got a new kitchen girl today. Brings plates down to them." Her smirk turns into a mischievous smile. "I locked her in a closet."

"What?"

She nods proudly as we stride into the hallway. "See, the hit on Beast is from Juan Juarez. I fucked that motherfucker, and he's nasty." She turns up her nose.

"What do you mean…nasty?" I'm pretty sure I might not want to know.

"Nasty like he gave me the clap."

Oy. So I was right. I didn't want to know.

"I've been looking for a way to get him back, and now I found it. See, he's got the Julios thinking he's a good replacement for Beast."

"What's a Julio?"

"Hispanic. There's the Mexicans—that's his people; Juarez is their man—and then a bunch of others, too. Like Puerto Ricans, Cubans. They're kind of separate, but they're kind of together. They're all Julios."

I nod slowly. That's why the men were chanting "Julio" at me the day I first came to the prison to talk to Holt. They assumed I was Hispanic.

"Is Beast considered a Julio, too?"

She shrugs. "They don't think of him as anything, not till Juarez got them thinking he and Beast are just alike. He says if Beast can't do the job, he'll fill in. And then yesterday, all of a sudden, he starts saying Beast is going down. Something about betrayal in the money market. That man is crazy."

I nod again as we turn a corner, and all of a sudden, there's a thick steel door, behind a door that's just a bunch of bars.

"This is it," she says, as if it's no big deal. "Solitary. Your Beast is right down the stairs."

I grab her arm. "You're not coming with me?"

"I can walk you down, but I can't stay. Tommy's code's okay for that, but I've got another job right now. If I don't put my code in over there, I'll be tracked."

"What's your other job?" I ask, feeling suddenly suspicious.

"I've gotta deal with something on Guerrilla row."

"What's Guerrilla row?"

"They're one of the black gangs. Mostly people from the inner city. Not war vets. Black war vets have got another group. Guerrillas are sneaky bastards. They can get in and out of anywhere. I think they're the most likely to escape." She holds her hand out. "Can I have my money now?"

"Put his pass code in first." I nod at the keypad to the right of the door. "I want to see it work. Then you can have the money. But before that, I've got a question." I nibble one of my nails. "Your friend, the one in the camera room— when does his shift end?"

"He's on all day."

"And even though he disabled that one camera, he can still see me in here, right?"

She nods. "But he's a lieutenant of Beast. Those two are like brothers, him and Nose."

She steps up to the key pad and starts to punch the number—then slides her gaze over to me. "You know how important this is?"

"How important what is?" I ask.

"I'm letting you into solitary. I don't know anybody who's ever been down there that shouldn't. Well, besides me, but that was just for sex. It's just me and you—Holt's girl. I must have lost my mind."

She nods at my bag. "You don't have a gun or something?"

"No. Of course not." Only Mace, but that's none of her business.

"Okay." She lets her breath out, then her fingers come in contact with the numbers on the pad. She punches in a few, and a small green light flashes. I'm shocked when the barred door retracts into the cement wall, and the steel door makes a hissing sound, as if it was pressurized and now it's not.

Maura presses on it somehow—I can't tell how—and, to my shock, it opens like something out of *Raiders of the Lost Ark*. On the other side of it is a small-looking staircase. As I step over to it and hesitantly start going down, I can see our destination is a long, ordinary-looking hall. I see a row of doors on each side. Unlike the doors on most of the regular cells upstairs, these doors don't have bars. They're solid steel.

Maura walks down ahead of me, and as she steps down onto the cement floor, one of the doors opens, and a guard steps out.

I gasp.

Maura laughs and turns to look at me. "Calm down, girl. He's on your side."

"He is?"

"This is Rocker Joe."

I blink. Rocker Joe is Mexican, with a moustache and a well-worked upper body on top of short, stout legs.

"He's in a Metallica cover band on weekends. They're amazing."

Rocker Joe grunts a little, then nods at me and goes back into the room he came from.

"He hates Juarez," Maura tells me. "The other guard down here today is on a break for two hours. So you're cool."

She waves down the short, narrow hall. "Six doors on the left, and six on the right. One he just went into is the office, others are all rooms. This one here—" she taps the one closest to us— "that's Beast." She looks down at her watch. "You good to go? I can have my money?"

With a cautious look around, I turn myself into the corner by Beast's room and dig into my bag. The last thing I want is to get caught paying her on camera. When I'm pretty sure I can't be seen, I slip her the wad of hundreds.

She bends down and slips it into her sock. When she stands back up, she looks a little more lighthearted.

"Come out the way you went in, no later than ten o'clock. After ten, it's shift change for some of the junior guards. I've only got it covered for the early morning."

She knocks me on the shoulder with a loose fist. "Try to talk to him. Try to get him to wake up. Tell him what's coming. No one will be in while Rocker's here. He'll keep everybody out."

I frown at the thought of relying on one of the guards to keep a bunch of other people out, and she says, "2-4-6-8-1. That's the pass code you just bought."

Maura tugs her gaze away from mine, and without looking back over her shoulder, she says, "Later, Julio."

I wave, then stand there staring at the door.

CHAPTER 6

Annabelle

I KNOW BEFORE I even punch the pass code in that it's going to be bad.

She told me without telling me. *Wake him up... Tell him what's going on...*

Those are bad things.

Those things make me scared to open the cell door.

I stand there with my legs locked tightly together, trying to keep my breaths slow and even. I feel like the ice skaters in Adrian's little ice rink toy—led across the ice by an unseen magnet underneath the plastic rink. I feel like I have no control over my feelings for him. Over the choices I'm making to help him.

For one crazy moment, the riot inside my head is so loud, I think of leaving.

You don't have to do this.

You could get in trouble.

He won't even care.

You don't even know him.

But I don't believe my conscience.

I think sometimes you can know someone even though you haven't been around them very much. Certain souls, when they encounter one another, throw out anchors, and their ropes get tangled and the anchors get hooked all together in a messy barb. And it holds. It doesn't make sense, but it just holds.

I'm going inside. I'm going to check on him, even if it's stupid and I only stay long enough to be sure he's alive and tell him about the Juarez hit. And if I'm going inside his cell, I might as well do it now.

I punch the pass code in and the door clicks open.

I push my face into the space between the door and door frame, tugging air into my lungs. I'm terrified that it will smell like mold or worse. It doesn't. The air is cool, and it smells clean. Like…antiseptic.

Prickly heat spreads down my chest and out through all of me. I step inside, and somehow, my wobbly legs actually carry me.

I don't know what I'm expecting. A rusty cot in the corner and a grimy, barred window? Rats on the floor? Brick walls with chains hanging out of them, and the business ends around his wrists?

I don't know what I'm expecting, but it can't be worse than what I find.

The room is empty.

It's a small, white room with no window, no cot, nothing. No one is in this room.

"WHAT THE EVERLOVING FUCK?"

I whirl around, infuriated, brutally disappointed, already thinking of what I'm going to do to Maura. That lying, stealing—

Strong arms wrap around me from behind, and I'm pulled up against his chest. I know it's him because it feels like him.

"Beast?"

"No. Just…fucking *no*," he growls into my ear.

His words are half-moaned, but his body, wrapped around mine, is strong enough to scare me as he carries me across the room, into one of the corners. The door slams shut behind us and I glance around, taking in the limits of my new captivity, even as he squeezes me against him.

As my eyes flicker around the room, I notice the ceiling. Holy shit, it's covered with pictures. Horrible pictures. Pictures from the wreck.

Bile sloshes up my throat as I remember these moments in the awful Technicolor of memory. I jerk my eyes down as

Beast sets me on my feet. He frowns, then grabs my hands and shuts his eyes.

"No," his hands squeeze mine. "Not you, too, Angel."

When his eyes peek open a second later, I hold his wild, dark gaze because I expect at any moment it'll turn lucid. Half a second, though, and I can tell it's not going to happen.

My eyes roll down him—hungry; scared; assessing.

He's nude. Leaner. His cheeks are lightly bearded, his hair long enough to shag around his ears. His strong, kissable lips are dry and cracked. But it's his eyes that get to me. They're so…wild. As they search my face, then roll down my body, his dick begins to harden.

"This shit is too much," he whispers. "You," he says as his hand moves to clench around my bicep, "are too much."

I grab his wrists. "Beast—how? What about me is too much?" My gaze implores his, trying to figure out what's wrong with him. Trying to find sanity there. "I don't get it," I say gently.

He crushes me into his arms and presses his lips against my hair. "I kept waiting for you. I begged them to see you…but you're not real." His voice drops a notch. "I don't want to see you dead, too."

"I'm not dead."

He shakes his head. I can feel his cheek against my hair. I can smell the heady, spicy scent of him.

"I'm not dead, Beast. *Look.*" I press my palms against his cheeks and drag his heavy head up. "Look at me. I'm me. I'm not dead."

His eyes meet mine. "They're all dead." His eyes flicker up to the ceiling, and I think I understand.

I grab his arm. My fingers walk down it, looking for bruises or red marks. When I don't see them there, I run my hand down his strong, hard abs and "v" of his hips, and down his thigh, which trembles slightly underneath my touch.

His mouth finds my neck as he presses his dick against me. "Angel."

I shiver at the touch of his lips on my skin, but I duck out of his grasp and look down at his thigh again.

Yes, I'm right. It's bruised: a bunch of little green and blue and yellow circles overlapping in one area. I wriggle out of his reach and tilt my head back, so I can see the full sick splendor of the ceiling.

Every last one of them is familiar: a picture quilt of images from that night. My hands grab onto his waist and slide down his thigh.

I look into his face. His eyes are wide, his mouth open.

"Angel." He bends down to kiss me again, and I can't seem to stop him. "You really are my Angel. Coming here. You don't look like the others. You still look alive," he murmurs in a low, scratchy voice.

I can feel his hands tremble against my waist…my belly. "God." His fingers struggle with the button of my jeans, and I help him undo it. His palm glides down my mound. His fingers find my folds and part them gently. I must be wet because he slides inside with ease.

"Oh God."

"If you're real," he murmurs, kneeling down, "you'll scream."

Beast

It's such a strange hell, this place. Every night—some nights?—he comes in here and has the thing to stop my cravings. No more gnashing of teeth or screaming in my sleep. It stings when he jabs the needle in but then I'm floating through heaven. For a few moments, at the start of every time, I think it's heaven.

And then I start to focus. Start to see what's really there.

Uma. Guy. Brody.

They're all dead and I can smell their blood. My blood? Their blood? I start getting restless but when I look around to find somewhere to go, it's never-ending, white eternity. I end up in the corner, hugging my knees, trying not to look up but I always get so tired. I'm on my back, I'm looking up, and Angel is nowhere nearby this time.

I killed them all. I understand why this hurts. It's because I killed them. Hell… This isn't heaven. This is hell.

I never sleep in hell. Every time my eyes are open I'm gritting my teeth and pulling at my hair and wanting things I can't even fucking see.

My chest feels hungry and my eyes are dry.

It's going on and on. I don't know for how long. All I know is I'm lying in a corner, by what I think might be a door. I've seen it before, but nothing makes a lot of sense right now. It never does lately.

And then Angel is here. She's down here with me, and she's not bloody, though I know she must be dead.

"I know you're dead, and you should go away," I murmur up against her thigh, "but I can't let you go yet. I just have to taste you first." I lick my way toward her cunt. "If you're still here when I'm done, I'm going to fuck you—hard."

I spread her with my fingers and I can smell her before I taste her. Sweet like fruit. A luscious, dripping fruit. I press my tongue and lips over her sweet pussy and start to lap her up.

"Oh God!"

I drag my tongue up, gliding slickly around the soft bud of her clit, teasing just enough so her legs give way and I'm easing her down onto the hardness of the floor. I spread her legs. I lift her legs over my shoulders, so I'm holding her up. Her ass is off the floor, her pussy lifted to my face like an Angel buffet.

I ease my tongue down in between her slit, over her warm, plump flesh and down to where the wetness pools. I push my tongue into her sweet center, and her legs grip me.

"Beast! Beast! Fuck!"

She's pulling my hair, and I like it. Fucking love it.

I've already got one finger shoved inside her. I push another finger in. She grunts. So full. I like her full of me.

I start to pump inside her, spreading my fingers out a little, getting her ready for my cock. It's been a while and I am jonesing for her.

Up and down and up and down. I drag my tongue smoothly over her, always flicking just inside her entrance—then skating over her smooth, smooth inner skin and up around her clit. She arches up. She's going wild, pinching my neck. She rocks into my face and I lick her like a succulent desert.

"God! I'm close!"

She hugs my head against her cunt and I fuck her ruthlessly with my fingers and my tongue. Working her up into a frenzy. Making her legs scissor atop my back. Making her ankles bend around my neck. My Angel grunts and groans and—yes—she even screams.

I feel her soft flesh spasm, and I lower her down to the cold floor. Push her legs open. And before she's even finished panting, I aim my cock head for her core, work my thickness into her, and give a mighty shove.

Now…this is heaven.

Annabelle

He splits me open with his huge sword of a cock, and I can feel my body meld around him. God, his dick is huge. So crazy big and hard he can barely fit as he pushes in so deep his balls are pressed against my taint.

"Shit. Oh shit!"

"You like this, Angel?" He grins vacantly over me. I don't care if he's drugged, if he's different. He still fucks me like Beast, and I still want him like I always do. I nod. I like it.

He drags himself out, moving so slowly I shudder, then rolls the full, plump head of him around my slickness and, when he's coated in my juices, he shoves back in.

I slide across the cement floor as he grabs onto my forearms and we start rocking.

"Oh Beast!"

"Say it, Angel." Two fingers grab my nipples, roll them. Tug them. "I want to hear you tell me who owns this sweet pussy."

He's thrusting faster. In and out. I'm drunk on lust, lifting my hips for him, letting the thick head and long, hard shaft move deeper into me than anyone before; his shaft parts my inner lips and rubs against them as his fingers roll over my clit. I'm so slick there. Swollen and ready for him.

"God, I missed this!"

In and out. When he's in, he seems to touch the very core of me. My mind blanks out, and all I am is a place for him to shove his cock. God, he's thick and hard. I'm so tight around him. Feel so stretched. My hips lift higher off the ground because I want to take in more of him.

"More," I murmur. "More please."

He's halfway out, but he drives back in and starts to find a brutal rhythm. As he leans over me, his fingers skate through the lake of silky liquid pooled around my clit, between my lips. Everywhere his cock has touched, I'm sopping wet. His fingers play in my folds, taking me to the edge so I'm gritting my teeth and hissing his name.

And then he moves them off of me.

I can feel his hand under my ass. Two fingers slide between my cheeks as his dick pounds me and my head hits the hard wall. I can feel a fingertip—damp from my pussy—probing gently.

"Yes! Oh yes!"

I want everything he has.

"Tell me you're alive," he grunts. "You like it when I fuck your pussy hard."

"I... I...like it..."

He stops, and my hips thrust up, burying him deeper as he gently slips a fingertip inside my tight bud.

"Say you like it when I fuck your pussy and your ass."

"I like it when you..." His finger slides a little deeper—"fuck...my pussy and my...ass." I gasp.

He grins. "That's right."

In and out and in and out and I'm so full of his cock I'm screaming. I thrash under him; I push against his fingers in my ass. I like his fingers in my ass. My cunt is lit up like a lightning bolt; so raw. "I'm close!" His fingers glide over my clit, teasing every nerve ending as his cock fucks me relentlessly. Slam in, pull out, slam in.

Inside my ass, his fingers curl. His shaft drags over my clit. I clench my body, hold my breath, and—

"You can come now," he says.

He drags himself out of me and mercilessly shoves back in, and I come in an exquisite wave of pleasure.

A second later, he pulls out, and warmth covers my belly.

CHAPTER 7

Annabelle

MOM DATED A LOT of addicts, and was one herself at times, so I know what it looks like when someone is coming down.

The way their eyes glass over and go soft and tired around the edges. The way they seem to fold into themselves: quiet and languid—for a moment. That's until the withdraw sets in. But we're not there yet. He's not there yet.

He's on his back and I'm lying in the crook of his arm. I open my eyes to be sure, in his semi-high state, he's not looking at those awful pictures on the ceiling. But I find his eyes are shut, his breathing slow.

As if my worries roused him, at that exact moment, his eyes flutter open and he blinks up at the photos taped onto the low ceiling. He turns his head away from me, and I reach out and wrap my arm around his neck, turning him back toward me. I press his face into my neck and stroke his hair, then drag my fingers slowly down his nape.

"They suffered...didn't they?" he murmurs. "All of them...suffered so much."

His voice is soft and broken. I wonder how many hours he's stared up at those photos while high on whatever they're giving him. Of course he didn't know what was going on when I showed up. Everyone he's seen these last few weeks is dead. It's sick. It's unforgiveable.

"I don't think so," I lie. "When I got there, two of them were already gone and the other one wasn't conscious."

Sometimes a lie is more compassionate than the truth. I've never been so committed to honesty that I was willing to hurt someone hurting already.

He shakes his head, and I continue stroking his neck. "It was an accident, Ricardo." I wrap my arm over his side, so his chest is pressed against my side, and try to rock his heavy body closer into mine. He doesn't move. I his neck and shoulders with my fingernails. "Try not to look up there again, okay. It's not real. Those are just pictures."

His breathing seems to slow for a second, and I rest my hand gently on his jaw. His cheek is pressed against my head. And then, a second later, he's rolling away from me. Rolling onto his other side, facing the other way. I hear him cough and gag. He's getting sick.

Shit.

I reach out for his back, then realize most people would probably be embarrassed, so I stay away as he heaves and gags, and I see sweat coat his broad back.

By the time he sags back on the floor, his face is damp and his chest is pumping with the speed of his breaths.

I crawl over to him. There's nothing on the floor beside him except liquid.

"God. Are you okay?"

He turns his head away from me. "I'm sorry. Angel. I don't know how you're here, but go. Please, Angel. Go on."

I rub his bicep with my hand. My palm is warm against the damp cool of his skin.

"I'm not leaving yet. Not until I know that you're okay. What are they giving you?" I touch my hand down on his thigh—the one without the scar—and he flinches a little.

"Ricardo…"

He turns away. "I'm not Ricardo." The words are muffled by a hand. He curls up a little more, giving me a view of his beautiful back and ass that heats me up and at the same time hurts to see.

"Who's doing this, Beast? It's the DA, isn't it?" I stroke his back. "Have you been high most of the time that you were here?"

He shakes his head. I think he's not going to answer—until he whispers, in a raspy voice, "I never did do well with drugs. I didn't like cocaine." His eyes flicker over mine, but it's brief—as if he wants to tell me more but won't allow himself. And after a moment, with his eyes on the wall in front of him, he says, "That night, we were pulled over. I did it for Uma."

"Did what?" I murmur.

"A bunch of blow." His eyes meet mine again, two deep brown pools, then quickly retreat. "We all did, in the car. Uma had a bunch of it, and she didn't want to get caught when someone pulled us over."

I nod slowly. "Wow. I never heard that said that way."

He makes a strange sound. "Yeah. In the stories I'm coked up, on a fucking binge." His lips curl up, morose and cold. "I don't even like that shit."

"And they're giving you something similar in here? Injecting it into you? How do they do it? How do they make you do it?" I frown at him, genuinely confused, because even half starved and out of shape, he's bigger than most of the guards here.

He turns his head to look at me full on. His eyes are empty. Bleak. "They don't have to make me, Angel. I beg. I get hungry for it. Whenever it's been too long…" he licks his lips. "A guard from the clinic comes down and gives it to me here." He turns back over on his back, touches his thigh with two fingertips. "It makes my heart beat fast, and I can't breathe well enough," he whispers, "so I always end up on my back."

He turns over on his side, giving me a full view of his blank, tired face, and I reach out and touch his shoulder. "I wish I could reach the ceiling and pull it all down."

The ceilings are low, but not that low. Even Beast can't reach him. Can he?

"I deserve to see them," he says quietly.

"Of course you don't." I wrap my arms around him and snuggle close to his body. He doesn't move. "You're coming down. You're tired and, I imagine pretty frayed and—God—

fucked up. Anyone would be. Can I hold you?" I ask. "Really hold you?"

I try to get my arms around him better, but he leans up on an elbow and shifts away from me.

All of a sudden, he looks angry. "What's the point? We hardly know each other, Annabelle. I'm never getting out of here. So what's the point?"

"Because I want to," I whisper. "I want to hold you for a second."

He presses his lips together and looks at me like I've just asked to drive a hammer into his thumb.

"I care about you, and I think you care about me, too."

His face hardens. "But I don't."

"Yes you do. I know you do, Ricardo."

"Don't call me Ricardo. I told you, nothing but Beast." He sits fully up, then grabs me around the waist and pushes my back against the wall. Sitting on his knees, with his hard cock jutting up against his belly, he lets his hands come down on either side of my head.

"Beast. *That's* who I am," he says.

"Okay. I can call you Beast."

His eyes drop to my breasts. I can feel his hunger. Not just in his cock, but pouring out of every part of him.

I caress his cheek. He closes his eyes.

His hand grabs mine and drags it down his pecs and abs, down his happy trail and to his dick. He rocks into my palm, and I lean down so I can suck him into my mouth.

CHAPTER 8

Beast

"WAIT."

She's got her mouth around my dick, but I pull gently out of it. "What are you doing here?"

I'm feeling a little less hazy now. The drugs I got however long ago are pretty much all out of me, leaving me tired and low. So very tired. It's hard to think much, but for her, I can.

"I don't want you hurt, Angel. You need to leave. This is not a good day for you to be here."

Her eyes narrow. "Why not?"

I can't tell her, of course. Juarez thinks he's going to off me today, and maybe he is. I stand up and pull her up beside me. Wrap my arm around her back, not because she needs me to, but because I can't keep myself from touching her. "You need to leave—right now, Angel."

"Do you know about it?" she whispers.

"What?"

"Someone— his group is Julios?"

"Juan Juarez." I sigh. "Yeah, I know about him. Thinks he's gonna kill me. Maybe he is. But you're not going to be here to see it, either way it goes."

I put my hands on her shoulders and walk her toward the door.

That tires me out. She notices me breathing hard.

"When do you get more?"

"Tomorrow, I think." I grit my teeth. "Today is the in-between day. I'm more aware of what's going on, but it's not a party."

"Why is this happening? Who's doing this?"

"I killed someone, Angel."

"I have to tell you, as ridiculous as this may sound, I find that a little hard to believe."

"I killed someone," I tell her harshly, "and more than likely, I'm going to be killed."

"Why?" Her eyes are wet. "I don't get it."

I kiss her tears.

"I want to go to someone. Appeal or something. Help you."

"You can't help me."

"Why?" Her tears are running down her cheeks. I wipe one away and do some quick thinking. Weighing things out

"Can you keep this to yourself, Angel?"

She nods. She grabs my arm. "Yes. Of course."

I don't see in the moment why I shouldn't tell her. I'm stuck in solitary, defenseless and waiting for my killers like an overthrown despot. Everything I tried to do here, all the work I did—it's meaningless. It's gone.

I've been a thug. An executioner. I've killed ten men since I came to this place—eight of them because I was asked to. Would it be so terrible to tell someone the truth?

I look into her eyes, and I don't even have to make a choice. The words just roll out of my mouth. "I was an informant, Angel. For the government. The other night after I made a hit for them, they turned on me."

I exhale deeply, and I look into her eyes. They're wide with shock.

"This probably won't mean anything to you," I tell her as I rub my itching eyes, "but I recently found out Juarez might not be the mastermind behind his family's drug cartel. The government must be dealing straight with him now, and if he's in charge of all the gang leaders at La Rosa instead of me, he'll probably take me out, no matter how hard I fight."

It's fucking weird to say so, but that's the position that I'm in. If I were upstairs, it would be a little less impossible, but in solitary? It's basically a done deal.

I dare a look at Angel and find her face blanched white, her lips pulled into a little 'o'. "No way. I won't let it be true. It can't be true. It isn't fair! Maybe you're wrong," she says quickly. "You don't know for sure."

I nod slowly, catching my lip between my teeth as I decide how much I should tell her. I reach the same conclusion I did a minute ago: If I'm a dead man by tonight, why hold anything back?

"When they decide it's over, it's over, Angel. Especially if you're stuck in a place like this. What do you think happened to Holt? He knew about my deal with him, and he and I ran this place for years. How do you think that fucker Robert Ryan, the DA, found out I had so much control?"

"The government? And by that do you mean the FBI?"

Not exactly—more like a smaller sub group under the general branch of Homeland Security—but I nod because it keeps things simpler. "When they want somebody out, they do it just like they do it overseas. Clean house, replace the old regime, take out the dictator."

I smile a little, because really, it's preposterous that I was ever a dictator here. My ability to do the most basic things is limited by where I am. Of course it is. Never more than now. That anyone here was kept under my thumb for any amount of time… If I was ever going to win an Oscar, it would be for this.

I lean over and kiss her lips.

"I love this mouth. That sweet cunt of yours. I love everything about you, Angel. But what I need is for you to go. This thing between us—consider it over the moment you walk through that door."

I grit my teeth against a sudden rush of emotion. I manage to keep my eyes from misting, but I can't stop my arms from reaching out for her. "For whatever reason, you're my angel. It's not just a nickname." I kiss her hair. Her cheek. Her soft lips. I'm hard again but it doesn't matter. "It means the world and some that you came here, but you've gotta go before you get caught. Go back out. Go to your car and drive away, Annabelle."

She kisses my mouth hard, then pulls away and looks into my eyes. "I'm not letting you get killed."

I smile at her—or try to. "Angel, I'm pretty fucking good with my hands and feet. I've got a fighting chance. But not with you here. You'll hinder me. Believe me when I tell you that."

Panic twists her face. "That's what people in this position always say!"

"You know a lot of people in this positon?" I

"In the movies, and in books. They tell the stupid woman, 'I can't fight with you here,' and the women leave them, and then they die tragically and become heroes." Her eyes glimmer.

"Angel." I hug her close again and kiss her head. "You've got this backwards. I'm the antihero. I think maybe you're the hero."

I think about the photos above our heads and feel so awful that I hope I do die, but her arms are around me and I'd like more of that, too.

Her hands crawl down my belly and I know where she's going.

"The hit is in three hours now. You need to go, Angel."

She leans down and licks her lips, then opens wide and points my cock toward her mouth. I can feel it swell and stiffen, getting longer and harder than it is already as her hand moves under my balls. She sucks me into her mouth, the head of me buried deep down in the velvet of her throat; my shaft caressed by her cheeks. Her tongue swirls around my base, and with her hand, she gently lifts and kneads my balls.

"*Angel!* Fucking evil little angel." I rock into her—my legs move on their own as bliss floods through me—and she deep-throats me. I moan, and that's the end of my resistance.

I let her lick and suck and tease me with her tongue and lips and throat until I've suken down onto my knees. She's on her knees, too, sucking me off with a zeal I wouldn't have thought possible.

I come with a low growl and lay her hips up across my lap to return the favor. When I've made her come two times—hard—I know I have to move fast. I lift her up and walk to the door.

"What's the pass code you used?" I ask her.

She tells me the number, and I punch it in to unlock the cell door.

I watch her eyes rove the hall curiously as I take her to the showers at the end. It's one shower a week for us down here, and mine was yesterday. I think.

I know Joe won't give a shit—he's one of the ones still loyal to me, despite everything—so I push through the door and step into one of the stalls and strip her clothes off and start the water.

"My room is dirty. I'm dirty. I'm gonna wash you off, and Joe will see you out."

If Juarez is the man in charge, reporting to the feds, they might have him off Bosman. It's a move I think they've been mulling for a while, but the Black Guerrillas don't like me. Ever since an incident last year, they like Juarez a little better.

That must be it, I think as I strip my Angel's clothes off. They've got McGuire dealt with, and I helped install someone more pliant. If Juarez leads things, helps them take out the guy who may really be in charge of the cartel, it's a double-win because they can also get Juarez to take out Bosman. It's so tidy, I wonder if I should have seen the whole thing coming.

"I can't take you getting killed," she says as she wraps her arms around my waist and presses her belly into my cock.

"I'd prefer to avoid it, too, Angel, but sometimes shit just happens."

CHAPTER 9

Annabelle

I SUCK HIS DICK AGAIN in the shower. He sinks down to his knees on the shower mat and puts his hands atop my head as the water rains down on us and steam tingles over my damp pussy.

He props me up against one of the cement divider walls and leans down to lick my pussy, putting my legs over his shoulders, even as he braces me against the wall, and I cling to his arms.

When I've finally stopped shuddering, he carries me out onto a disposable mat and helps me dry with a dark green, shrink-wrapped towel. He dries my hair and helps me into my clothes, and every second that his hands tend to me, I feel a little sicker.

When he's finished helping me dress, he grabs a pale blue, shrink-wrapped jumpsuit from a shelf and I help him get into it.

I stand back and look at him, suddenly understanding the phrase 'my heart is in my throat'. My throat feels so full, I can't even breathe. My heart is pounding everywhere.

"Now you leave, okay?" he says.

I nod, but I don't mean it. I can't leave him here.

"Maybe I could break you out," I whisper.

"Angel, don't get arrogant. It's a fucking miracle that you got in here." If it weren't for the role he played here these last few years, I wouldn't have gotten by with it.

He takes my hand in his and tugs me toward the hall.

"We've gotta hurry, okay?"

I nod, and say a silent prayer: "Please, God. Please. Please save him. I'll give up anything but Adrian."

Beast kisses me once more on my damp hair. Then he opens the door into the hall. He steps out before me, and he stops in place immediately, causing me to bump into his back.

When I see what's stopped him, I flush of hot sweat pops out all over me.

There is Robert Ryan, the renegade DA. He's got a small gun pointed at Beast's chest. On the end is a long, black silencer.

This is how it happens when your life changes.

Something starts things off. Some kind of trigger. A stupid decision—or a bold one? A desperate prayer? I don't know.

All I know is, I promise you, before Beast kicks the gun out of Ryan's hand—

Before Ryan rushes forward and stabs Beast in the neck with a long needle—

Before Beast hits the floor with a smack and clutches his neck, and starts breathing really, *really* fast—

Before he gasps, "Oh fuck. Angel."—

Before one of his hands reaches up toward me as a dying look crosses his face—

I know already that I'm going to grab the gun and use it.

It doesn't happen so straightforwardly, of course.

When Beast starts gasping and the DA scoops his gun up off the floor, I jump on Ryan's back and jerk his neck as hard as I can. He grunts and drops the gun, and I jump down off his back, scooping it off the floor faster than I even knew that I could move.

I take a few steps back. For a moment, I am stunned by Beast's loud gasping. It sends a flood of adrenaline through my veins, which helps me hold the gun steady as I lift it and point it at Ryan's face.

"You little bitch. You wouldn't," he taunts.

The truth is, I don't think I can pull the trigger, but I want to scare him. To make him leave.

"You're sick," I start. My outstretched arms tremble, but I don't move the gun from where it's aimed. "Hanging these horrific pictures everywhere. It's immoral and disgusting! Now, get him some help!" I wave the gun at Beast. His wide eyes cling to mine.

Then the DA dives for me, and my fingers just react. The gun goes off.

Beast is up. I'm screaming. I'm being lifted into his strong arms. Blood is on him and me. Blood, just like the night we met.

He looks down at me, and I know what will happen now as well.

We run.

BEAST

Volume 4

CHAPTER 1

Beast

I STEP THROUGH THE DOORWAY from the showers into the hall, and there he is: Robert Ryan, pointing a gun at my head.

My synapses fire, registering his presence and working to make sense of it. My brain flips frantically through possibilities, and the first I entertain is that I'm dreaming. This thing with Angel—fucking her in solitary, after I've been ousted by the Agency—is nothing but a medicated dream.

I reach behind me, torn between hoping she's there and praying she's not.

My fingers touch soft skin, and my pulse goes haywire.

There've been times when Ryan came into my cell alone—with a syringe, with a club, with pepper spray—but this is different.

Angel is here.

I've got to protect her!

I kick the gun out of his hands, and it clatters to the floor behind him. His eyes bulge, and he lunges for me. My instinct is to dodge, but Angel is behind me. *I've got to protect her!* I hesitate a fraction of a second, and Ryan plunges a needle into my neck...

Tugged under and tossed backward. Static fills my head. My body tingles like I'm nothing but a bunch of dust, floating in a stream of sunlight.

Something…

There's something going on! I try to look around, but all I see is white. White walls? White ceiling? Where am I?

My heart is flopping like a fucking fish. My lungs pump frantically, but I'm not getting any air. My head throbs and my chest feels too tight, but the rest of my body is still dust.

I drift beside her as she points the gun at Ryan.

Oh, *her*.

I blink up at her, and I feel tugged toward this pretty woman—Angel.

I want to cry, I shouldn't cry but I could cry, because there's something wrong—so wrong. I'm fucking worried—so fucking worried about what she's doing here, but it's hard to figure out what's going on when my heart is beating *so fast*.

Milliseconds later, my body manages to process a little of whatever was in the syringe, and GAME ON, BABY.

I push up on my elbows, lifting my head and shoulders off the floor. I'm still numb, but I feel strong and powerful. Unbreakable.

I'm sitting up, pulling one knee up to my chest, marveling at how strange and indestructible I feel, when Angel's face tightens, her outstretched arms jolt, and Ryan hits the floor in front of me in a spray of blood.

Goddamnittheblood!

It's spreading out around his ruined head, dark and thick. I'm on my feet before it touches me.

Somewhere vague and far away, I hear Angel sobbing and it troubles me. My dazed eyes bounce around the hall and find her on the floor right by me, clutching the gun and wailing.

I wrench it from her hands and rip the top of my jumpsuit off my shoulders, using it to wipe away her prints.

HAWK HUNT.

The words tumble into my mind before their meaning, leaving me grasping… Looking down at Angel.

There's blood on her pretty face. From Ryan's head. She's really upset and HAWK HUNT.

I don't—

HAWK HUNT.

A tidal wave of dread washed over me.

I remember something Mack, another of the solitary guards, told me recently. About how the new warden was uneasy about Ryan's frequent visits, worried he'd get caught letting the DA fuck with me.

"He's sorta a stickler," the guard told me.

Which means when the new warden finds out what just happened, there's gonna be a hawk hunt.

A hawk hunt is when trouble prisoners get killed. Usually when bad shit goes down, and the bosses need to cover their asses. Guilt and innocence don't matter in a hawk hunt. Anybody involved in the incident—anybody who might tell a story that could cause the prison staff to get in trouble—is put down.

Angel is here. I'm here. Both of us can—will—blow this Ryan thing up.

Angel just did. I blink at the blood pooling around him, struggling to think.

The Agency was using him to take me out. If they hadn't been, he'd never have been able to throw me down here into solitary. I had too much power for that before they turned on me.

But they wanted me out. They wanted Juarez in charge.

Rocker strolls out of the guard station. The cameras are off, so he didn't see what happened, and the gunshot was silent, so he didn't hear it either. It must've been Angel's sobs that drew him away from computer solitaire.

Rocker gets a good look at the blood bath in the hall and his eyes bulge.

And then I snap out of my stupor and I kick him in the fucking face.

He goes down like a sack of flour and I throw Angel over my shoulder, wrapping one arm around her back and wielding Ryan's gun with the other. The weight of her in my arms cuts through the numbness. Makes my chest ache. Makes me want to scream. But there's no time for that. My iron legs race up the stairs.

As I reach the door that divides solitary from the rest of La Rosa, I catch the scent of blood. It almost gets me, but I'm juiced up now. My body sings *benzoylmethylecgonine* as I punch pass codes into the keypad by the door, striking out once, twice, three times before my mind spits out one that works.

The door clicks its acquiescence, and I throw it open. Angel is still wailing, so I hiss "Quiet" before I tighten my grip on her and run toward the library.

I'm energized by the thought that I can fix this. I can save my Angel. All I have to do is get us out the emergency library exit and hotwire a car in the employee parking lot. If I can get Angel home before anyone notices I've gone…

If I can get Angel off the prison grounds…

I don't care what happens to me.

I'm already fucking dead.

Annabelle

I'm nothing but my terror. Not a person, not a body, not even a soul. Nothing but pure, animal terror.

I cling to Beast as he rushes through the halls. My hands are clamped around his shoulders. My heart is beating like a drum.

I killed someone.

I might have killed a district attorney.

Will I be in prison soon?

Who will raise Adrian?

The questions come like pop-up ads on a computer screen, and I "x" them away.

I think I've stopped screaming. Yes, my mouth is shut.

I wonder if Beast can get us out of here.

I brush a tangle out of my face, and I feel the stickiness of blood on my cheeks and in my eyes. I can even taste it.

And—oh shit. My stomach heaves, and I'm puking over Beast's shoulder, sobbing as he hauls me down the hall.

CHAPTER 2

Beast

I'M IN SIGHT OF THE library door when the static comes over the intercom. A new warden trying to figure out how to issue an SOS? A new warden knocking the intercom mouthpiece off its holder as he reaches for the circuit board to issue a lockdown?

My fingers tremble as I tuck the gun under my arm and punch the working pass code in. The library door clicks, and we hurry through it.

The partially constructed room is quiet and empty. I shift Angel down off of my shoulder, into my arms. Her face is blood-splattered, streaked with tears. I can't feel anything because I'm so strung out, but I know on a cerebral level that I hate her sadness. It isn't right. I'm going to fix it.

Her name rolls off my heavy tongue. "Angel."

Tears well in her eyes, and I pull her close to me, because I think that's what she needs. She's scared. She's scared and it's my fault that she's scared.

I'm going to fix this.

I squeeze her hand, then turn to lead her to the emergency exit door. This is the moment that the sirens start to scream. All the keypads and cameras around the room start flashing bright red. Which means the exit door in front of us won't work.

FUCK!

I whip toward one of the bay windows.

Goddamn—*plastic!*

I let go of Angel and dash to a pile of junk where I keep some industrial pliers. I was here when the windows were installed, I remember how they're skewered into the pane. I grab the pliers and jump onto the window seat, moving like the fucking Flash.

Using both my left hand and the pliers, I start tearing out the sheetrock all around the wooden window pane.

The joists are right where I thought they were. I cut through three before I realize this window isn't budging.

Down off the window seat. Angel runs at me. She's sobbing, clinging to me, but I push her off. I need to get us outside *right now*.

I grab her by the arm and haul her with me to the door. Her hands on my shoulder. Her arms around my waist. I push her off again and start punching passcodes in.

9-2-5-6-1.

Nothing!

0-1-3-5-2.

Fuck!

8-2-6-1-5.

"FUCK!"

My fingertips sweat.

8-1-8-0-0.

Fuck!

On a crazy whim I try my own pass code. The keypad flashes red.

"FUCK ME!"

I whirl toward the door to the hallway, where I think I hear the sound of boots.

Angel is clinging to my waist. I look down at her bloody face and see pure terror.

Stuck here.

We're stuck here.

Goddamnit!

I dash to a work bench, grab a coil of rope. I snatch Angel's wrists in front of her and twine the rope around them—fast. I tug it tighter than I should, because I want to be convincing. Then I grab onto her elbows and look into her eyes.

"Play along, Angel. I killed Ryan. When they come through the door, struggle against me and run to them for help. You heard what was going on with Ryan and me. You came to check on me and saw me kill him."

Her eyes widen. "He's dead?"

I stroke my thumbs over her cheeks. "Don't think about that, Angel. Do what I say and get yourself out of here."

"No." Tears fall off her chin as she shakes her head. "I'm not doing that to you."

"Yes—you *are*. In just a second. Do what I say, Angel. I fucking mean it."

I'm right in front of the exit door and she's facing me, so her back's to the hall door. It's me who sees them first—the group of guards as they burst into the room, guns drawn and pointed. My gaze bounces over familiar faces, friends and foes.

"Struggle," I hiss.

A look of uncertainty passes over her face, but it's gone an instant later. She wrenches her shoulders out of my grasp, and I can see the confusion flicker over the guards' faces. The adrenaline and blow leave my blood stream in an instant. My muscles start to tremble. I'm not even breathing as I hiss, "*fight*." I grab her arm and shove her up against the wall. She head-butts my shoulder, then kicks me in the thigh, then runs toward the group of guards.

Relief streams through me, so I'm a half second delayed in dashing after her. The guards engulf her before I can reach her, and three of them split off and come for me. I hold up my hands to avoid the fucking Taser, and as I do, a few gears shift inside my head: 9-9-9-9-1. *The riot password.*

I bet the riot password would've worked on the exit door!

I bet no one thought to change it after Holt left.

The guards grab my arms, and I feel the familiar shape of a Taser pressed against the back of my neck. I barely care. I'm watching Angel as one of the new guards puts his hands on her shoulders. I can see her crying. Another guard, Terry—one of the ones who used to readily take my payoffs—cuts through the rope around her hands. I see them shaking their heads and looking stern. I hear her voice, but I can't track it. My head is buzzing.

I wonder dimly what will happen to me now, but I can't summon the emotion to go along with it. All I want is to know she is safely gone and is never coming back. I'm consumed by thoughts of Angel at her house, cuddling her younger sister. Watching over her sick Mom.

So I'm a little slow to comprehend what's going on when I see Angel waving her arms around. When I see her run at me.

It takes me a full second and the horror on their faces to realize she's fucked it up.

I gave her an out, and Angel didn't take it.

Annabelle

I was going to do what he said. I told myself I couldn't help him if I was in prison, too. I told myself—I didn't have to tell myself—that Ad needs me. It happened so fast, there was no time for me to think.

I ran to them.

I had no trouble acting scared. I was scared out of my wits.

And then they shouted, "slow down," and asked "what happened," and I couldn't do it. I just couldn't let him take the fall for something I did.

I sob, "I shot the DA. It was self-defense."

Then I dart across the room to Beast.

My eyes are too blurry to see the reaction on his face, but I know he's opening his arms to me.

He grabs me tightly and spins around, putting me between him and the wall as every guard in the room starts rushing at us. I'm caught up in the scuffle, pushed and pulled. And then Beast tugs me out the door.

CHAPTER 3

Beast

YEARS AGO, I USED to dream of this moment.

Before prison, I would use the family jet to travel everywhere. Anywhere. When things got to be too much, I'd just go. I had a yacht called *Mistress of the Seas.* One year, I sailed her all the way to Greece.

I don't think I ever spent more than a few weeks in one city until the start of my sentence at La Rosa. The first few months, I used to wake up at night, checking my ceiling for patterns. Expecting to see the popcorn ceiling of my suite on *Mistress*, the dramatic indention where a chandler hung in my room at my house in Napa. The smooth beige of the Ritz in Central Park. Instead, there was this crack running the length of the room I shared with a man named Poohbar. My first reaction to it would be to freeze, because the only way I'd be sleeping in a building with structural problems was if an earthquake wrecked the foundation while I slept. Then I'd get thrown off, because things *were* shaking. But it wasn't the floor. It was me.

I lunge out of the emergency exit, and when my bare feet smack the cool dirt it's such a shock I almost freeze.

I don't, of course, but I think it slows me down.

This isn't good, because when the first guard hits the ground behind us, bullets start zipping by.

For the first few dozen yards, they're rubber bullets. I know their sound, having heard them fired at other inmates many times, and even once at myself, by a guard who didn't know that I was Beast and never to be fucked with.

Still, rubber bullets hurt, and the last thing Angel needs is to be hit by one. I sweep her into my arms, press her head against my chest, and run so fast I might as well be flying.

I run in a zig-zag pattern with Ryan's gun out, hoping none of the new hires can shoot for shit—or run fast. We've got maybe a twenty yard lead on them, but it might not be enough.

I run into a copse of trees that frames the parking lot, and hear real bullets slice the air around me as the footsteps on my tail grow louder.

I reach behind me and fire a few shots blind.

I lead them away from the parking lot, then cut back toward it. I realize they're too close, so I drop Angel and go at the guard behind me. He fires a shot that hits me in the shoulder, but the pain only pisses me the fuck off. I scoop Angel under my arm and after shooting another guard in the neck, I run toward the back of the parking lot, still trying to stay hidden in the trees.

All I think of as I move is her.

I have to protect her like she protected me.

We're found again when we get near the parking lot. I'm a fuck good shot—lots of target-practice for action roles—so it's not hard to shoot the guard in the hip.

I notice as I move that there are sirens coming from the prison. I know the exit gate is on lockdown, but it's the staff gate, and I think I have the codes.

No one knows what codes I have, so they don't know to disable all of them. I bet these dumbasses haven't even disabled the riot code I used to get out.

I run into the parking lot, toss Angel under a truck, and bust the driver's side window out of a car across the way. I go slick with sweat in my panic to hotwire the car—it's been years—but I manage, though I get pinged again in the hip and have to shoot two more guards. I scoop Angel up as a half-dozen guards run out of the grove, and bullets start to flow again.

I throw her in the passenger's seat and hit the gas so hard we clip another car as I turn toward the gate.

I fly, then hit the brakes at the pass code tower before glancing up and realizing the big gate is pushed back. The idiots left it open on default, and there's only a white and yellow plastic arm in front of us.

I punch through it as one of the guards whizzes up behind us in his truck, but I chose a Pontiac Grand Am and I know I'll outrun them.

We fly for a minute, and they drop way behind.

"Buckle up," I tell Angel, and she's screaming something, but I can't hear what. "Buckle up!" I scream louder, because I just hit one oh five and she hasn't done it yet and *memories*.

I think I see her snap her belt out of the corner of my eye, and I go faster. It doesn't matter that she buckled, though. My stomach is churning. I think I might be sick but I can't be sick, I'm not going to be sick, I'm not going to crash.

Handling the wheel and working the gas and brakes sobers me some, strips my apathetic, drug-hazed armor off.

I can't look over at her, but that doesn't stop my mouth from moving. "Sorry, Angel. Christ, I'm so damn sorry. I'm so sorry. We had to leave. In the library they said— there is this code word— they were gonna shoot us."

I glance over at her and find her clutching her stomach with one hand, the door with the other.

Her face is pale and still stained with Ryan's blood. Her eyes are horrified. Traumatized.

I'm shocked to feel my throat tighten, then swell. My eyes burn, but I'm fucking driving. I've got to fucking drive.

I turn some music up and focus on the road and my speedometer.

"Where are we going?" she cries over the music.

"We've gotta hide."

We get maybe another mile without seeing anybody. Then, right at the horizon line, I see red and blue lights coming at us. I try to slow the car, so I can run off the road, into the scrubby trees on either side of it. I try, but we're going too fast, and I'm not willing to risk spinning out.

The police cars are moving fast as fuck, because before I know it, the first one of them is on us. The pig does what I think he or she will do—this maneuver where they throw the car in front of us, spinning so we clip their tail. I've seen it dozens of times in action movies and in real car chases, so I'm halfway expecting it. I loop around them with some ease.

The second cruiser passes us, does a violent-looking U, and gets up on our ass. Angel starts crying. I keep my eyes on the road in front of us until I see them: spikes.

One of my characters, an HBO sex offender named Samuel Irons, was stopped this way.

I jerk the wheel hard right, swerving onto the dirt beside the road. A second later, the car behind us drops way back. They ran over their own spikes.

I laugh, and Angel starts laughing with me. We cackle until I see another light show: a wicked swarm of red and blue, maybe a half a mile ahead. And suddenly, there's another one behind us. He sidles up beside me, almost scrubbing my door, and I hit the brakes. He sails ahead, and I note the landscape on either side of the road. Lots of trees here. Lots of trees for California desert land.

I'm still watching him, feeling out my next move, when his car shudders, then stops.

More spikes.

The line of red and blue lights ahead is closer now. Close enough that I can make out individual light bars on the tops of the cruisers. Close enough that in another mile or two, they'll be right on us.

I make a split-second decision and jerk off the road, gassing the car as we drive into the trees. It's the biggest gamble of my life.

Almost immediately, I'm faced with an even bigger one, as I realize I'm driving straight toward a pond.

I punch the pedal and shout, "hold on!"

Then I plunge us into the water.

CHAPTER 4

Annabelle

I CAN'T SWIM.

It's one of my dirty little secrets

When our car hits the water, I learn what it means to see your life flash before your eyes. I see Adrian and Mom, and I feel my body under Beast's that day he took me in the library. I see myself dancing in Mom's room with Ad, holding her hands as we swing to U2, weaving between Mom's beeping machines.

I feel desire so sharp it takes my breath away.

Desire for life.

I can't die now!

I haven't done enough.

The chill of the water seeping through the floor, up my shins, snaps me out of it.

"Oh my God! Shit! Fuck!" I curl into a ball in my seat, waving my arms and sobbing because I CAN'T SWIM AND THERE'S WATER EVERYWHERE.

Then Beast is unbuckling me, pulling me into his lap. He turns me around to face him and grabs my face, forcing me to look into his eyes.

"Hold on, Angel. Try to calm down." His gaze clings to mine, penetrating my terror. His hand around my jaw is stroking as he speaks. "I'm going to push you through the window and shove you toward the surface. Kick your feet.

That's all you have to do. I'll come right behind and push you up."

In addition to the water seeping up through the floor, a mini waterfall is pouring in the cracked driver's side window behind Beast, sloshing over our laps.

The water coming from the floor is rising, too, now up to the bottom of our seats. I shake my head and clutch his neck. "I can't! I can't swim!"

"You won't be swimming," he says sternly. "I'll be pushing you." He strokes my damp hair off my head and mimes a deep breath as water rushes everywhere around us. "Breathe, Angel. You can fucking do this. Do this for me."

His voice is low and hypnotic. His beautiful eyes are a beacon in my haze of terror.

"Pull your shoes off," he orders.

I reach into the cold water and toss them off, then look back him for more instruction.

"I'll push you out first, and I'll be right behind you. There will only be a moment when you don't feel my hands on you, and that will be right after I push you out the window. Hold your breath. This pond isn't deep, baby." He nods toward the windshield, where I see a cloud of dirt and dark plant sludge.

I look down, suddenly realizing that the water is up to my breasts. I think the car is moving.

"Come on, Angel. We've got to go."

"Okay," I cry. "Okay, I will!"

Still, he has to peel me off of him. He shifts his body between mine and the partially broken driver's side window, fiddling with it as I lift my head toward the car's ceiling and try to breathe.

"I'm going to break the rest of the window out. In just a second, I'm about to grab you and thrust you through the window. Kick your feet and hold your breath. That's all you have to do."

With no further warning, he thrusts his elbow through the remainder of the glass. I don't hear it shatter, but I know it does because more water floods in. I'm scooting back toward the passenger's seat, fleeing it instinctively, when his hands come around my waist.

"Hold your breath," he snaps, but I already am. Cold water is covering my face. It's all I can do not to scream or pass out as I feel my body shoved forward. I grab the metallic window pane and try to thrust myself out. Then I feel a hard push on my butt, and I'm lost in mud-brown water.

Kick, Annabelle!

I'm supposed to kick!

I do, and the amber light ahead of me grows brighter. I wave my arms, but my lungs are screaming. I can't breathe!

Something hard comes around my waist, and I startle, blowing out some of the air I'm holding in my lungs.

It's okay.

It's Beast!

He's got his arms around my waist. He's dragging me up toward the light, kicking hard enough for both of us. I wrap my arms around the thickness of his torso, clinging desperately, then belatedly wonder if I should be kicking, too.

It doesn't matter. I get a split-second glimpse of the shiny underside of the surface, then I burst through, gasping.

His arm comes around my neck, and I struggle against him until I realize he's scooping my chin into the crook of his elbow to keep my head afloat while he treads water with his other arm and tries to look around.

I can feel him kicking, hear him panting as he works to keep me afloat.

After a minute or so of watching him look around, I whisper, "Is there anybody here?"

"It looks clear, but not sure yet," he murmurs.

He starts toward the grassy edge of the pond, stretching his right arm out in front of him and kicking his long, strong legs. His left arm holds me: keeping my face toward the blue sky as my body drags through the water behind me.

I'm so afraid of drowning, it's all I can do to keep from crying. I try to focus on the blue of the sky—how smooth it is, how unknowing; it doesn't care what happened today. *I don't need to think about what happened today.*

I can feel it when Beast's feet touch ground. He shifts me around to the front of him, wrapping an arm around my waist, so my back is pressed against his chest and my butt is propped against his hip. We rise out of the water, and my eyes fly around, eager to find out where we are and if we're alone.

It looks like we're maybe a half mile from the road, emerging from an oval-shaped pond about the size of a football-field. Our side of the pond stretches underneath a couple of big trees. Around the trees and pond is lots of thick green grass—thick enough to maybe be some kind of pasture.

I run my gaze along the highway out in front of us, but I don't see anything.

Is it possible that we would be so lucky?

Beast seems to read my mind. "Well, Angel, looks like we may have run into some luck."

He hoists me over his shoulder and hurries into the middle of the grove of trees, where about a dozen thick tree trunks offer some shelter.

He sets me down on my butt, in the dirt amidst the trees' big roots, then nods at a pile of what looks like dry, gray dirt a few feet away.

"That's old, dry cow dung," he says, standing over me. His broad, glistening chest is free of the white jumpsuit; it hangs from his hips, melding to his lower body.

The first thing he's going to say to me after what we just went through is "that's old, dry cow dung." I actually laugh a little. "There are cows here?"

"From the looks of that, not anytime recently. This is probably a grazing pasture." I look around us, at the flat, grassy field.

"If this is a grazing pasture, then where are they?"

He kneels down beside me. "When people graze cows, they switch up where they put them. This field is probably out of rotation. Which means it may be the perfect place for us to lay low for a little while." He stands again, looking around with squinted eyes, as if he's worried he missed something.

I find myself unable, even in this dire situation, to keep my eyes from roving his body. Which is how I notice his white pants have a red stain. A quick once-over reveals his whole left arm is red.

"Oh my God." My eyes fly to the elbow he used to break the glass. It's got a small gash, but… "Your shoulder!"

I jump up, and he takes what seems to be an instinctive step back. He turns his head to get a look at his left shoulder. On the outside of it, around the same spot my high school friend Todd had a scar from rotator cuff surgery, there's a crazy huge gash—like, five inches big. Blood is pouring from it down to his elbow, then dripping off his elbow onto his pants.

"Did you get shot?"

His lips press together as his eyebrows arch. "Looks like it."

I glance left and right, and left again, looking for I don't even know what. There's nothing but a field and the little highway out in front of us for what seems like miles. "What do we do? You're bleeding a lot!"

He frowns, looking around distractedly. "I'm okay." He walks from one tree to the other, dripping blood as he surveys the land around us.

"I think we made it about to Covington."

I nod slowly. "Yeah—it looks kind of like that."

If we're in Covington, a little dairy farming community, we're only a few miles from the wreck site.

"What do we do now? Where will we go? They're going to find us—right?" I sink back down onto one of the larger roots and wrap my arms around myself. Even contemplating the question hikes my adrenaline up a notch. I'm shaking slightly as I wonder what if Mom dies today. What if I get hauled to jail for shooting Ryan? I don't want Beast to take the fall for something I did, but Adrian needs me, badly.

"Oh my God," I moan. I clutch my head as fear twists through me.

A second later, I feel Beast kneeling in front of me.

"Angel," he murmurs. He pulls me up against his chest and buries his face in the softness between my shoulder and my throat.

"I'm so sorry. So very, very sorry, Angel." He pulls away and looks up at me. "Are you okay? Are you hurt—physically?"

I shake my head as tears fill my eyes. "I don't think so."

I watch his face tighten, so much he looks almost mad at me. A second later, he walks over to one of the other tree trunks, leaning his right shoulder against it. I can see his shoulders rise and fall as he breathes. Angry? Upset?

What's he feeling? What's he thinking?

I remember how I found him in his cell. The sick collage on the ceiling. Needle marks on the inside of his thigh. What have the last few weeks been like for him? The last two months…

I walk over to him, unsure what he needs but unwilling to stand around and do nothing. I step over the roots so I'm right behind him and press my palm against his back.

He flinches, then turns around with hard eyes.

"Sorry," I whisper. I take a small step back.

He whirls to face me. "Don't be sorry. Never say you're sorry—not to me, Angel. I'm the one who's goddamned sorry." He clenches his jaw and gives a brief shake of his head. "I didn't keep you safe. I…" He inhales deeply, exhales hard, and bites the inside of his cheek as he dips his head down. For half a breath, his face twists painfully. Then his eyes meet mine. They're red around the edges. "I'm really fucking sorry that I ever met you."

CHAPTER 5

Annabelle

"DO YOU REALLY WISH THAT?"

He looks away and shakes his head a little. "Don't you, Angel?"

"No."

"Then you're not thinking about it right." He rubs his eyes. "I ruined your life today."

"What did you do specifically do wrong today to ruin my life?" He presses his lips together, so I keep talking. "When the DA got the drop on you, he did because you didn't dodge him. If you had, he'd have gotten me instead. Since then, you tried to take the fall for something you didn't even do. You tried to let me of the hook for…murder." I choke the word out, but I keep talking, holding his gaze as my body vibrates with adrenaline and emotion.

I step closer to him. So close we're almost touching, and I can see every line of his face. "You did nothing wrong. Nothing with me, anyway. Things were fucked up there. Fucked up," I say again. "You were being fucked with, you were in solitary, and that's really, really wrong and really scary."

"And now you're caught up in this shit—and that's wrong, too." He runs his hand back through his dark, wet hair, then brings his gaze to mine. "I'm going to get you out of this. All I need is a phone. Do you have your phone?"

I shake my head. It got left back at the prison.

"It's okay. I can find another phone. Can call." His eyes take on a glazed look as he speaks, and some of the color blanches out of his cheeks. "I'll get you home," he mumbles.

He blinks a few times fast, then crouches. He shifts from a crouch into a sitting position, with his butt in the dirt and his long legs stretched out in front of him.

"Are you okay?" I step over to him and watch him rip his left pants leg along the seam on the side. As I kneel beside him, he rips it all the way off.

His eyes tug up to mine. "Can you tie this around my shoulder? Tie it tight."

"Okay. Yeah, sure." I take the swatch of fabric and, using my teeth, tear it in half again, so I have two long strips.

I move around to his left side, which I feel bad I didn't notice is looking a lot worse. His whole left side is bathed in blood.

"Tie it under your arm, kinda up against your pec?"

"Sure," he says, resting his head on his knees. "Just do it tight."

I tie the bandages tightly and he grits his teeth as I knot them.

I come around in front of him and put a hand on his knee. "Is there something I can do?"

"Can you check the road?" he says, not lifting his head.

"Of course."

I get up and walk to the edge of the trees so I can look out at the road. I see nothing. Hear nothing. Which is good, but what the hell am I going to do about him? What if he passes out? I walk back over to him and crouch back down. "We're okay. There's no one there."

He doesn't respond, and I start to worry. Then he lifts his head so he can look at me with dark, tired eyes. "Why didn't you do what I said, Angel?"

He doesn't expound, but then, he doesn't have to.

"I just couldn't," I whisper, sitting down in front of him. "I couldn't do that to you."

He groans. "I wish to hell I'd never asked you to come back that first day."

"I'm glad you did, or you would still be in solitary. I came back this last time—and the times before, it, too—because I wanted to." My voice cracks unexpectedly. "I'm sorry I messed things up today. I didn't mean to shoot him! I meant to, but I didn't want anyone to die. I'm glad I killed him, if I killed him. He was…tormenting you. But it feels so weird. To be a killer." I cover my mouth with both hands and let out a sob.

"You're not a killer, Angel." He scoots closer to me, close enough so he can touch my knee. "You're not a killer. Don't say it again."

He strokes my knee with gentle fingers. "You're innocent, Angel. Innocent people come out okay."

"They *shot* you. They were torturing you."

He laughs, low and hollow. "I'm not innocent." He shuts his eyes and rests his head on his knee again. "If there was any way to cut you loose... But I'll protect you—this time," he adds softly. "I just need a phone. I'm worried, though…" He runs his unhurt hand over his hair, which I'm beginning to see he does when he's nervous. "I'm worried that I won't get far. My face…" He lifts it up to look at me again.

"Someone will recognize you, you mean."

"Not if you hit me." His eyes widen. "You think you can bruise me up a little?" He waves at his cheek. "Just enough to make me look like…not Cal Hammond?"

I laugh. "Are you insane? No way. I don't think it would work, anyway. Your skin is hardly the only thing that makes you look like Cal."

He lowers his head, then props it up in the palm of his good hand, as if he's getting tired, and holding up his head is just too much.

"Forget about hitting me," he murmurs. "I'll figure it out."

"Who are you calling?"

He shakes his head. "I don't want you to worry about it, Angel. Can you trust me? To get you home? I can do it, Angel." His eyebrows lift a little, as if he's just remembered: "How's your mom?"

I bite my cheek and look away, but it's not enough to stop the tears from spilling down my cheeks.

He scoots over to me and wraps me in his arms. He kisses my hair, my cheeks, and then my mouth. He kisses me with a strange kind of abandon borne of feeling so bad, I guess. His forehead brushes mine. His cheeks and nose stroke over mine, almost a caress. His lips are gentle and surprisingly sweet, conveying just the right amount of sadness and care.

He pulls away and kisses my throat. "I'm sorry, Angel."

"Don't apologize." I sniff and wipe my eyes. "It's not your fault. In fact, the money you gave me has kinda helped a little. Ad enjoyed the things I bought her."

I try to smile, because God knows, we don't need another thing to worry about right now, but the harder I try to just chill out, the more hysterical I feel. If Mom dies and I'm not there for Ad…

I inhale deeply.

And, as these things seem to go, it's that moment that we hear the helicopter.

I freeze, literally petrified.

Ricardo stands up quickly and tilts his head back, looking up at the trees' big limbs and trembling leaves. After a long moment, during which the thumping of the chopper's blades grows fainter, then louder, then more distant again, he mutters, "I think we're okay here."

He pulls a gun out of his pants—the one I used to…—and starts pacing the dirt.

Shirtless and blood-smeared, with his rock-hard ass and thighs evident through his wet pants, he looks like exactly what he is: a man with movie star-good looks—and an escaped convict.

It's funny that he has two such unusual distinctions, and neither one of them explains at all what he is to me.

Our lives are linked in ways I don't think I'll ever understand.

I need him in ways that don't make sense. They never have.

I listen to the helicopter rumble in the distance, and I watch him pace. I can't help admire his broad, taut body. Can't help care for him. Can't help want him.

My thoughts circle pretty quickly back around to Mom and Ad, but I try my best to focus on his body as he stands near the edge of the grove, looking out over the fields. I just can't go there—to worrying about what's going on at home. I think I'll go insane if I do.

The helicopter's thumping, which had grown distant for a few moments, gets louder again, and for the first time, I see it in the distance. It's small and green and prowling the area for us. Looking out at it makes me feel like I'm going to hurl.

"Will you talk to me?" I whisper to Ricardo's back.

He turns around. "About what, Ang?"

I smile a little at my new nickname. "It can be anything. I just need a distraction."

After one more glance in the direction in which the helicopter just disappeared, he steps over to me, lowers himself down to the dirt, and reaches out, so the fingers of his right hand are brushing my shin through my pants.

"Are you scared?" I whisper.

He shakes his head, and starts stroking me with gentle fingers as his eyes hold mine. "If something happens, we'll both surrender, okay? I don't have a problem surrendering, or explaining that what happened today was all on me. We ran because…" He presses his lips together and looks away from me. I watch his jaw clench before his eyes come back to mine. "It's complicated, Angel, how justice in a prison works, but let's just say if we get found before I put my phone call through, we'll get a fairer shake out here. Especially you."

"And you, too, right? Everyone loves you, Cal." I'm teasing, using his old movie star name, but he doesn't smile. His lips twist down and his brows knit together. He looks down at his hand, playing on my leg. "I don't think that's true."

"Trust me, it is. People are waiting for you to get out of prison and be in more movies."

He looks out at the field as he pulls my foot into his lap and starts to stroke the arch of my foot. "Are they?" he says.

"You're a really good actor. Which seems stupid to tell you, because obviously you know. Do you think you'll ever go back to that?" I blurt out, "Holt told me your sentence got lengthened."

He just keeps rubbing my foot, looking out at the field, and after a few more moments, his neutral silence becomes melancholy silence by virtue of its length.

"I'm sorry," I say quietly.

He looks at me. "Don't feel sorry for me, Angel. I made my own choices. Every choice that got me to this point was mine."

I shake my head. "You didn't choose to have the wreck. You told me the cocaine was Uma's and you were snorting it to help her."

His eyes narrow. "When did I say that?"

"Back in your cell. It was when I first came down to see you in solitary, earlier today. You were kind of out of it."

"Yes," he says. "I guess I was."

I look at his fingers, smoothing down my arch. I watch their repetitive motion while I listen for the helicopter. When I decide for sure I can't hear it anymore, the anxiety of sitting here—just waiting to be caught—pushes more questions up out of me.

"What was that in the syringe?" I ask.

"I'm not sure," he says, avoiding my eyes. "Probably cocaine or something like it."

"Ryan was playing around with that because of the wreck, right?"

He rubs his head. "I don't want to talk about that anymore." He lets go of my foot and stands up, wincing a little as he moves, then craning his neck to get a good look at his bandaged shoulder.

"Do you think it's bleeding less?" I ask.

"Seems like it," he says. His voice is gruff, and I can tell he wants some space, because he walks farther from me than he's been since we got here, over to the tree that's closest to the highway, and stands there for a few minutes, just breathing with his jaw flexed.

He's still standing there when I notice the three big dots in the sky out above the highway, getting bigger as they come our way.

CHAPTER 6

Annabelle

THREE GREEN HELICOPTERS. That's what they are. Three green helicopters flying low over the road. So low I can almost read the words painted on the side of each one. They're flying in a row, but as I watch, they split, with one following the road, one going over the land on the opposite side of the road, and one coming our way.

The one on our side of the road starts to comb the fields, moving perpendicular to the road, flying so low I bet someone could jump out of it and not be badly hurt.

When I manage to comprehend just how *fucked* we are, I gasp. "Beast, what do we do?"

He walks to me and takes my hands in his. "Calm down, Angel. I don't think they can see us through these trees."

"What if they have infrared technology?" I wail.

"They don't."

"How do you know?"

"The state's not that wealthy. Also, the one that flew over earlier didn't notice us."

"It wasn't green. That one was black!"

"Look into my eyes, Angel."

I do.

"If we were to get caught—and I don't think we are, I'm only supposing for your benefit—we would hold our hands up. Drama-free surrender. Tell whoever finds us that I shot Ryan."

I open my mouth to protest, and he presses a silencing finger against my lips. "Do you think I have a reason to shoot him? A justifiable reason?" I start to speak again, and he shakes his head. "No—scratch that. Do you think most people would feel that it was reasonable for me to shoot him, had I do so?"

I nod. "Yeah…I guess I do."

"So this isn't such a big deal, is it?"

"Yes," I cry, "it is! Because it wasn't you who did it, it was me! And I did other bad things, too. Like sneaking into solitary. That's got to be some kind of mega crime!"

He cups my cheek. "One you committed because you were worried about me, right, Angel? You'd heard I was being treated badly—hadn't you?"

I nod.

"Why did we run?" he asks.

I shake my head. I've never been very good at prompts.

"Because we were worried I'd never get a fair shake at La Rosa again. I worked for the FBI, and they turned on me; you can say that, too. Say that I got sold out. Who would blame you for sneaking in to check on me?"

"I can say that to whoever catches us? Even if it's just a regular police officer?" I chew on my lower lip. "Wouldn't that get you in trouble with the FBI?"

"No." His lips twist up in a cross between a smirk and a smile as the chopper behind him grows louder. "It wouldn't get me in trouble—I don't think—because I don't think anyone would believe you. They would think I lied to you, most likely. But it would make your coming to see me a little more justifiable."

I agree with him well enough, so I jump subjects to another one that's bothering me. "I don't want to lie. I want to say I shot Ryan, because I did, and you shouldn't have to take the fall for me. It isn't fair."

"Please don't, Angel. That would be a very bad idea for you."

Over Beast's shoulders, the helicopter looms. Its big, long blades blow the grass flat; bend the smaller branches on the trees above us.

How close is it now? Seventy yards? Fifty?

I squeeze his fingers. “Can we talk about something else for a minute? Something more…distracting?”

He sits down in between the tree roots, half pulling me with him. Propping my back against his chest and wrapping his arms around me. He leans his back against a tree truck, and we both watch the helicopter, hovering not even half a football field away.

I can’t breathe. My pulse gallops, and my head feels light.

I can feel every contour of Beast’s chest against my back. I can feel his warmth. I try to focus on that even as my eyes drip tears. “What do you want to talk about?” his low voice asks into my ear.

“Movies,” I half-shout.

He chuckles in my ear. “Not mine.”

“No?” I lean back so I can see his face.

He’s giving me a painful smirk. “No one likes to hear an actor talk about himself in movies.”

“I do.” I’ve started to sweat, and I can barely speak I’m so afraid. The helicopter is right above us, just hovering. It takes every iota of willpower I can muster to turn around so that I’m facing him and look into his eyes and talk like normal—albeit a little louder. “I want to know what it was like. Every single detail. Cough it up.”

“What part?” He gives me a small, sad-looking smile. I can’t tell if it’s because he’s scared as badly as I am or because talking about his lost career makes him unhappy.

“I don’t want to make you talk about it if it makes you sad.”

He leans a little closer to me, and surprises me by pressing his mouth against my cheek. “Talking to you could never make me sad.” He licks his lips, and I swear to God, I think the helicopter starts to scoot on by.

“I liked ‘The Rise and Fall of Henry Dockett.’ It was shot on an island off Australia, and I liked where I stayed. It was beautiful. Lots of palm trees and crystalline, clear water.”

His hand rearranges itself around mine. The motion is so gentle. Then his thumb begins to stroke the top of my knuckles. He leans more heavily against me and kisses my lips slowly as—yes!—the helicopter moves along.

I notice one of us is shaking. Me, I think.

His hands knead my shoulders. "Let's keep talking," he urges.

I nod. "What's your favorite movie?" I half-shout. "All movies, not just yours."

"I like 'The Godfather,'" he says, "because the theme is beautiful, and Brando's performance is elegant." He kisses under my jaw. "Sparse," he adds, his breath grazing my earlobe.

"It's leaving," I squeak, looking out at the field, where the awful thing hovers, sweeping left and right, but moving on, back toward La Rosa.

He doesn't turn around to look, but instead kisses my lips, a feather-gentle sweep of his soft mouth over mine.

"Forget about them," he murmurs against my cheek.

"What if they—"

He strokes my hair out of my face. "We have a plan," he says softly. "And they haven't found us." He looks into my eyes as if he's waiting for me to agree, so I nod slowly.

"Good girl."

His mouth finds my collar bone. He kisses me there, then looks into my eyes as his free hand lifts the bottom of my shirt.

"It might…not work," I whisper as he tugs it over my head. I think there's a good chance I'm too scared to have an orgasm right now.

"Let me worry about that."

My shirt is off, and now my pants are coming off. I tremble as he tugs them down my legs, spreads my shirt out on the ground, and sets me on it. Then he leans me back against a tree trunk.

I'm naked, only a few hundred yards from the road where the police are gathering to look for us. Only a dozen or two yards from the green helicopter.

I could be found in a few minutes. I could be shot here with him. Naked.

His hands part my knees. His mouth touches down on my pussy, and it's gentler than anything I've ever felt in my life. His tongue slips between my folds with delicate precision, finds my clit, and laps gingerly over it.

I'm expecting to feel nothing, so I'm surprised when my ass lifts off the ground. I can feel wetness pooling in my center.

I can feel the empty neediness, the raw desire for him to fill me with his cock.

Instead, he slides two fingers in. When I moan and thrust against his face, he adds a third.

"Oh God."

He's stretching me. Stretching until I feel so full. His mouth is driving me into oblivion. Up and down my dripping slit, smearing my slickness over my clit. It's throbbing now. Ignited by his skillful tongue, stroking all around it, trembling over it, baring down a little harder—as his fingers push up way inside me, and his thumb parts my swollen lips and drags moisture from my sopping cunt toward my clit.

With his pinkie, he teases my asshole, dragging it over me as he sinks his fingers deep inside my cunt, and his mouth worships my pulsing clit.

I cry, "more," and he pulls his fingers out of me, rubs his damp knuckles over my ass, and licks my taint, then flicks his tongue over my asshole.

"Push against me when I try to come inside."

He drags his tongue in circles around my clit, then in between my sensitive pussy lips. He laps his tongue around his fingers, shoved inside my cunt.

"You taste so good, beautiful."

His three fingers inside me thrust in and out in a rhythm that makes my eyes roll back into my head. All I know is him. The velvet tongue alighting nerve endings as his fingers pump in and out, making me feel filled up. Making me feel fucked.

Then, when I'm dripping and my legs tremble from wanting to rock against him— When my fingers are tugging his dark hair, gripping his neck and shoulders— When my juices are rolling down my ass, he pushes his pinkie into my ass, and I scream.

My scream seems to energize Beast: his fingers stretching and pumping, reaching deeper into me, where my walls throb against them, pulsing and needing. His mouth on my cunt teases till I'm trembling, and the finger in my asshole makes me feel invaded from every entrance. I'm a mad woman, nothing but a pulsing pussy.

He drags his tongue around my clit and laps at my finger-stuffed cunt, and straightens the pinkie in my ass so it's pushed in deeper.

"Come for me," he orders as I shatter.

When I'm finished, he's leaning over me, stroking my hair and cupping my cheek. His face looks strained and tired, but it's impossible to miss the stiff cock stretching against his pants.

I sit up and kiss his lips. I look around. The road is empty. The noise of the helicopters is gone for now.

I laugh a little. "Thank you! That was incredible, a hell of a distraction." I grin. "They didn't get us."

"No."

I close my hand around his head and rub my palm down his huge, hard shaft. "Let me suck this for you. If we're not leaving this spot until it gets dark anyway…let me make you forget for a few minutes."

He shakes his head and surprises me by getting up, walking to the edge of the grove. I follow him to where he stops, between two trees, and come around in front of him.

"Why not let me make you feel good?"

He lifts his gaze to mine. "I wanted to pleasure you, Angel. I don't want pleasure myself."

Because he feels bad about what happened. That we're here. I'm here.

I sink down to my knees and wrap my arms around his legs, and his hands come down on my hair. I tug on the fingers of his unhurt arm, and he allows himself to be pulled down beside me.

I stick my lower lip out.

"It's not a good idea," he says. "I need to be alert."

I push on his chest and spread his legs, then lean down and nip at where his balls are behind the fabric of his pants. I try to suck his balls into my mouth, despite the fabric barrier in place. I mouth his dick and breathe hot breath around the head of him.

My teasing ministrations have the desired effect. I'm able to pull his pants off a few minutes later. I do what he did, spreading his pants out under him. Then I shove him down onto his back and promise that I'll look around.

"You don't have a choice," I say. "You're mine."

I pull his cock up off his belly, lick around the head and shaft.

He starts panting. His hands lock onto my shoulders and he groans my name.

I flick my tongue along the underside of his cock. I suck him into my mouth, taking him as deep as I can, and he starts to tremble.

“Sit on my cock,” he moans. “Please—Angel. I want to be inside you.”

I position his head at my center, then slide it up and down through my moisture. His breathing grows ragged. I cup my palm around his balls.

“Let Angel take care of you, you sexy Beast.”

CHAPTER 7

Annabelle

I PULL HIS DICK UP, so it's pointing toward the treetops, then ease it in between my lips and sit down on his cock, taking him so deep, I feel like I'm split open. He groans. I rise up on my knees, dragging him out of me, then sink back down with a little bounce. His hands grab hold of my waist, locking me down atop him as he rocks his hips against me. Until he's buried so deep inside me, my pussy is kissing his balls.

As I sink down and rise up, he starts to thrust his hips.

He thrusts so hard I'm bouncing on top of him. His gorgeous face is dirty and sweat-slick and perfect. I lean over to kiss his lips, and he pushes me back.

"I want to," I pout.

"Not unless I tell you."

I feel a stab of hurt until his fingers find my clit and start rubbing. Then I'm panting harder, my legs shaking as I bob up and down on him. I enjoy the thrust of us together, the way his huge cock makes me ache with fullness; the way I draw him out of me a little, then bounce back down, so the thickness of his head slams deep into me, his mighty shaft stretching me deliciously, and his nimble fingers stroking over my clit. I reach behind me and tickle his balls. They're rock hard, drawn up and ready.

We find a rhythm. His hands around my waist, my hand cupping his heavy balls and the other clutching his hard hip.

When I rub my fingertips over the taut skin of his balls, his face goes rapt. His fingers on my clit are gentle, unsteady.

I slide him almost all the way out, then slam back down on him.

He comes with a shout and tries to pull me off his dick, but I stay there, loving the way he spurts, warm inside me.

His eyes shut and every part of him except his dick goes limp. So limp, in fact, that at first I fear he might have passed out. I rise up off him and lie in the dirt beside him, so limp and tired I don't care that I'm lying on dirt where a cow has probably stood.

Beast is moving his arm to pull me to his side when his eyes stretch wide.

"Oh fuck, I didn't pull out."

"I didn't want you to. I'm on the pill."

His face tightens, but he says nothing, just opens his arm for me so I can lie against him. Our racing hearts slow down together as we lie in silence, listening for the humming of cars and the thomping of helicopter blades. After a few minutes of stillness from him, he squeezes me a little closer still and kisses my cheek.

I put my arm over him and kiss his pec.

"Angel," he rumbles.

I feel his lips in my hair.

"You're beautiful," he murmurs, "and I love your cunt."

"My cunt loves your cock. Forever."

He nods, squeezing me a little, and I hear him mumble something about this being a bad idea. "Keep me awake," he warns me in a muzzy voice. But when, a couple minutes later, I feel his body jerk, I let him fall asleep.

I hold him while he sleeps, and listen to the road and sky.

Nothing.

We're locked here in the trees, in a bubble that separates us from the rest of the universe. Maybe that's the only way the two of us can be together—in the most improbable of times and places. Maybe the universe conspired to give us this moment, and the only way that it could happen was the way it did.

But no.

Because I shot someone today.

The reality of it sinks in slowly as I lie there, until it's a weight pressed on my chest and I can't breathe, and I want to stand up but I don't want to wake Beast—Ricardo. He's not Beast anymore, because he's not in prison. Not now, anyway.

I lie there on my back, looking up at the kaleidoscope of leaves and sky, and I want to know how he's doing. The DA. Even though he's vile and horrible, I want to know for sure if he's alive or dead.

I didn't want to kill him.

If I killed him, he all but goaded me into it. That means he deserved it.

No one deserves that, my conscious protets.

But who cares about 'deserve'? Ricardo didn't deserve what went on in solitary, either. It was horrible, and it was Ryan's fault.

And the fact remains, any way I try to spin it: I shot someone today. As I'm lying here right now, coming down from sex of all things, his family might be mourning his loss.

It's disgusting, and it's horrible, and I roll away from Beast and actually gag into the dirt because the thought of me shooting someone—even someone as horrible as Ryan—makes me sick.

The sickness stays with me, and it won't go. It makes me feel so dirty, so stained.

I tell myself Ryan isn't dead. He's only hurt, and that makes me feel better because he hurt Ricardo. He deserves to be hurt. It's not hard to tell myself he does.

Beast seems to be sleeping off his comedown, so he's very still. I, on the other hand, can't stand to be still any longer, so I get up, squeeze myself back into my wet clothes, and walk around for a few minutes, looking at the road and sky. Waiting for another round of torture.

I walk back over to Beast and ease myself to the ground. His breathing is light and steady. I slide back under his arm and lie there, still as a doll, thinking of Ad and Mom, wondering what kind of phone call Beast—Ricardo—wants to make. Wondering more about his gig with the FBI. Wondering if there's any way we can actually come out of this okay.

I end up thinking about the first time I met him, at the house party the night I had the idea I'd lose my V-card to him. How harshly he tried to warn me off at first. As if he knew, on some mystical, cosmic level that he should avoid me, lest we tie our fates together.

It's melodramatic, I know, but it still rings a little true.

I lie beside him as he sleeps, listening to every rustle of the leaves, eventually pushing myself up on my elbow so I can look around the field. When he wakes up, and hour or two later, he's edgy and harsh and strained. He rolls me over on my back, positions me atop what remains of his jumpsuit, strips my pants off, and fucks me hard.

Until I'm aching from his thrusts and creaming all around his dick. Until my ass hurts from the ground and I'm clawing his pecs and twisting his nipples.

Until he's hard enough to dig through diamonds with that big, beautiful cock. Until he's shoved so deep inside me, I don't where he ends and where I start.

I feel him spurt inside me before I see the sweet relief on his face. He comes down on top of me, collapsing with his chest against my breasts. His fingers stroke my face. His eyes are heavy.

He shifts atop me and pulls his dick out, and my pussy feels sore and empty. He's still half hard, bigger than any man I've ever seen. He gets back into his ragged, stained white pants and ties them around his hips.

He dresses me as I lie there, and then he kisses my pussy.

"Thank you."

I lean up to kiss his cheek, and he ducks his head. "No, Angel."

I don't understand.

He says it once more: *"No."*

He goes and sits on the other side of the tree as night falls down around us.

CHAPTER 8

Beast

MY PLAN IS RISKY AT BEST.

My plan to get Angel out of this nightmare is risky at motherfucking best.

I drop my head into my hands, because rubbing my forehead and temples is better than pulling my fucking hair out.

Fucking Ryan.

Fucking whatever was in that fucking syringe.

I pretty much know it was some kind of cocaine derivative, because shit, I remember this comedown from my acting days. It's all I've known the last—few weeks? I'm not even fucking sure.

I stand up and start to pace around, hoping Angel won't come over here to me. I need to think. Need to try to find a way to calm my racing mind.

I've felt regret before, but this is different. The night of the wreck, I did something stupid, but I didn't do it with any sort of premeditation. Uma wanted us to help her get rid of the blow, so I helped her. I drove fast, but when I did, I didn't think that I would lose control. It was an accident.

You know what wasn't a fucking accident? Playing games with Angel to get her to come see me at La Rosa. Scaring her that day I kicked Holt's ass. Getting her to fuck me in the library. Those things weren't a fucking accident. That was me being selfish, taking what I wanted, and now— damnit!

My guilty mind screams that I didn't know I'd be double-crossed by the Agency. How could I have known?

But it doesn't matter. It doesn't change anything about what's going on right now, and it does nothing to ease the weight of guilt on my chest.

I rub my hands back through my hair and I can feel Angel coming up beside me.

"Go away," I tell her.

I'm in a foul ass mood, and she deserves some warning.

Of course, Angel being the angel that she is, she sits down beside me and leans her head against my shoulder. She drapes an arm around my back as if I'm not half an inch from losing my shit and murmurs in my ear, "You all right? Not feeling well?"

I freeze for a second, because no one's asked me how I feel in a very long ass time.

"I'm fucking fine."

An asshole. Sick with asshole-itis.

Her hand kneads my shoulder. "You sure?"

I nod. I'm gritting my teeth.

"Can you take some deeper breaths?"

I look up at her. "What?"

There's an edge to my voice—one that I'm not proud of.

"Like this." She inhales deeply, sitting straighter. Then she slowly lets it out. "Breathe in through your mouth, hold it in for a second or two, and out through your nose."

I frown. "What makes you think I need to do that?"

"You sound a little strained." She presses her lips together. "Whatever he gave you must have been an amphetamine for sure. I've never seen someone move as fast as you did, getting us out of there." She reaches for my face and gives me a small, slight smile. "You look a little rough around the edges so you must be coming down."

Her gentle hand touches down on my cheek.

I can't bring myself to tell her not to touch me, so I try my best to smile back at her. "You saying I look like shit, Angel?"

"You could never look like shit. You know it, too. You're handsome even in prison clothes."

"It's called a jumpsuit."

"Okay, then. Even in a jumpsuit."

Her hand starts stroking up and down my back. I don't realize till this second, but my left shoulder, where the bullet went through, hurts pretty fucking bad. Her gentle hand diverts my attention, giving me a little relief.

I let my head hang between my shoulders. I want to say *thank you.* I want to say a dozen things, but I can't make my mouth open.

What do you say to someone who's given you everything? What do you say to someone who's killed for you?

My throat feels thick, so I do the thing she said, sucking air in through my nose.

"Does this feel good, what I'm doing?" she asks as I let my breath out. "I want to make you feel better."

I swallow. Clench my jaw.

I lift my head and turn toward her, and all the badness I've been holding in comes pouring out. "You understand I fucked you, right? Asking you to come and visit me? Fucking around with you that day and telling you that you had to or I'd fuck with Holt, just because I wanted you? That's a fucking asshole move, and I'm an asshole, Angel. You should save your fingers the effort."

"And stop rubbing your back?" Again, that smile. The tired, kind, understanding one. "I'm not doing that. I knew Holt was okay when I came back to La Rosa. It was my choice, because I wanted to get to know you better. Try to quit worrying about things for a second. You said you had a plan."

Oh, right. My plan.

My immediate overlord at the Agency is Thom Ford. I don't think he knew about my ouster in advance because he hates Juarez. Tom was always friendly with me. He was a fan of my movies.

So there's a chance that I could bargain with the Agency. Make a deal with them. If they put Juan Juarez in charge, it was because they realized (or strongly suspected) he wasn't in charge of his family's cartel any longer. If Juan isn't in charge of the cartel, any control I had over him was meaningless. They needed to overthrow the person currently in charge—my guess is Juan's younger brother, Emanuel—and not only plant Juan back at the helm of things, but endear him to them, too. Giving

Juan control of La Rosa puts him in their pocket. And if the whole thing went kaput, if Juan refused to do what they wanted, the Agency could have him killed.

That's how it works.

When gang leaders are in prison, they're vulnerable in a way they never would be on the outside, surrounded by their soldiers. They can so easily be bought.

Look at me. They got me to kill in exchange for...what? Creature comforts? A big cell and control of other people's fates? The assurance that I'd always be on top. The illusion that I'm not a prisoner, but some sort of fucking secret agent?

Even now, after they ousted me via Ryan and my hellish trip to solitary, I'm considering killing for them again.

I would off Emanuel Juarez in a heartbeat if it would win me favor with the Agency. If they could guarantee Angel's extrication from this mess.

It would probably be a suicide mission, but what do I care? I've got no better options. My sentence has been extended. If I'm sent back to La Rosa, which I almost certainly will be if—no, *when*—the police catch us, I'll be killed.

The Agency has power. Lots of power. Enough of it to ensure that Angel's life goes back to normal after this.

The only other option for getting her out of this is much dirtier and riskier, and involves blackmailing the Agency. Using my famous face and my old connections to expose their involvement in the gang wars. Giving some kind of exclusive interview about what I did in prison. How I was sold out.

But that's a long shot. There's no guarantee anyone would believe my sordid tale. There's little chance they'd care. The last time I talked to my old publicist, about a year after my sentence began, she told me I would never have a career again.

"The public won't forget."

I killed three friends, and I was amped up when I wrecked.

So I'm relying on the Agency needing my help offing Emanuel Juarez. I think there's a reasonably good chance that, if I can reach Thom Ford, I can get Angel out of this.

"I do have a plan," I tell her as she strokes my back. "I'll take care of you this time, Angel."

I wrap an arm around her back and hug her close—because she's being good to me, and I convince myself, for just a moment, that I should pay her back by being good to her as well. My body responds as quickly as it ever has, cock hardening, mouth watering for a taste of her sweet pussy. I kiss her forehead, because I just can't stop myself, and then I remember looking up at her from the floor of the solitary unit as she held Ryan's gun out.

She shot someone today because of me.

Haven't I done enough to damage her?

I get up and walk away from her, vowing to keep my distance until we part.

CHAPTER 9

Annabelle

THERE ARE A FEW MORE scares just after dusk. Movement on the road from police cars—some driving toward the prison, others away. Movement in the air as the helicopters circle over us a few more times, shining their spotlights into the fields as night starts falling.

Beast is quiet. *Ricardo*. I need to start thinking of him as Ricardo, because that's who he is. Beast was a twisted, addictive fantasy of mine. A choice I made that was stupid, brave, and ultimately so compelling, it almost didn't feel like a conscious choice at all. My obsession with Beast started as obsession with Cal Hammond, movie star. But he's gone, too. The man I'm with tonight is nothing but Ricardo. Gun-shot, blood-streaked, sweaty, tired, and worried—he's not a dream I conjured. He's a real man.

I think that's what scares me the most. Now that he is real to me, my feelings haven't ebbed at all.

I want him as much or more than I ever have, even after he walks away from me and starts acting cooler toward me.

He's quiet and moody even in the times he has to talk to me, and I know some of it is the comedown. And some of it isn't. I'm convinced he's acting distant because he cares about me. Every time he touches me, his fingers say it, even though his mouth won't dare.

I imagine he feels guilty.

What happened today—he would blame himself for it. At least I'm pretty sure he does.

So I try not to let his silence hurt my feelings.

I try not to dwell on how lost and lonely I feel. How much I wish that he would touch me, just to reassure me with his body that things will be okay.

I'm desperate for word of Mom and Ad. Terrified that Mom picked this day to die.

What will happen to Ad if I somehow don't come home at all? If I'm arrested and held without bail—or, God forbid, worse?

I try hard not to dwell on that, but not thinking about the future means living in the moment, and that's not a cake walk, either.

My clothes are blood-stained. My hair is dirty and matted. I'm tired enough to pass out, and every time we hear the whoosh of traffic from the road, or the thumping of helicopter blades, I feel like I'm going to hurl.

Just before we leave our little grove, Ricardo tells me again that if we're caught, we'll both surrender without a fuss. He explains that he probably wouldn't be taken directly back to La Rosa; he'd go to a holding facility, where they'd investigate his escape and probably the prison's (mis)management, too. Before that, though, I bet he'll go to the hospital for that shoulder wound.

Me—I'm not so sure. He tries to tell me I'll be free and clear, especially since I didn't shoot Ryan, he did. But I'm not sure I can let him take the blame for that. Even if I decided that I could, for Adrian's sake, I'm pretty sure forensics is advanced enough these days that they can tell who fired the shot. Ricardo is a good bit taller than me; that's just one of many problems with his idea that he can get me off the hook.

It's tough to comprehend that my life is probably forever changed. That there's a chance whoever hears our story won't be as sympathetic as I'm hoping, and I won't be raising Ad. The thought fills me with anxiety and dread.

By the time we start walking—through the grassy field, about a quarter of a mile from the road—we have a more immediate problem: thirst. It's been hours since either of us has had anything to drink.

Every step I take makes me thirstier. The vast, star-scattered sky reminds me of water. The dew on the grass reminds me of water. I lick my lips and swallow to fool my body into thinking it's not dry and gross, but my need for water drives me to a painful place.

Ricardo walks beside me, occasionally touching my arm or my back, but rarely speaking, probably because he's as worn out as I am.

When it feels like we've been walking for several hours, he stops. He reaches out and touches my arm. "Angel," he rasps. "Over there."

It takes me a minute to see that he's pointing, not toward the road but deeper into the field.

My heart hammers. "Someone?" I choke.

"No. I think it's a water trough. For cattle."

He reaches for my hand, and we make our way toward a large metal structure shaped kind of like a big spider. It's got buckets arranged at different heights, and as we near it, I hear a low-pitched "moooo."

"Holy shit!"

Ricardo laughs and pulls me close. "I think we found the cows."

"Will they like…attack and stuff?"

He snickers. "Cows are lazy. No—they won't attack, Angel."

He reaches the trough a half-step before I do and sticks his hand inside. I hear him murmur a curse, and my throat constricts.

"It's feed."

We don't speak as we make our way around the structure, and Ricardo sticks his hand inside each trough.

They're filled with food.

Cow food.

I want to cry. Okay—maybe I do cry. Just one tiny little sob. Ricardo's fingers, twined through mind, squeeze gently, and he tugs me toward him.

He's walking backward as he does, and I hear a thunking sound, followed by "fuck." Followed by laughter as he turns around.

"Water."

He bumped into a round, metal water trough.

We stand over it. My mouth stings with the need to drink, but I think the trough looks cloudy.

"How often do you think they refresh it?" I ask.

"Probably don't," he says. "Probably just rain water."

"Is that safe?"

"Maybe, maybe not. It probably won't hurt us in the immediate."

He leans over and drinks right from it, then straightens up and wipes his mouth. "Not as bad as I thought. You interested?"

I nod, because seriously, my body isn't giving me a choice.

Ricardo cups his hands and dips them into the trough, filling them with water, bringing it up to my mouth. I mouth his palm, slurping as my lips stroke him. A few sips, and I'm pretty sure I feel his erection against my belly.

I drink a little more before deciding the water tastes too bad for even one more sip. When his hands return to my mouth, nudge his fingers away. "Thank you, but I think I've had enough."

He clasps my hand as we resume walking, but a few steps later, he lets it go, as if he suddenly remembered he's not supposed to be too friendly with me.

The next hour or so is brutal on my tired, sore body. I wish for the shoes I left back in the sunken car. My feet are scraped and sore, and I know Ricardo's must be, too. I don't think he was wearing shoes when we left the prison.

He stays half a step ahead of me, pointing out fallen limbs and, once, an electric fence. Just as I'm thinking I can't believe we haven't seen any police cars on the road out beside us, or any helicopters with spotlights, I hear the thumping of a chopper approaching fast.

It scares me so much, I jump on Ricardo. He jerks me down to the ground and lies on top of me.

"They're going to see us!" There are no trees around, or anything else to offer us shelter.

My heart pounds so hard, and when I try to inhale, my lungs feel frozen.

"Ric," I whisper.

"It's okay," he murmurs. "We've got this, Ang."

The helicopter swoops over us, its spotlight whirling through the field, but never landing on us. When the horrible, thumping sound fades, we lie still for a few more minutes before he pulls me up and we start walking again, this time faster.

I can tell his shoulder must be sore because he moves stiffly on that side. He says almost nothing to me, leaving me alone with my thoughts again—my thoughts of Mom and Ad and whether the district attorney is dead.

My thoughts of Beast. Ricardo. Cal.

It's weird to be walking through a bunch of pastures with him. Total non-fantasy material.

And then, with no warning, we're out of pasture and it's just desert dirt and scrubby trees. Another hour. Two? Time spreads out, and I'm so tired, I can't tell how long I've been walking.

When we hear the helicopter approaching this time, it seems headed straight for us. Ricardo grabs me, and we hide under a scrubby little tree. I clutch him as tightly as I can as it flies overhead, makes a circle, and heads back by us.

"I hate this so much," I whimper.

He holds me close to him and rubs his cheek against the top of my head. I watch the spotlight as it fades into the vast, dark sky.

"Definitely no infrared," I say as we get moving again.

"Yeah. That's a good thing." He smiles a little, and I catch his hand. I'm irrationally, pathetically thrilled when he doesn't pull away.

"Are you okay? How is your shoulder?"

"It's alright," he says.

"Where are we going exactly? A gas station or something? I just realized I don't even know."

"Anywhere we can find a phone," he says.

"There's a gas station soon, I think. I remember a few as I'm driving to La Rosa."

He nods.

"What do you think is the best way to get our hands on a phone—assuming there's no payphone, anyway?"

"You'll ask to borrow their phone, and find a way to come outside with it, so I can use it," he says simply.

"Who are you going to call?"

"Someone I worked with at the Agency," he says after a moment.

"Are you serious?"

"Yep."

"Do you really think they'll help us?"

"You don't need to worry, Angel. Really." His gaze flickers over me. "I know I've fucked things up before, but this time, I'll make all this right."

I don't trust him necessarily, but I'm not sure what to say. I go with "thank you."

Time drags as we walk. One of my soles feels damp, and stings, so I assume it's started bleeding.

Finally, we start to see more buildings by the roadside. We cut a little closer to the road, where a sidewalk runs now, and where street lights shine in the darkness. A mile of this, or maybe two—during which we both startle every time a car passes—and there it is: a lovely, pristine B.P. station on the right side of the road. We run across when no cars are coming, and Ricardo finds a water faucet on the back side of the building. We both drink our fill and then I leave him there and go inside.

I go straight to the desk and ask the cashier, a thin woman with magenta hair, if I can borrow her phone.

Her green eyes pop open wide as she looks my blood-stained self over. "You're that woman with Cal Hammond?"

"What?" I frown. "Cal Hammond? Isn't he in prison?"

"He escaped, girl. How did you miss a thing like that?" She shows me on her phone. They're using an old picture of me, back from sophomore year of college when my hair was shorter.

"Sorry to tell you, but I'd never wear my hair like that," I snark at her.

She frowns at me. "But you'd go around like that?"

I roll my eyes, because seriously, I'm too tired to think of an answer for her. "So what happened?" I ask. "With Cal?"

"He broke out," she says conspiratorially. "First thing people was saying was Cal Hammond shot the district attorney, but there's some people used to work at the prison saying there was something more going on. The DA's granddaughter was Uma, the girl in the car back when he had that wreck that got him sent to prison in the first place."

I can't breathe. Can't even speak. My mouth is hanging open, but I can't get words out.

"You okay, doll?"

I nod slowly. "He killed a district attorney?"

"Yep. Shot him on the prison grounds. Turned off the cameras first. People say that he was powerful at prison. Kind a leader."

My chest feels hot and full. My hands shake. "Wow, that's crazy. My sister had a baby today, so I've been busy there and not watching the news. Then my car broke down like…miles ago. I went through hell to get here."

She raises her eyebrows. "Boy or girl?" she asks me.

"A little boy. They named him Oliver."

She says she likes the name, and I ask again. "Do you mind if I use your phone?"

She shakes her head. "We have a pay phone, but it doesn't work." She slides her hand into the pocket of her khakis and draws out a black Android. She sets it on the counter and slides it to me. "Careful with the 'send' button. It's kinda shaky."

"Thank you." I scoop it up, then turn away from her and flip it open; raise it to my ear. I frown and draw it down so I can see the screen. I walk around the gas station for just a moment before telling her, "I can't seem to get more than one bar."

"Sometimes it's like that in here. You can step outside if you want to. Just don't run off."

"Perfect," I ramble. "I've got my own baby out there waiting for me," I tell her, hoping every false detail will throw her more fully off.

"Aww, a baby! I love babies. How old?"

"Mine is ten months now. Little girl. Sarah." I step into the doorway and wave. "I'll bring your phone right back. Thanks."

I grin hugely, and when I'm out the door, I run into the trees to Beast.

CHAPTER 10

Beast

I HAVE ANGEL CALL, in the slim chance someone else has Thom's phone. My voice is probably still memorable—at least to some people. Angel could be anyone.

I watch her face, lit by the dim parking lot lamps, as she bites her lips and waits for him to answer.

If he doesn't answer "Thom here," or "Thom Ford," I've told her she'll need to end the call.

I can tell when he picks up, because she stops breathing, then quickly says, "Is this Ricardo's friend?"

He must tell her *yes*.

She thrusts the phone at me, and I feel a rush of nausea as I bring it to my ear. "Thom."

"I'm sorry, Beast. It wasn't my idea."

Anger bubbles up inside me; I channel it the way I used to for my roles. "Yeah," I sneer. "You fucking should be. I gave you years and this is how I get repaid?"

"I know," he says. "And I'm sorry. It really wasn't me. I wasn't even asked. Believe it or not, I'm not the most important person here."

"You guys got Juan Juarez running the show now, don't you?"

"He'd been talking shit to you," Thom says. "Juan's no longer leading the cartel. His younger brother Emanuel is. We need to get him back in charge, so we've got aour finger on the pulse of things. You know the mission."

"Yeah," I snap.

"We've gotta rearrange things so his cousin Tito takes control on the outside, and Tito's reporting back to Juan. We had to give him some incentive. Make him feel we value him."

So in other words, I was left for dead because the Agency wants to install a more friendly Juarez Cartel head. Someone more willing to work with them. Because Juan Juarez suddenly could do more for them than I could.

"Robert Ryan?" I spit. "Was that a 'had to,' too?" I'm surprised by how bitter I sound.

"It wasn't my call. It was Brown." His boss.

"You been updated on today?" I ask. I glance left and right, because there's no way Thom's not tracing the shit out of my call. It's one of the risks of calling him.

"You shot Ryan," Thom says, "although there's a conflicting report from prison staff that a woman did it. Annabelle Mitchell. Holt's daughter? You must be one hell of an all-star pussy eater, Beast."

I guess he thinks that's the only way I could motivate someone like Angel to help me. And what the hell—maybe it is. Or "maybe she just fucking *cares*," I hiss, stepping away from her. "Do you know what the last few weeks have been like for me? *Ryan*, Tom? You could have just fucking had me hanged."

I take another few steps away from Angel, and I drop may voice a notch.

"She didn't do it. I did, Thom. She was with me, but I shot that sick fuck, and I don't regret it, either. I'm calling now because I need to get her home and get some assurance that her dalliance with me won't end up on her record."

He makes a thoughtful sound. "You must really care for her."

I ignore the statement, and his warm, interested tone. At this point, he's not fooling me. Thom's as cold as anyone else at the agency. He'll use anyone he can if it helps further his goals. "I don't want her found with me. Can you help with that?" I ask.

"Well… It's kind of hard to say right now."

"What if I could help you out. Take care of something on the outside while I'm here?"

I imagine his lips curling up into a smile. "That might be easier to organize. I'll talk and let you know."

"Fuck no," I say. "I'm throwing the phone away in two seconds. This is your only chance, if you want to get rid of E.J."— Emanuel Juarez.

I can almost hear Thom thinking through the line. His fast reply lets me know for sure he just lied to me. His boss doesn't call all the shots. Thom is not an entry level fucker. "I need you down at San Diego Bay by ten o'clock tomorrow night. Drop your girl off somewhere in L.A., and I'll have someone take her home. And Beast? She better know *nothing*."

I snicker. "Obviously." I rub my eyes. "I'll need a car and a gun that doesn't belong to Ryan. You can pick me up if you want. Or leave me something somewhere that doesn't sound like a setup."

"Where are you now? At that little B.P. station?"

"You're pretty fucking good," I say. Of course, he's got the FBI's firepower behind him.

"Give me a few minutes."

"No way."

"Two."

I lower the phone and turn back around to face Angel. She's standing with her arms folded across herself, looking tired and beautiful and stressed.

A second later, Thom is back. I take another step away, and turn around, putting my back to Angel.

"I'll have a car for you at Desert Campers and RVs in an hour," he says quickly. "Black Honda Accord. Desert Campers is two miles down from where you are. Same side of the road. Keys will be atop the right rear tire, firearm in the glove box. Drive down to San Diego not tonight, but tomorrow. Can you kill some time tonight? Lay low, stay out of sight? Maybe drive somewhere outside the city? I'll include a fake ID and credit card. More detailed instructions will be under the car's passenger seat."

"Where will I leave Annabelle?" I ask.

I hear her shift behind me and imagine a nervous expression on her face.

"I'll leave you instructions for that, too."

"Make it somewhere public. Somewhere I can trust that you won't fuck with her."

"How about a hospital?" he asks. "Cedars Siani, main entrance. I'll leave some cash with one of the bell hops and she can call her own cab."

"Thom?"

"Yes?"

"If you double-cross me when it comes to her, I'll kill you with my bare hands."

I hear smile. "Duly noted, Beast."

"It's Ricardo, asshole."

Annabelle

"So what are we going to do?" I ask after I emerge from the gas station. We're standing in some trees, about ten yards behind an air pump machine on the rear side of the parking lot.

The conversation he just had seemed intense, and I'm worried about him. He talked quietly, and he turned his back to me, but I could tell he was making some kind of deal.

"Right now, we're going to a car," he says matter of factly. "We're going to stay out of the metro area tonight, and then tomorrow, I'll drop you off at Cedars Siani Hospital, you'll get some cash from a bell hop, and you can get a cab home. It's a public place, so you'll be safe."

"Where will you go?"

I can tell I'm right to be worried, because he doesn't look me in the eye. In fact, he turns away and starts walking away from the gas station, moving deeper into the trees.

I hurry to catch up, and when I do, he still won't look at me.

"If I go home, what will you do?"

"I've got something to do on my own," he says after a moment.

"What kind of something?"

I can hear traffic on the road that runs alongside us—a reminder that we're still in danger. Both of us.

"What I do is not your problem, Angel. All that matters is getting you home to your mom and your sister. Focus on that."

He still won't look into my eyes.

My stomach twists. "It's the FBI, isn't it? You're doing something for them. It's the only way you could get us out of trouble this bad." I let out the breath that I didn't realize I'd been holding. "Bea— Ricardo, I *want* to know. Maybe it's not 'my problem', but it matters to me. What will you have to do, and what do you get in return?" He pulls back a limb for me, and I pass by in front of him, but he doesn't answer. "Will you have to kill someone? Will they give you shelter, or clear your name or something if you do?"

"Don't worry about me, Angel. Please." He stops moving and turns around to look me in the eye. There's a pleading quality to his expression, as if he's given this a lot of thought and there is only one outcome. "I'm doing what I have to do, based on the situation that I'm in."

"You didn't *have* to do anything. You could just keep running," I say hopefully. I'm not sure what I think the end result of that would be, but it makes me feel less nervous than being dropped off at the hospital tomorrow while he goes off to do God knows what.

"When you were talking, it sounded like you mentioned me."

"I told you, you'll be cleared of all this shit. Stop worrying about it, Angel. This is the plan we're going with—one where you go home and forget about today."

"Oh, right! Like I can just forget it. Okay, cool. I shoot people every day!"

He's on me in a millisecond, pressing his hand over my mouth and pulling me back against his chest.

"Quiet," he hisses into my ear. "You're putting yourself in jeopardy."

He moves his hand off my mouth, but keeps his arm wrapped around me. I look over my shoulder, up at him. "Looks like we have that in common!"

He clenches his jaw, looking pissed off, and I turn around to face him fully. "You've got a lot of nerve, acting like you can just do whatever you want to save the day and I'll just go home and live in a fantasy land. Do you think that I don't care about you? That I won't want to know what happened to you after you drop me at the effing hospital? That I'll just...magically forget about today, and all the shit before it? Ricardo, you're my...*mine.* You're my...I don't know, my cosmic fucking destiny or something! I tried to forget you years ago and failed, and you failed, too." He opens his mouth, looking outright angry now, so I preempt whatever bullshit he might spout. "I remember the pictures," I say, "so don't you dare pretend that you don't give a shit about me, too."

"I give a shit about you," he says. "Yes. That's why I have to insist you lower your fucking voice and forget whatever you think there is between us. I was curious about you, and you the same. We've got chemistry, I'm not denying that."

He starts walking again, and I stride after him. "Is that why you called that night you killed the Aryan? You called me to your room, where you were laid up, having been stabbed, because we have 'some chemistry'?"

He glances my way. "I fucked you, didn't I?"

"So I'm a booty call."

"Don't tell me you didn't know that."

I inhale deeply through my nose and work to keep from screaming. "If you want to minimize this, you can go for it. But you're not rewriting history, and you're damn sure not fooling me. You're lying to yourself so that it's easier when we say 'bye' tomorrow. Fine. But let me tell you this: I care about you. And if it's the FBI you're working with, then you shouldn't! Aren't they the reason you got thrown in solitary? Why are you trusting them? I didn't kill to protect you, so you could turn around and die!"

He stops mid-stride and turns to me with wide eyes.

"Yeah. Ryan died. I am a killer." I grit my teeth as hard as I can, because I'm not going to cry, damnit!

Beast reaches out and pulls me into his arms. "Angel…" I feel his mouth against my hair; the warmth of his breath. I shut my eyes and feel the rising of his chest. "I'm sorry, Angel."

"I found out in the gas station," I whisper to his chest.

He pulls away a little, so he can see my face—and I can see his. I can see the way his jaw clenches and his eyes narrow on mine. I can see him fighting with himself. "You're right," he whispers finally. "But it doesn't matter, Angel."

His voice is so bitter, so totally filled with pessimism and defeat; I surprise myself by letting out a sob.

He wraps his arms around me. "Don't cry. Please don't cry, Angel. It wasn't your fault. It was *my* fault. Everything was my fault," he whispers. "I just can't seem to keep myself from you."

Tingly heat runs through my body. "I can't stay away from you either."

I cling to his shoulders, and I feel his erection press against my belly. I lean up and kiss the one part of him I can reach: his chin. He leans down and welcomes my lips into a warm, slow, gentle kiss. I deepen the kiss and immediately feel wet and needy. I rock myself against his dick. "Beast…"

He steps back, running one hand down my arm and catching may fingers in his.

"We need to keep walking, Angel. Make it to the car."

But he holds my hand as we move. Strokes my fingers.

"I'm worried for you," I whisper.

"Please don't be."

And, after a long time walking silently, listening to the traffic on the road to our left, he murmurs, "Would you talk to me? I'm tired of fighting." I'm about to ask what he means—we haven't exactly been 'fighting'—when he looks down at me and whispers: "Fighting what I want." He strokes my cheek with his free hand and looks into my eyes. "I want you, Angel. It's fucking stupid, and it's dangerous and wrong. But I have you…just for one night. I'm gonna use you if you let me. I don't have the discipline to let you go unspoiled."

My body heats to its boiling point. "What would you like to talk about?" I choke.

He shrugs. "You. I want to know the story that goes along all with my pictures."

I squeeze his fingers. "I still can't believe you had those taken."

"I needed them."

"Why?"

He slows, and I notice we've reached a fence around what looks to be an RV sales place. "I needed to know that someone in this world was good, and living a good life."

"And that was *me*?"

"That's you." He strokes my hair. "That night of the wreck…" His eyes flicker over mine. "You really were an angel to me."

The words are whispered hoarsely. They're a gift.

He pulls me close for a moment and kisses the top of my head, and I squeeze him around the waist.

"Think about tonight," he tells me as he leads me up to the fence.

"I don't need to think. I want you, like I always have."

"You really shouldn't," he says.

"That doesn't always matter."

He helps me over the fence, and climbs over himself, and I oblige him by talking about college as we walk to a black car parked behind the building, and he gets a key off one of the wheels and lets us in. He drives through a gate that opens automatically as we approach it, then headed south, and, with continued prompting, I move on to grad school and my desire to be a therapist.

"I like teaching people new things," I tell him as he drives toward us down a dark highway. "Things to help people be more confident and less afraid. I really like PTSD. I mean, helping people who have it." I roll my eyes.

I feel kind of silly for misspeaking, but he doesn't even look my way. He's staring at the road like it holds the answers to the universe's mysteries.

After a minute or so, I touch his elbow, and he jumps.

He looks over at me, and I can tell he's tired and trying not to be. "What kind of things do you do for these people?" he asks.

I shrug. "Relaxation techniques. Visualization." I reach across and touch his knee. "Let's wait until we lie down for the night, and I'll help you relax. I think you'd really benefit."

He smirks a little. "My stress level is higher than you like?"

"Much higher," I say. "I also want to stop at a pharmacy and get something for your shoulder. How is it?"

He shrugs, one-sided, as if to emphasize the point. "Could be worse." His eyes find mine, and they go molten. "I already told you, Angel, I'll take anything you're offering tonight."

CHAPTER 11

Beast

ANGEL RISKS A QUICK trip into a rural Walgreens, where she gets a blanket, cheap scrubs for us both, basic first aid supplies, and a bunch of food and drinks. She feeds me powered donuts as I drive toward the country home of my late manger, whose wife, I read in a celebrity gossip rag online, has recently been moved into a nursing home.

I bounce us down the long, dirt drive and pull into a swatch of forest that folds around the house. I've barely got the car in park before I start to tear Angel's clothes off.

Her shirt goes first, and then her bra, so I can suck her breasts into my mouth. I taste them both, then recline the passenger's seat and turn her around so that she's hugging the head rest. "Stay like that, and stick your ass out for me."

I climb over into the floorboard behind her and yank her pants down. I rip her panties ruthlessly, so that she's bare before me, wet and fragrant, ready for my mouth.

I lean down and plunge my tongue into her cunt, and she gasps my name—not Beast, *Ricardo.*

All I need on earth is to drag my tongue between her pussy lips. Drive my fingers into her wet cunt. Make her squirm and pant my name, and when she's dripping wet and ready, toss her into the back seat and push my cock so deep inside her, she's screaming.

So that's exactly what I do.

When I've got her on the verge of coming from my tongue and fingers, I lift her into the back seat, then climb into it behind her. I'm hard and pulsing, ready to bury myself to the hilt. Instead, I'm greeted by her hands yanking down my pants and her warm mouth sealing, hot and wet, around my cock.

She sucks me for a minute as I groan, and then she pushes me down onto my back, so I'm lying belly-up across the seat. She climbs astride my thighs, rubbing her pussy on my leg and pushing my knees apart so she can take my dick in both her hands and guide her mouth down over my head.

"Goddamn, Angel." I twist my hips and tug her hair.

She sucks me hard, taking my head way down into the velvet softness of her throat. Taking every centimeter of me, down to the base, then sucking me in and easing me out, licking me like a lollipop until my balls are drawing up and I can feel my orgasm roaring down the tracks.

I moan and grip her hair, and come into her throat. I sit up and kiss her lips, and then I flip her over, pushing her torso against the door and pulling her ass up with my hands gripping her hips. I nudge her legs wider with one of my knees and punch inside her. Her cunt is hot and wet and swollen, pulling on my taut head and stiff erection like a dream.

I squeeze her ass and shove myself inside, tracing around her clit with my damp fingers as I fuck her doggy style with the biggest erection I've ever had.

We come together, and when I try to pull out, she reaches behind her and grabs my hand—telling me not to pull out.

I come inside her like a fucking prince, and when I'm done, she grins and kisses me.

After that, she bandages my shoulder. God, she's gentle. So gentle and sweet and soft, and despite everything, I fucking swear she smells good. I love having her in my lap. Having her hands on my skin.

It's been so long since I was touched this way.

She has to clean my shoulder with alcohol, which hurts like a bitch, and when she's done bandaging it and it's throbbing, she eases me into a corner and snuggles up beside me. She drapes her leg over my lap and wraps my unhurt arm around her shoulders, pressing her soft, warm breasts against my chest.

I'm so tired, I can almost feel my eyes rolling back into my head, but I fight sleep, because I want so much to be with her. I stroke her back and let my fingers play in her hair. When she smiles at me, I smile at her and say, "I fucking love having you close."

She strokes gently up and down my abs, making me hard again. Making me throb with needing her.

I groan and thrust my dick up toward her hand. A few minutes later, I end up with her ass in my face. She's bouncing on my cock, letting me impale her. Sliding on and off me like fucking is a sport and she's a goddamn Olympian.

It's perfect sex, and when it's done, I spread her out in the back seat and suck her pussy till she comes again on my face.

I lean back against the fabric seats, grabbing deep, fulfilling breaths.

She pastes herself against my side and strokes her fingers through my hair.

"Are you tired yet?" She smiles.

"No." I kiss her mouth. "I want to talk some more. For you to tell me more."

That's what keeps me up, with Angel sitting in my lap, my arms around her back, her cheek against my chest, like we're a couple of high schoolers, yapping through the night in puppy love.

Annabelle

"What did you want to do when you were young?"

His cheek presses against my hair as I listen to his heart beat through his warm, thick chest. "I don't know," he says after a short silence. "I was always an actor. I did my first commercial for Fisher Price when I was eighteen months old." He smiles a little. "It was that red and yellow coup."

"Were you glad about that? When you got older, I mean?" I stroke my fingers up and down his hurt arm, the way he said was good for distracting from the pain of his shoulder.

He makes a sleep, rumbly noise in his throat, and I wonder if he's finally going to conk out—but a moment later, he murmurs, "I don't know how to tell if I did or didn't. It was just what I did." He strokes my cheek. "What about you?"

I laugh. "I wanted to be a singer—like Mariah Carey."

He chuckles, and in a soft, pitch-perfect baritone, sings: "'Cause you'll always be my Angel…"

"And you'll linger on… Time can't erase a feeling this strong!" I catch his eye and start laughing, because I've got a bad voice. Really bad. I nuzzle my forehead against the stubble on his chin. "You see why I never made the cut for 'American Idol'?"

"You tried out?" he grins.

I giggle. "No. Simon Cowell would have laughed me off the stage."

"He's not so bad."

"All that meanness is for show?"

He shrugs, a lazy movement of his warm, hard body, like a continental shift beneath me. "I don't know anymore. I don't watch that much TV."

"What did you miss the most in there?" I whisper. "At La Rosa?"

Maybe I shouldn't be asking questions like that, but the truth is, I want to know everything about him.

His lips twist as he peers down at me. "What did I not miss? A good merlot. Dancing with a beautiful woman." He drops a kiss on my temple. "The smell of the ocean down in Santa Barbara. Miles Davis, played as loud as the house system can play him."

I smile, imagining that. "You're a jazz fan?"

"The biggest," he says.

My fingers wander over his cock, which I'm not surprised is hard. I start to stroke it through the Walgreens 'on sale' scrubs he's wearing.

"I can go with a little Miles Davis on a Sunday afternoon."

"Why Sunday?" he asks. He shifts his hips so I can have better access, and as I work him up and down through his pants, his face tightens.

I shrug. "Just seems like jazz should be played on Sunday."

"Jazz should be played every day," he breathes.

He shifts his hips a little, making his erection tent his pants. I continue teasing him with my fingers and palm, eager to see his face relax with his release.

"Before I plow into your sweet cunt, Angel, I've got a question," he says.

I squeeze his head gently. "Okay."

But his face is serious. "Why are you alone?" he asks. "Did something happen? Is there a reason why you…?"

"Why I'm still single?" I smile and shake my head. "Just the busyness of grad school and the strain of taking care of Mom and Ad. No time for romance really. Definitely not with most of the guys I know."

I must have given the answer he wanted, because as soon as I finish speaking, he pulls me onto his lap, facing me away from him, so my ass is pressed against his cockhead. I rub my butt in circles till he groans.

"Maybe I was waiting for you," I whisper as he starts to kiss my ear and rock below me.

"I don't think that it's a maybe," he says.

Then he takes my hot pink, Walgreens, scrubs pants down, lifts his cock out of his pants, and pushes it between my warm, slick pussy lips.

My legs shake as I sink down on him, letting him stretch me, letting him fill me thoroughly, letting him ruin me for anyone else, ever.

CHAPTER 12

Beast

FOR A WEALTHY MAN, I'm not very educated. I never studied music in a college class, because I never went to college. I don't know the proper names of musical things—not much at all beyond your basic notes and stanzas. I didn't start listening to Mr. Davis until I got to prison. I told Angel wrong on that. What I truly missed was the chance to hear his music on a real sound system. The kind installed in walls and ceilings. Not a little box inside a cell.

But what I do know, despite my lack of formal education, is that I enjoy jazz because it's constantly finding and re-finding its rhythm. A lot of it is improv, and improv, I understand. I love the way jazz shifts, so something goes from soft to loud with no warning, and no warning is needed, because when you can make a sound flow so well, there's no point in prior notice, in the subtle signaling of intentions; you can take it anywhere and it will still be beautiful.

The way I feel for Angel reminds me of a Davis song called "So What." When I would listen to it on the prison's old boom box, I'd turn the volume all the way up, and I could hardly hear a thing when the song started. For the first minute or so, the first few times I played it, I thought the volume was broken. The notes rise on their own accord, and find consistency and steadiness in an unexpected way.

And suddenly, it's loud. Downright fucking loud, and wonderful.

I'm holding Angel after our fifth fuck in this car. I'm looking out the window, looking at the hazy outline of the trees in the night. My hands are on her soft, warm arms and shoulders. My legs are arranged to cradle her. Her hair is in my face. I'm breathing in the scent of her. I'm remembering the way her cunt clings to my cock, and even as I love her smell and feel, the way she breathes, the rhythm of her pulse— Even as I marvel at her beauty, the song of my soul is silent.

And all at once, she reaches out in sleep to grab onto me, and things get loud.

I'm looking down at her, only instead of sitting in this car, I imagine us in a chair on the deck of my yacht. And all around us is the sound of Miles Davis.

And I know we're celebrating out at sea because I married her.

In another life, a better life, a different life, I marry Angel, not because it makes a fucking bit of sense—but just because I want to, and I can.

And it's autumn and we're walking Central Park and she's got on a huge coat, tied around her awkwardly, and under it, her soft belly is growing big and round.

It makes my dick hard. Thinking about Angel with my baby growing inside her makes me hard as a motherfucking rock.

Because I love her.

This woman in my arms—I love her. Angel. She's my other half. My compliment. She makes me not care what the future holds for me. If I can see her, even once a year, I want to be here for it.

I sit there with my heart slamming against my sternum, bathed in the scent of her, warmed by her soft, slender body, worshipping every single cell of hers—this woman who is infinitely better than every specimen that's come before her.

And I think that maybe Davis would appreciate the tragedy.

Because tomorrow, I'm probably going to die. And there will never be a chance to tell her how I feel.

There are some things I *can* do, so as she sleeps, I do them.

I write down my bank account information. I've got a few accounts that no one knows about. I use the phone under the driver's seat to call those banks, which are open, because they're located in Switzerland.

Through a series of elaborate emergency questions, I prove my identity, and designate Angel as the accounts' new beneficiary. My photographic memory knows her social security number, and for that reason alone, I'm able to complete my task. Just before the sun comes up, I risk one more call to a man named Hebert Frank, my financial attorney.

I give him verbal instructions that if something happens to me, if I'm deceased or unable to make medical decisions for myself, I'd like Annabelle Mitchell to receive my royalties.

"Ric—how much of them? Er, what percentage?" he asks in that stalwart voice of his, which has yet to sound surprised by my call.

"All of them."

I nestle Angel into the blanket she bought at the pharmacy and drive carefully toward the city. And when she wakes up, rosy-cheeked and bathed in the sunlight that spills around L.A.'s cityscape, she climbs into the front seat and kisses me on the lips.

I pull the car into a car wash, fuck her twice, and eat her pussy twice after, crouched in the passenger's seat floorboard with her legs over my shoulders. Then I buckle her back up, give her the paper from Thom specifying a contact at each applicable law enforcement agency, should any problems arise for her, and speed toward Cedars Siani.

We find out on the radio that her mother's still alive—at least as far as the public knows, and I can see the relief on her face. A little of it ebbs away when an analyst explains that I kidnapped her from prison.

When I frown, she says, "I don't want people thinking that's what happened."

I clasp her hand. "Don't worry, Angel. No more worrying. I want you to promise."

Annabelle

"You must think I'm either a heartless bitch, or some kind of robot. Ricardo, I'm going to worry. I'll be worried until you call me later tonight. You are still doing that, right?"

He nods, his eyes flickering over mine, then returning to the road, where L.A. traffic is starting to thicken.

"I'll call you as soon as I've finished what I'm doing," he says. "Phone number 555-155-2398."

I nod. "You better call me. I still don't like this. Do you really think they could get your sentence shortened back to how it was?"

He told me that this morning—that, according to his handlers in the FBI, he could probably get the extension removed—and it's filled me with elation ever since.

"I think it's possible," he says.

"It needs to happen. But if it doesn't, I can still see you?"

He nods. "In exchange for the favor I'm about to do them, I'm going to be just another prisoner. Juan Juarez might run things on the inside, but I'll be segregated, and his instructions will be to leave me the fuck alone."

I catch his hand in mine. "I'm so glad. I just wish they had done this sooner."

He shrugs. "Sometimes you have to give to get, especially when it comes to pricks like them."

"Give and get." I grin. "I'm already a horny girl again."

"Come see me next week."

Hope bubbles around inside my chest. "I will, for sure."

He checks the phone in his hand. "We should be about eighteen minutes from the hospital." His fingers squeeze mine. "You're not gonna give me any trouble, are you? Getting out and going? You know I need you to go so I can do what I have to do."

I nod. "I know. I don't want to, but I will."

"Good girl."

As he brakes for traffic, he leans over and kisses my lips.

I have to turn my gaze away from him and focus out the window, because I'm starting to feel like I might cry.

Ten minutes later, he takes the exit for the hospital, and I do cry.

He pulls over at a fast food joint. Walks around the car, opens my door, and gathers me into his arms.

"Don't cry, Angel. Everything will be okay. You'll see."

"I just don't want you to go. I'm scared." I cling to him.

"I promise you will be okay."

"And you?"

He smiles a little. "I can take care of myself. No need to worry."

He kisses my eyes and cheeks and lips, then eases me back into the car.

"You're sure about this plan? Like—totally sure?"

He nods. "Go home to your sister and your mom, Angel. Don't think about me until I call you."

"I'll never stop," I whisper.

His fingers stroke mine, and we turn into the hospital's vast parking lots.

He pulls up at the main entrance and stops. He grabs my mouth and kisses me, so hard and hungry. He keeps it brief, and fast, then comes around and lets me out. He walks me up the stairs, where a uniformed man greets me.

"Are you Annabelle Mitchell?"

"I am."

Beast tugs me into his arms abruptly, and we rock together, hugging. He's holding both my hands as I look back to the bell hop.

"I've got an envelope for you, ma'am."

He hands it to me, and Ricardo releases my hands.

He kisses my forehead, then my cheek, and finally my lips. I throw my arms around him, holding tight until he steps away and holds his hand up. "Bye, Angel."

I follow him down the cement steps, and he laughs at me. "Go back up and call your cab."

"I love you," I say as he opens his car door.

He freezes and his face loses its expression.

He gets inside and drives away, and I cry as I call my cab.

Several minutes later, a yellow van pulls up. I get inside, already preparing to ugly cry in privacy.

That's when someone grabs me from behind.

Beast

I know Angel's home address. I looked it up. So when the van she gets into turns the other way out of the hospital parking lot, I know my sixth sense about Thom was right. Just not quite in the way I thought. Thom isn't going to let me get killed by the Juarez Cartel and help Angel live happily ever after. He's going to get us both. Remove all threats.

I speed after her, following the van as it drives toward LAX.

CHAPTER 13

Annabelle

UGLY CRY, I DO.

I cry so hard, my captors seem a little bit afraid.

In the driver's seat is Glasses, a short man of indeterminate nationality. Then there's Hairy, an American-seeming man with a long, gray beard; and Pervy, a man who might be Indian, who leans over me every time the van hits a bump and tries to adjust my seatbelt but instead ends up touching my boobs.

Yes, that's right—I'm buckled in, in the middle seat on the back row.

My mouth is bound with a long strip of tape, and my wrists are bound together in front of me by that same gray tape.

From the moment they grabbed me, as we careened out of the hospital parking lot, to right now, as we're bouncing down the interstate, I've been sobbing like a mental case. I'm blowing snot bubbles out my nose, so I can barely breathe. Instead of calming me, my snotty state makes me sob harder.

I strain my hips and abs to stay upright as the van makes yet another hairpin turn, and in the whirl of our momentum, I think I see a sign for the airport. I sob harder still, because this is just my fucking luck! And a mile or so later, harder still, because we're definitely going to the airport. Finally, just as I have to slow my sobbing roll because my nose is so stopped up I literally can't breathe, Hairy leans back and holds a cell phone to my ear.

"When your mother passes, we will see nothing but the best for your sister Adrian. It's not your fault you know what you know," says the man who answered the call I made for Ricardo last night. "You'll be going to Pakistan to be a rich man's companion. No sex. Only business, lunches, and dinners. Play along if you want your Beast to live."

The line goes dead, and Hairy raises his eyebrows.

No more crying for me. I sit numbly, trying to process that unlike last night, when my fate was still fluid, it's sealed now. I may never see Mom, Ad, or Ricardo again.

A minute or an hour later, in what looks, to my blood-shot, puffy eyes to be an airport parking lot, Hairy picks me up and hauls me into another van—this one the boxy, European style. I'm thrown into the floor space between the two pilot seats in the middle of the van, where I lay while the three men pile in with me.

I'm too stunned to cry or even move as we shoot off moving again. Glasses turns up a National Public Radio program that seems to be about the cultural importance of pigs, and I hear a woman talking about how more and more people are keeping them as pets.

I start to tremble as my situation begins to feel more real, and immediately I begin imagining Ricardo's hands on me. I imagine he said he loved me when we parted at the hospital. I imagine him stroking my hair. I imagine us somewhere far away, tucked into a bed. The bed is soft and warm. I'm in that bed, not here. I can handle anything that happens to me now, because Ricardo will be right back.

There's a fine line between positive visualization and outright denial, and I don't give a fuck where that line is.

I keep my eyes shut, even when Pervy's boot repeatedly nudges my thigh, and I try my best to feel Ricardo's fingers stroking through my hair.

I picture Adrian's face, not premeditating the logic of this move, and of course, the mere thought of my poor sister sends me into a fresh wave of hysterics.

My sobs ebb and flow as the men in the seats over me talk in a foreign language. I picture myself wearing strange lingerie, carrying a tray with martini glasses balanced on top. I'm going to be a sex slave.

I can't believe this is my fate.

A low whine comes from my nose, followed by a bunch of snot, and Hairy says, "Stop!"

I think he's talking to me, but he must be talking to Glasses, because instantly, the van jerks to a stop.

Pervy looks down at me and says something in that other language: Pakistani?

Then they're all moving at once. This time, both Pervy and Hairy grab one of my shoulders. They thrust me out the door so hard, when they startle and let go of me, I fall face-first to the asphalt, busting my nose, which promptly starts to pour blood.

Lots of blood.

Or maybe that's not my blood.

I kick my legs hard enough to roll over and blink up into the bright sun. I squint, because it's bright, and all I can see is shadows. Warring shadows.

I think I hear Ricardo's voice, and I make a mental note that if I ever am a therapist, I'll need to warn my patients that positive visualization can lead to a mental break a little faster than one might expect.

Then I see the glint of a knife.

Ricardo has Hairy on the ground beside me and is prying a huge knife from his hands. He stabs Hairy in the chest, then whirls and slashes Pervy across the neck. Pervy's knees hit the ground, and blood gushes everywhere—and yet, this is my fairy tale come true.

I'm sobbing again, happy tears this time, as Ricardo kicks both Pervy and Hairy, and the sound of their moaning fills this new airport parking lot.

Beast looks down at me—Ricardo. He says, "I love you, Angel."

Then he opens the driver's door, pulls Glasses out, and starts to kick his ass. And it's perfect—absolutely perfect—until I see something glisten in Glasses' hand, and Ricardo is clutching his chest as Glasses stabs him once, twice, three times, four times. Ricardo hits the ground beside me, pouring blood, and Glasses stabs him three more times before the van speeds off.

I'm screaming, but no one can hear.

I long to touch him, but my hands are tied.

Warm blood leaks out of him, penetrating my clothes. His eyes are shut. His face is white. His body limp.

I can't even sob. I drag myself to him and lie my head against his arm, as blood soaks through my hair.

I don't know when or how, but an ambulance arrives. Paramedics wearing blue scrubs much like ours jump out and start barking questions. They jerk the tape off my mouth, and cut the tape binding my wrists, and I start screaming. I grab at Ricardo, frantic to check on him, but they put him on a stretcher and whisk him up over me faster than I can even get a glimpse of him.

I jump into the ambulance behind him, and I hear one of the EMTs say "Cal Hammond" while another one says "dead."

Someone yells something, and the female EMT is pushing paddles against his chest. She yells again, and I watch in horror as his torso comes up off the cot.

He's dead, he's dead…he's dead. He's dead!

She does it again, and I clutch my stomach. And again.

"Last time," she says, and the other paramedic is speaking quickly into a little phone. I hear her say, "actor."

I jump on Ricardo. I grab his leg, and a male paramedic yells and jerks me off, but I've got my idea and I'm not backing away. I start screaming.

"BEAST, HELP ME! BAD GUYS HAVE ME AND I'M HURT!"

"Miss, you need to—"

"Beast, PLEASE! PLEASE help! I NEED YOUR HELP!"

"You need to—"

"BEAST, RICARDO, PLEASE! Please, please!" My screams die out as sobs punch through me. I collapse into a bucket seat, wailing so loud it startles me at first.

A paramedic hovers over me, telling me something I can't understand because I'm screaming. He keeps repeating himself, over and over, the same words from his lips; his eyes are wide, but I don't care. The other two are moving all around Ricardo's pale, dead body, holding onto the sides of the ambulance as we whip through traffic.

I'm sobbing so hard I can't breathe, sobbing so hard I'm deaf and blind to everything except my pain.

One of the women cleaning blood off Ricardo grabs my arm, and I just sob harder—until she yells, "HE'S NOT DEAD! He's hanging on for now! So shut your mouth, please, and quit disturbing my patient."

I stop sobbing, instead gulping huge breaths back, and things go fuzzy as someone puts something plastic over my nose.

CHAPTER 14

Annabelle

I'M IN A HOSPITAL BED when I wake up, and an unfamiliar man is standing by my bed. For the first few seconds, my mind tries hard to make him into Beast, but this man's coloring is so different that it's impossible, even for my addled mind.

"Who are you?" I croak. My eyes can't seem to focus. They flit from his lightly bearded face to an IV sticking out of my arm.

Some time passes, no more than a minute or two as I try to get my bearings. He sits in a gray plastic chair beside my bed, which I notice is surrounded by curtains.

"Do you know where you are, Annabelle?"

I shake my head. "Where's Ricardo? I came here with…" I swallow, and find my throat is dry. So dry. My head feels dried out, too. It aches, and it's so hard to think.

I came here with Ricardo, didn't I?

I hold my hand out in front of me, and that's when I notice: there's blood caked in my fingernails.

My heart pounds hard. "I came here with him."

"With who," the man beside me prompts—and something clicks inside my head.

That voice…

"You're Thom."

He nods, and I pass out again.

FIVE DAYS LATER

I can't take Adrian to the hospital with me. In the three days since Mom passed, every time I close my eyes, she starts to cry. The trick is, letting her go to sleep first and then nodding off beside her, so if she wakes up before me, there's no lag time between the moment she wakes up in her bed and the length of time it takes her to run into my room and be sure I'm still alive.

To me, she doesn't seem to be doing very well, but the hospice counselors tell me that all of this is normal for a kid her age.

Without Holly helping me watch Ad, I have no idea what I would do. The only thing that keeps me from feeling totally guilty for monopolizing all of Holly's time is, two nights after Mom died, when she stayed over to help me with Ad, I got her to agree to let me pay for some community college courses she's been wanting to take.

That makes me feel good, especially considering I've been spending four or five hours a day sitting by Ricardo's bed.

Today, when I go, I've got my binder with me. It's mostly filled with paperwork I don't understand, but sometimes when I come visit, I bring the binder with me, and I try to understand the charts and graphs.

It's not easy.

Ninety million dollars is a lot of money, and until he wakes up again, they tell me all of it is mine.

Just another twist in this strange fairy tale of ours.

I've been sitting by his bed for an hour, staring at the binder, when I realize I haven't read a word of it today.

I'm just…staring.

Tears start falling down my cheeks before I even know exactly what I'm crying about. Mom? Ricardo? Ad? The empty, sick feeling that never seems to leave my stomach, and gets worse when the doctors come in, with their nasty clipboards and their mean white coats, and their sympathetic nods and vague prognoses? I cry especially over Dr. Haberman, otherwise known as Dr. Doom, who's told me more than once he can't guarantee Ricardo will wake up at all.

When he got to the hospital that day, he'd lost almost all his blood volume, and when they started giving him a blood transfusion, his body reacted badly to it, which triggered a minor heart attack.

His coma isn't medically induced. It's real.

Most of the doctors think there's every reason to be optimistic, especially given his age and health status, and the good news he's got coming when he does wake up. But me…

That's just not enough for me.

I need fucking guarantees.

I need to see his eyes and hear his voice. I need to feel his hands on me. I need to climb in bed with him and hold him.

My heart pounds so hard I feel like I'm having a heart attack myself, and after a quick glance around the private ICU room, I take a deep breath, put the bed rail down, pull the blankets back, and break every rule in the book by climbing into bed with him.

There are wires and tubes everywhere, but I don't care. I duck under some and rearrange others so there's nothing but my green dress, his pale blue gown, and a bunch of bandages and sensors keeping us from being skin-to-skin.

He got stabbed almost everywhere on his upper body—thirteen times, much more than I actually saw—so the layers of bandages around his chest are thick enough that I can see them through his gown.

There's oxygen tubing taped to his cheeks and IVs in his arms, but there's a spot between his shoulder and his jaw—a small spot of real, Ricardo skin that I can nuzzle up to. And I do.

My pulse slows almost instantly as my cheek strokes his neck. The tightness in my chest that makes every breath feel strained eases a little. I kiss his smooth skin and inhale deeply, and I swear, I can smell him. Not the acrid scents of a hospital room, but him—my Beast. My Ricardo.

I look around—there are cameras hanging from the ceiling—then look at the door, but no one's come yet, so I decide I'm going to enjoy this.

I kiss his cheek and stroke his hand and start to whisper to him, telling him about my mom, about Thom, about La Rosa and the Juarez Cartel, and the *New York Times*, and his re-sentencing results, and the yacht I'm going to buy.

I tell him how much I love him, how much I miss him, and even though I promised myself that I'd be strong, I end up crying, begging him to wake up.

"I need you. Please. I really need you. I know it's wrong to…pressure you. The nurses say it…isn't good, but please," I sob. I lace my fingers through his. "Please wake up. I miss you so much, Beast. I miss you so much."

And maybe they're usually right, those nurses. Maybe usually, it is bad to pressure a coma patient into waking up.

But most patients aren't Ricardo. And most people doing the pressuring aren't kissing all over the person they're threatening.

Maybe my tears have magic, as they do in fairy tales.

All I know is, when I open my streaming eyes again, his eyes greet me.

"Beast!"

He coughs, then smiles, a little hazily, and mouths, "Ricardo."

"Yes, Ricardo. I love you so much. Thank you for waking up. I was starting to lose it here."

He clutches my dress, and I stroke his hair and kiss his temple, and do everything I can to touch him, so he feels my love and wants to stay.

He stays.

That night, we talk. And three weeks later, we go home to our new mansion on the coast of Santa Barbara.

EPILOGUE

Ricardo
TWO MONTHS LATER

I STEP OFF THE TREADMILL and almost trip over Adrian, who's got herself wedged between two exercise bikes, curled up with a Beauty & The Beast coloring book and the little velvet box.

She draws her feet underneath her and gives me a funny look.

"Sorry, Ad. I didn't see you there."

She stands up, balancing the box in her palm.

"That's because you're nervous."

I narrow my eyes at her, exaggerating the expression until she smiles. "Nervous? I'm not nervous."

She nods. "You're nervous. Remember, you told me! You said you're nervous about this box."

She holds it out, and I pluck it from her palm.

"Nervous you're going to lose it, little girl."

She shakes her head. "That's not what my mama said."

My lungs seize up. "Did you tell your mama, Ad?"

She shakes her pigtailed head again. "No."

"Are you sure?" I watch her nod in the reflection of the wall of mirrors in the yacht's new gym.

"Are you positive?" I run my towel over my face, watching her as she twists her arms together and bats her pretty eyes.

"Yep."

"Then why did Mama say I'm nervous?"

Adrian grins. "She says you're all rusted, and you really want to be the booker from Tall Street!"

Whew. I laugh, and Ad laughs with me; then she scampers off down the hall, probably headed toward the longue where her nanny, Holly, likes to study.

I'm tempted to follow her, but the sound system starts playing Miles Davis, and I need to do my stretches anyway.

If she runs into trouble, there's help everywhere. The new yacht has two dozen staff, and at least three of them are sort of backup nannies.

I lie on my back on the rubber mat, enjoying the cool rubber against my sweaty skin. I start my stretches, moving carefully at first, because my chest is still tight in some places and zingy in others.

There are lots of scars, not fully healed, and even though I'm running now and starting to get back on the bench, I'm a long way from fully healed.

I put the little velvet box just above my navel as I stretch. It's kind of stupid, but I like to have it in my sights.

I've been toting it around since two days after I woke up, after I found out about the scandal and the campaign for my release, which went viral and set a new record for Twitter retweets in the first three days I was in my coma.

I've been waiting for the perfect time, but no time seems perfect enough. Angel and I drove up to L.A. yesterday, so I could audition for the part of a Wall Street banker in a new Scorsese project.

I smirk a little. That little beastling Ad is right. I am pretty fucking nervous.

The door to the workout room opens, and I jump. I grunt a little in my struggle to stuff the box under my ass before Angel glides inside. That's how she seems to me, in her soft, red yoga outfit, with her hair pulled back and diamonds in her ears. Just like a real angel…she glides.

I must have a weird expression on her face, because she laughs at me.

"What?" I sit up, raising my leg to hide the black box.

She laughs. "Just…you. You look so funny doing your exercises."

I arch a brow. "Funny how?"

"I don't know." She shrugs. "Just grumpy."

I stand up, expertly hiding the box behind my back. After all, I've been doing it almost constantly for two months now.

"I am grumpy," I say as I slide my arm around her waist and brush her cheek with my lips. "I'm tired of doing PT all the time and ready," I say, lowering my voice, "to use our new private room."

She grins. "Me, too. The doctor said just another two weeks."

I lower my forehead to hers and lick my lips. "Two weeks is two too long." I want to tie her up. To spank her, to restrain her. To really play. But for now, I have to take it easy. No lifting Ang.

Which is why I'm so lucky she plants her palms against my chest and pushes me against the mirrors. My dick is hard already, but it juts up, making a tent of my work out shorts.

She pulls back the elastic and sinks down to her knees. Takes me deep in her throat and starts to suck me off.

It feels amazing. So incredible, my knees feel unsteady after only a few strokes of her hot mouth over my shaft. So incredible, I want to touch her, too. My hands move to stroke her neck, to knead her breasts, but I make a pivotal mistake.

I forget what I'm holding.

The little box falls to the floor, and I stiffen, waiting for her eyes to find the shiny, eleven carat ruby. But my Angel is good. She never even opens her eyes as she blows me. As I come into her throat and pick her up and lie her down on the soft, rubber mat and peel her pants off. As I spread her soft thighs and start to eat her pussy.

She does everything right. The perfect little groans. The sexiest thrusting of her hips. The way she pushes her sweet pussy into my face, urging me to get her off *right now*. So of course, I take my time and make her scream.

As I'm bringing her to orgasm, my mind spins back through the events of the last few months. The way I almost lost her, because Thom's boss betrayed his word. The way Thom spoke out, telling a reporter the truth about what happened with me, Angel, and Ryan. The way the Juarez Cartel went down, and almost everyone with a Twitter account called for my release. And then a judge agreed. The look on Angel's face when she told me I was free, and that she'd bought a yacht.

The first time I fucked her, in my hospital bed.

God, I love her. So fucking much.

And when I'm loving her, I grip her hands, and slide the ring on her finger. She comes screaming my name, and climbs on top of me because she wants my cock inside her pussy.

She bounces on me a few times, and then she screams.

I grin, still hard as nails inside her hot cunt.

"Do you like it?"

"Is this a ring?"

I laugh as she keeps on rising and falling on my dick.

"It's an engagement ring, Angel. What do you say? Will you marry this beat up, out of work actor who loves you?"

Her knees stop moving. She falls all the way down on me, and my dick throbs as she takes it deep into her pussy.

"Yes!" She bounces on my dick. "Yes, Ricardo! YES! I will."

I roll her over and I fuck her from on top. And Angel comes. And cries. And when I carry her out of the workout room, breaking the doctors' rules as I spirit her to our room, I have to wipe a small tear from my cheek as well.

"Perfection," I whisper to her after we fuck two more times in our bed. "Our life is perfection."

She grins. "Yeah, it really is."

Made in the USA
Middletown, DE
05 March 2017